network — caf
<u>Bourdie</u>

Panofsky — See <u>Gothic Architecture and Scholasticism</u>
translated by Bourdieu.

707211

Bourdieu's Game of Life:
Using Simulation to
Facilitate Understanding
of Complex Theories

by Lauren Miller Griffith

The Craft of Sociology
Epistemological Preliminaries

Pierre Bourdieu
Jean-Claude Chamboredon
Jean-Claude Passeron

Edited by Beate Krais
Translated by Richard Nice

Walter de Gruyter · Berlin · New York 1991

Pierre Bourdieu
Professor at the Collège de France, Director of Studies at the École des Hautes Études en Sciences Sociales, Director of the Center for European Sociology, Paris, France

Jean-Claude Chamboredon
Director of Studies at the École des Hautes Études en Sciences Sociales, Paris, France

Jean-Claude Passeron
Director of Studies at the École des Hautes Études en Sciences Sociales, Paris, France

Beate Krais
Max-Planck-Institut für Bildungsforschung, Berlin, Germany

© 1968 École des Hautes Études en Sciences Sociales and Mouton Éditeurs Title of the French edition: le métier de sociologue

Translated by Richard Nice, University of Surrey, Great Britain

Library of Congress Cataloging-in-Publication Data

Bourdieu, Pierre.
  [Métier de sociologue. English]
  the craft of sociology: epistemological preliminaries / Pierre Bourdieu,
Jean-Claude Chamboredon, Jean-Claude Passeron: translated by Richard Nice. —
English ed. / by Beate Krais. XVI, 272, p. 23 × 15 cm.
    Translation of : Le métier de sociologue. Includes bibliographical references.
    ISBN 0–89925–870–0 (U.S.) (alk. paper)
    ISBN 0–89925–555–8 (U.S.) (pbk.)
    1. Sociology—Methodology. I. Chamboredon, J.C. II. Passeron, Jean-Claude.
III. Krais, Beate. IV. Title.
HM24.B67213 1991   90–24390
301'.01—dc20   CIP

Deutsche Bibliothek Cataloging in Publication Data

The craft of sociology: epistemological preliminaries / Pierre Bourdieu;
Jean-Claude Chamboredon; Jean-Claude Passeron. Engl.ed. by Beate Krais.
Transl. by Richard Nice. – Berlin; New York: de Gruyter, 1991
    Einheitssacht.: Le métier de sociologue ‹engl.›
    ISBN 3–11–011940–04
NE: Bourdieu, Pierre; Chamboredon, Jean-Claude; Passeron, Jean-Claude;
    Krais, Beate [Hrsg.]; EST

⊗ Printed on acid-free paper which falls within the guidelines of the ANSI to ensure permanence and durability.

© Copyright 1991 by Walter de Gruyter & Co., D-1000 Berlin 30.—

Printed in Germany
Typesetting: Wyvern Typesetting Ltd, Bristol, GB—Printing: WB-Druck GmbH, Rieden a/Forggensee—Binding: Lüderitz & Bauer GmbH, 1000 Berlin 61—Cover design: Johannes Rother, 1000 Berlin 21.

Preface to the English edition

This book was initially designed for teaching purposes, to enable students of sociology to become better equipped to cope with the pitfalls of sociological research. But it is not just a primer setting out the difficulties and risks of scientific work in sociology with the aid of illustrative texts drawn from the whole range of the human sciences; it is also a contribution in its own right to the epistemology of the social sciences. In accordance with the initial didactic intention, it was originally planned as the first part of a three-volume text-book, which was to deal not only with the epistemological foundations of the science of sociology but also with the major questions this science puts to itself and with the methodological resources of empirical sociological research. This original intention was not fulfilled, as is explained in the Preface to the second French edition and also in the interview with Pierre Bourdieu in this new edition.

The first French edition was published in 1968,[1] at a time when empirical social research in European sociology had already become an integral and recognized part of the discipline. Although it was far from being as developed and differentiated as it has now become, it was able to point to some interesting findings and was characterised by intensive discussion of its methods. In the context of Pierre Bourdieu's wide-ranging production, the epistemological reflection presented in this book can be situated at a precise point in his development as a sociologist — and much the same could be said of empirical social science in general. Bourdieu, like his co-authors, was already able to look back on a rich experience in sociological research. By 1968, some of his major works had been published — the studies on Algeria, the studies in the sociology of art (on photography and museums), and a number of works on the functioning of the educational system.[2] However, the major part of his oeuvre was still to come. Perhaps it is exactly that moment in the development of a discipline, when research routines, specializations, and the accompanying

---

[1] This translation is based on the second French edition of 1972, in which the first edition was slightly revised and the number of illustrative texts was reduced.

[2] P. Bourdieu, *The Algerians*, Boston: Beacon Press, 1962; P. Bourdieu, A. Darbel, J.-P. Rivet, & C. Seibel, *Travail et travailleurs en Algérie*, Paris and The Hague: Mouton, 1963; [partially translated as: *Algeria 1960*, Cambridge: C.U.P., & Paris: Maison des Sciences de l'Homme, 1978]; P. Bourdieu & A. Sayad, *Le Déracinement: la crise de l'agriculture traditionnelle en Algérie*, Paris, Éditions de Minuit, 1964; P. Bourdieu, L. Boltanksi, R. Castel, & J.-C. Chamboredon, *Un Art moyen: essai sur les usages de la photographie*, Paris: Éditions de Minuit, 1965; P. Bourdieu, A. Darbel, & D. Schnapper, *L'Amour de l'art: les musées d'art européens et leur public*, Paris: Éditions de Minuit, 1966; P. Bourdieu, J.-C. Passeron, *Les Héritiers: les étudiants et leurs études*, Paris and The Hague: Mouton, 1964 [translated as *The Inheritors: French Students and their Relation to Culture*, Chicago: Chicago University Press, 1979]; P. Bourdieu, J.-C. Passeron, M. de Saint-Martin, *Rapport pédagogique et communication*, Paris and The Hague: Mouton, 1965.

self-evidence of methods and techniques are not yet fully developed, that
makes it a matter of particular urgency to take stock of one's own procedures.
Thus, in West Germany, the 1960s were the years of the *Positivismusstreit*, a
controversy which evolved from the need felt by sociologists to establish
clearly the methodological position of a changing discipline. It has to be said
that, at the 1961 conference of the German Sociological Association, neither
the papers given by Adorno and Popper, nor the ensuing discussion, led to a
more precise definition of epistemological positions, thus disappointing the
expectations of many participants, as Ralf Dahrendorf writes in his report on
the conference.[3] As regards the "clear establishment of the relationships of
theory and empirical research, of construction, analysis and data-gathering",[4]
it is perhaps not surprising that the speakers — as well as the opponents,
Albert and Habermas, in the continuation of the controversy — achieved
relatively little in their endeavour to resolve these problems. They were problems that were of little or no consequence for their research practice.
   They are, however, exactly the questions with which a sociologist as
strongly influenced by empirical work as Bourdieu was, saw and still sees
himself confronted. Thus the epistemological reflection in *The Craft of Sociology*, which is, above all, self-reflection, emphasizes quite different aspects
than the German *Positivismusstreit*, despite its closeness in time. The question
now is why a book such as this is still of interest today — an interest that goes
beyond the fact that it expounds the epistemological foundation of the work of
one of the most innovative contemporary sociologists, a sociologist who has
shed new light on the nature of the social world. Since the book was first
published, empirical social research has developed enormously, which has led
to a significant change in sociology; and epistemological discussion has con-
tinued. What then are the reasons today for reading this book and translating
it?
   The epistemological position set out in *The Craft of Sociology* is in at least
two respects still new for sociology. Firstly, a central concern of the book is an
aspect of research logic which is seldom discussed, namely the logic of discovery as opposed to the logic of validation — so far as that distinction can be
sustained. The rigorous demarcation of two distinct logics which the research
process follows in its different stages, assigns a major aspect of scientific work
— hypothesis-building, the scientific "idea", the generation of ideas guiding
research, or whatever name one gives to these aspects of the research process
that are generally placed outside the logic of validation, which is regarded as
scientific in the strict sense — to the realm of chance, intuition, the purely
individual and non-rational. One can safely assume a consensus within the

[3] Cf. R. Dahrendorf, "Anmerkungen zur Diskussion der Referate von Karl R. Popper und
   Theodor W. Adorno", in : T. W. Adorno et al., *Der Positivismusstreit in der deutschen
   Soziologie*. Darmstadt and Neuwied: Luchterhand 1980, pp. 145-153.
[4] R. Dahrendorf, *op. cit.*, p. 153.

scientific community that, as Max Weber wrote in "Science as a Vocation", the "inspiration", the "idea", is the decisive factor in winning accomplishments for science.[5] After adding that "normally .. an 'idea' is prepared only on the soil of very hard work", Weber dismisses the problem; and this aspect of the research process has been excluded from subsequent discussions of scientific procedures, which are based on the distinction between the context of validation and the context of discovery. More recent studies in the sociology of science, however, show that the actual research process does not manifest this distinction. The process of validating scientifically generated knowledge extends far back into the context of discovery and cannot be separated from it. Pierre Bourdieu and his co-authors are explicitly concerned to remove the scientific "notion", the "idea", the "process of hypothesis-building", from the realm of intuition, and to make it amenable to reason in an *ars inveniendi*. They speak of scientific "invention", thereby recalling a figure of classical rhetoric.

Central to this *ars inveniendi* is the construction of the scientific object, and this is the second, and essential, reason that makes this book so stimulating to read. Discussing the construction of the scientific object involves two aspects: on the one hand, the "constructedness" of knowledge; on the other, the construction of a specific scientific object. Scientifically grounded knowledge does not appear as a faithful reflection of a "reality", but as a fabricated knowledge, generated only through the work of the scientist, in other words a constructed knowledge. In the construction of the scientific object it is of prime importance to break free from the representations, questions and problem formulations of common-sense understanding, i.e., as the authors themselves write, to break with "pre-notions" and "preconcepts", and to develop instead an autonomous object area which has systematic foundations and which formulates its own questions. A constructivist position such as this is by no means self-evident in contemporary sociology; even discussion about it has only just begun.[7] It is rather the case that sociology is to a large extent characterized by the fact that it simply takes over prescientific definitions of problems, often from the political sphere. In the interview included in this volume, Bourdieu cites examples of the simple taking-over of prescientific problem definitions. He points out that some "sociologies-of . . . ." mainly owe their existence to the public salience of certain social problems, and

[5] M. Weber, "Science as a Vocation", in *From Max Weber: Essays in Sociology*, trans. H. H. Gerth and C. W. Mills, London: Routledge & Kegan Paul, 1948, pp. 129–56. (The quotation is from p. 135.)

[6] Cf. K. D. Knorr, *The Manufacture of Knowledge: An Essay on the Constructivist and Contextual Nature of Science*, Oxford: Blackwell, 1980, and B. Latour and S. Woolgar, *Laboratory Life: The Social Construction of Scientific Facts*, London: Sage, 1979.

[7] In a recent article, written from the standpoint of the sociology of knowledge, K. Knorr-Cetina outlines the prospects for constructivism in sociology ("Spielarten des Konstruktivismus", *Soziale Welt*, Vol. 40, 1989, no. 1–2, pp. 86–96).

achieve no status beyond that of "public-concern" sociologies or technocratic management, so long as they remain within the confines of common-sense problem formulations. Only this break, the move beyond prescientific concepts and questions, can, incidentally, succeed in placing a systematic barrier against *ex-cathedra* prophesying, a temptation that sociologists cannot resist (except with the aid of their personal scruples) so long as they move in the same prescientific realm as the wider public. The authors discuss this problem in the first part of the book, which is devoted to the "break".

The above is not intended to bolster the misapprehension that scientificity is characterized above all by the use of complex technical terminologies, and by the distance between research and the problems of practice; and it does not claim that social agents are blind with regard to their social practice. The common-sense knowledge of the agents, their "practical sense",[8] is the starting point for any sociological understanding. This knowledge is, however, limited, and to that extent sociological knowledge, which strives to overcome these limitations, is always a clarification of social practice. But this clarification cannot be achieved simply by reproducing the promptings of practical sense or common-sense understanding. One needs analysis which shows — constructs — the relationships and connections that remain hidden within the wealth of appearances and actions of everyday life. In their argument, Bourdieu, Chamboredon and Passeron link up with an epistemological tradition which evolved mainly in France and is represented by names like Alexandre Koyré, Gaston Bachelard and Georges Canguilhem. With the exception of the work of Koyré, this tradition has so far largely been ignored in both Anglo-American and German sociological discussion. This volume includes several illustrative texts by Bachelard and Canguilhem. The conception of science put forward in this book was decisively influenced by these thinkers' work in the history of science, which is centred on the "epistemological obstacles", as Bachelard calls them — the social and mental obstacles standing in the way of scientific knowledge — and also on the construction of the autonomous scientific object.

Those who know Pierre Bourdieu's work will easily recognize how his understanding of the social world parallels his understanding of science. Society, social practice, the social facts or social structures and institutions with which sociology deals, are something that the subjects themselves make, something that, as Bourdieu constantly points out, they constitute, realize, modify and transform through their activity: nothing social exists outside the action of the subjects. To avoid a subjectivist reading of this position, it should be noted that in his understanding of the social world Bourdieu echoes Marx: he does not confine the social to interactions, but insists on the autonomy of institutions and social structures as against the intentions and will of the

[8] Cf. P. Bourdieu, *The Logic of Practice*, Oxford: Polity Press, 1990 [*Le Sens pratique*, Paris: Éditions de Minuit, 1980].

subjects. However, his main concern, in contrast to Marx, is not with these autonomous entities, the consolidated product of the social activity of individuals, but rather with the "practical operators" which reproduce and transform through their practice the social constructions encountered by each generation.[9] Here the concept of the habitus, the key concept in Bourdieu's work, has its origin and its distinctive value: being itself structured through social relations, it functions as the practical operator through which the action of the subjects becomes social action, the practical construction of the social world. And sociology, as the science which is concerned with the understanding of the social world, is a product of construction, construction of knowledge about an object which is itself already a construct.

It is tempting, in the case of sociology, to speak of a double construction — construction at the level of the agents, and scientific meta-construction. But that approach would fail to grasp the understanding of sociology and sociological methods presented in this book. Sociologists do not stand outside the social world they analyse, or look down on it from above; they are themselves agents in the social process. What enables them — to some extent — to analyse this process, i.e. to constitute objects for scientific understanding — is quite simply scientific method, but not a fundamental difference in their position from that of other social agents. So Bourdieu and his co-authors are quite consistent when, in the final pages of their book, they emphasize the importance, for sociological knowledge, of a sociology of sociology. The authors are following Bachelard when they state that one of the basic elements of "epistemological vigilance" is reflection by the scientific subject on his or her own social relations, a reflection which not only applies to the fact that sociologists are subject to the ebbs and flows of the Zeitgeist, that they carry ways of thinking and prejudices that they owe to their social origin, the social position they have acquired, and their specific roles as intellectuals, but also to the social order within their own scientific community and their own position within it. Thus, the quality of sociological research depends, as it does in other sciences, on the organization and functioning of the scientific community, on the social practice of those who have science as a vocation.

[9] Whereas Marx and Engels, in their confrontation with the idealistic view of history, write that, in history, "at each stage there is found a material result: a sum of productive forces, an historically created relation of individuals to nature and to one another, which is handed down to each generation from its predecessor; a mass of productive forces, capital funds and conditions, which, on the one hand, is indeed modified by the new generation, but also prescribes for it its conditions of life and gives it a definite development, a special character [....] circumstances make men as much as men make circumstances" (K. Marx & F. Engels, The German Ideology, in Collected Works, Vol. 5, London: Lawrence & Wishart, 1976, p. 50), Bourdieu stresses the mechanism or process through which, in practices, in "practical life", as Marx and Engels put it, those "circumstances" are constructed. While the meaning of social activity is objectified in institutions, it is the existence and functioning of the habitus, embodied history, "that makes it possible to inhabit institutions, to appropriate them practically, and so to keep them in activity, continuously pulling them from the state of dead letters, reviving the sense deposited in them, at the same time imposing on them the revisions and transformations that reactivation entails" (P. Bourdieu, op. cit., 1990, p. 57).

Preface to the second French edition

This volume on the *Epistemological preliminaries* was originally intended to be followed by a second volume on the construction of the sociological object and a third volume giving a critical review of the conceptual and technical tools of research. The preparation of this abridged second edition has been an opportunity to reconsider that original intention. In the end, it seemed to us that in those other areas it was impossible to perform the work of construction that was made both possible and necessary by the non-existence of an epistemology of the social sciences. In such crowded, not to say over-crowded, domains, the stance of deliberate naïveté could not be sustained; but we were equally unwilling to resign ourselves to the even-handed discussion of prevailing theories and concepts which the university tradition has established as the preliminary to any theoretical discussion.

We might have been more tempted to revise these *Epistemological preliminaries* so as to bring the exposition more into line with the didactic intention, which is very imperfectly fulfilled in the present state of the work. Each of the principles might have been translated into precepts or, at least, into exercises designed to internalize the posture. For example, in order to draw out all the heuristic potential of a principle such as the primacy of relations, we would have had to show with concrete examples (as one can in a seminar, or better in a research group, by examining the construction of a sample, the design of a questionnaire or the analysis of a series of statistical tables) how this principle governs the technical choices made in research work (constructing series of populations separated by differences pertinent in respect of the relations being considered; devising questions which, while secondary as regards the sociography of the population itself, enable one to situate the particular case in a system of cases in which it takes on its full meaning; using graphic and mechanical techniques to provide a synoptic and exhaustive view of the system of relations linking the relations revealed by a set of statistical tables, etc.).

We were dissuaded from doing so, among other reasons by the fear that, owing to the limits of written communication, this effort at didactic clarification might lead to the very negation of the teaching of research conceived as the teaching of invention, by encouraging the canonization of the routinized precepts of a new methodology or, worse still, a new theoretical tradition. The risk is a real one: the critique of positivist empiricism and methodological abstraction, which was heretical in its day, now has every chance of being confused with the eternally preliminary discourses of a new vulgate that still manages to defer science by substituting the point of honour of theoretical purity for the obsession of methodological impeccability.

September 1972

Contents

Introduction—Epistemology and methodology

Part One—The break

Part Two—Constructing the object

Part Three—Applied rationalism

Conclusion—Sociology of knowledge and epistemology

Illustrative Texts

Introduction—Epistemology and methodology

Part One—The break

Part Two—Constructing the object

Part Three—Applied rationalism

Conclusion—Sociology of knowledge and epistemology

Contents

The illustrative texts that make up the second part of this book (pp. 79–245) should be read in conjunction with the analyses in the course of which they are used or explained. Cross-references to these texts, in the first part of the book (in italics, in square brackets), give the author's name and the number of the text.

Introduction
Epistemology and methodology

"Method," wrote Auguste Comte, "does not admit of being studied apart from the research in which it is used; or, at all events, it is only a lifeless study, incapable of fertilizing the mind which resorts to it. Looking at it in that abstract way, the only real information you can give about it amounts to no more than a few general propositions, so vague that they can have no influence on mental habits. When we have thoroughly established as a logical thesis that all our knowledge must be founded upon observation, that we must proceed sometimes from facts to principles, at other times from principles to facts, and some other similar aphorisms, we still know method far less clearly than he who, even without any philosophical purpose in view, has studied at all completely a single positive science. It is because they have failed to recognize this essential fact that our psychologists have been led to take their reveries for science, in the belief that they understood the positive method because they have read the precepts of Bacon or the discourse of Descartes. I do not know if, in the future, it will become possible to construct by *a priori* reasoning a genuine course on method, wholly independent of the philosophical study of the sciences; but I am quite convinced that it cannot be done at present, for the great logical methods cannot be explained with sufficient precision apart from their applications. I venture to add, moreover, that, even if such an enterprise could be carried out eventually, which is conceivable, it would nevertheless be only through the study of regular applications of scientific methods that we could succeed in forming a good system of intellectual habits; this is, however, the essential object to be gained by studying method."[1]

There would be nothing to add to this text, which refuses to dissociate method from practice and rejects in advance all discourses on method, if there were not already a whole discourse around method which, in the absence of any serious challenge, is liable to force on researchers a split image of scientific work. Whether they are prophets who fulminate against the original impurity of the empirical—though it is not clear whether they regard the menial tasks of scientific routine as offensive to the dignity of the object they assign to them-

[1] A. Comte, *Introduction to Positive Philosophy*, ed. with introdn. and rev. transln. by F. Ferré, Indianapolis: Bobbs-Merrill, 1970, p. 23. As Georges Canguilhem points out, it is not easy to resist the impulses of vocabulary, which "constantly lead us back to an idea of method as something that can be separated from the research in which it is implemented: Comte teaches in the first lesson of the *Cours de philosophie positive* that 'method cannot be studied apart from the research in which it is *used*'—which implies that use of a method presupposes prior possession of the method" (G. Canguilhem, "Théorie et technique de l'expérimentation chez Claude Bernard", *Colloque du centenaire de la publication de l'Introduction à l'étude de la médecine expérimentale*, Paris: Masson, 1967, p. 24).

selves or of the scientific mind they seek to incarnate—or high priests of method who would gladly make all researchers spend the rest of their lives on the benches of the methodological catechism, those who pontificate on the art of being a sociologist or the scientific way of conducting sociological science often have in common the fact that they dissociate method, or theory (not to mention the theory of method or the theory of theory) from the operations of research. Our aim in this book, arising from our experience of research and its everyday difficúlties, is simply to make explicit, for the purpose in hand, a "system of intellectual habits". It is addressed to those who have embarked on the practice of empirical sociology and have no need to be reminded of the necessity of measurement and all its theoretical and technical apparatus. They will immediately grant us what we ourselves assume, because it goes without saying: for example, the need to neglect none of the conceptual or theoretical tools that enable one to give experimental verification its full rigour and its full force. Only those who do not have or do not want experience of research will see this work, which seeks to put sociological practice to the question, as calling empirical sociology into question.[2]

If it is true that the teaching of research requires both its teachers and its students to make constant and direct reference to personal experience of practice, then "the vogue in unapplied methodology, programmes for hypothetically superior research, evaluatory surveys of work done by others... and all such instruments and occasions for methodological pronouncements"[3] can be no substitute for reflection on the correct relation to techniques and for even a risky effort to transmit principles that cannot present themselves as *a priori* truths because they are the principle of the search for truths. And if it is true that methods are distinguished from techniques at least insofar as they are "sufficiently general to be common to all sciences, or to a significant part of them",[4] then this reflection on method must also take the risk of retracing the most classic analyses of the epistemology of the natural sciences: but perhaps sociologists need to agree on the elementary principles that are truisms for

---

[2] The division of the intellectual field in accordance with the logic of opposing couples (see Part Three) and the intellectual traditions which treat all reflection as pure speculation, making it impossible to see the technical function of a reflection on the relation to techniques, give a very high probability to the misunderstanding which we are here trying to prevent. In this dualistic organization of epistemological positions, any attempt to reinsert technical operations into the hierarchy of epistemological acts will almost inevitably be interpreted as an attack on technique and technicians. Whether we like it or not—and we would acknowledge here the important contribution which the methodologists, and in particular Paul F. Lazarsfeld, have made to the rationalization of sociological practice—, we realize that we are likely to be classified among the "Fads and Foibles of American Sociology" rather than "The Language of Social Research".

[3] R. Needham, *Structure and Sentiment: A Test-case in Social Anthropology*, Chicago & London: Chicago University Press, 1962, p. vii.

[4] A. Kaplan, *The Conduct of Inquiry: Methodology of Behavioral Science*, San Francisco: Chandler, 1964, p. 23. The same author expresses regret that "technology" already has a specialized meaning, since it could otherwise well be used to describe a good number of "methodological studies" (*ibid.*, p. 19).

natural scientists or philosophers of science in order to escape from the conceptual anarchy to which they are condemned by their indifference to epistemological reflection. In reality, the effort to interrogate a particular science with the aid of the general principles that are provided by this epistemological heritage is particularly justified and necessary in the case of sociology. Here everything encourages neglect of that heritage, from the humanist stereotype of the irreducibility of the human sciences, to the characteristics of the recruitment and training of researchers, not to mention the existence of a corps of methodologists specializing in selective reinterpretation of the heritage of the other sciences. So we must subject the operations of sociological practice to the polemics of epistemological reason in order to define and, if possible, inculcate an attitude of vigilance that can use adequate knowledge of error and the mechanisms that can induce it as one of the means of overcoming it. The intention of giving the researcher the means of taking on the oversight of his own scientific work is quite different from the calls to order by censors whose peremptory negativism can only inspire the mortal fear of error and a resigned recourse to a technology invested with the function of exorcism.

As the whole *œuvre* of Gaston Bachelard shows, epistemology differs from abstract methodology inasmuch as it strives to grasp the logic of error in order to construct the logic of the discovery of truth as a polemic against error and as an endeavour to subject the approximated truths of science and the methods it uses to methodical, permanent rectification [*Canguilhem, text no. 1*]. But the polemical action of scientific reason cannot be given its full force unless the "psychoanalysis of the scientific mind" is taken further by an analysis of the social conditions in which sociological works are produced: the sociologist may find an exceptionally valuable instrument of epistemological vigilance in the sociology of knowledge, a means of enhancing and clarifying knowledge of error and the conditions that make it possible and sometimes inevitable [*Bachelard, text no. 2*]. It follows that any residues of what may seem to be *ad hominem* polemics that remain here are simply due to the limits of sociological understanding of the conditions of error. An epistemology that appeals to a sociology of knowledge is less entitled than any other to impute errors to subjects who are never entirely the authors of those errors. If, to paraphrase a famous text by Marx, "we have not painted a rosy picture" of the empiricist, the intuitionist, or the methodologist, we have never thought of the "persons except insofar as they are the personification" of epistemological positions that can only be fully understood in the social field in which they are put forward.

Teaching research

The form and content of this work are defined by its function. Research training which aims to set out the principles of professional practice and simultaneously to inculcate a particular relationship to that practice, i.e. to give both the tools that are indispensable for the sociological treatment of the object and an active disposition to use them adequately, has to break with the routines of pedagogic discourse and restore their full heuristic force to the concepts and operations that have been most completely "neutralized" by the ritual of canonical exposition. That is why this work, which aims to teach the most practical acts of sociological practice, starts with a reflection that seeks to systematize and underline the implications of all practice, good or bad, and to specify the principle of epistemological vigilance in the form of practical precepts (Volume 1).[5] We shall then be in a position to try to define the function and conditions of application of the theoretical schemes to which sociology has to resort in order to construct its object — without claiming to present these first principles of specifically sociological inquiry as a complete theory of sociological knowledge, still less as a general and universal theory of the social system (Volume 2).[5] Empirical research has no need to implement such a theory in order to escape from empiricism, provided that, in each of its operations, it effectively realizes the principles that constitute it as a science by giving it an object endowed with a degree of theoretical coherence. On that condition, concepts or methods can be treated as *tools* that can be removed from their original context and put to new uses (Volume 3).[5] By associating the presentation of each intellectual instrument with examples of its use, we shall seek to prevent sociological knowledge from appearing as a catalogue of techniques, or a bank of concepts, separate or separable from their use in research.

If we have taken it upon ourselves to extract both the theoretical principles and the technical procedures bequeathed by the history of sociological science from the "order of reasons" to which they belonged, this was not done simply to break the linkages of the didactic order which only renounces academic indulgence towards the history of doctrines or concepts in order to grant diplomatic recognition to the values consecrated by tradition or fashion. Nor was it done merely to liberate heuristic potentialities that are often greater than academic usages would suggest. We have done so, above all, for the sake of a conception of the theory of sociological knowledge that makes this theory the system of principles defining the conditions of possibility of all distinctively sociological acts and discourses and only these, whatever the theories of the social system specific to those who produce or have produced sociological works in the name of these principles. The question of the affiliation of a piece of sociological research to a particular theory of the social system, that of Marx, or Weber, or Durkheim, for example, is always secondary to the question of whether that research belongs to sociological science. The only criterion of this is whether it implements the fundamental principles of the theory of sociological knowledge which, as such, in no way separates authors

---

[5] See above, Preface to the second French edition.

who differ in every respect as regards their theory of the social system. Even if most authors have been led to identify their particular theory of the social system with the theory of sociological knowledge that they involve, implicitly at least, in their sociological practice, the epistemological project can nonetheless use this preliminary distinction as a basis for juxtaposing authors whose doctrinal oppositions mask an epistemological agreement.

It might be feared that this undertaking will lead to an amalgam of principles borrowed from different theoretical traditions or to the establishment of a set of recipes dissociated from the principles that underlie them. But this would be to forget that the reconciliation whose principles we seek to make explicit really occurs in the authentic exercise of the sociologist's practice, or rather his "craft" — the *habitus*, which, as a system of more or less well-assimilated and more or less transposable schemes of thought, is nothing other than the internalization of the principles of the theory of sociological knowledge. The endlessly renewed temptation to transform the precepts of method into scientific recipes or laboratory gadgets can only be resisted by constant training in the scientific vigilance which, by subordinating the use of techniques and concepts to an examination of the conditions and limits of their validity, rules out the short cuts offered by automatic application of tried and tested procedures, and which teaches that even the most routine operation has to be rethought, both in itself and in relation to the particular case. Only a magical reinterpretation of the demands of measurement can lead one simultaneously to overestimate the importance of operations that are ultimately no more than tricks of the trade and — transforming methodological prudence into sacred reverence — never to use instruments that ought to be judged only by their use, or to use them only with trembling hands, for fear of falling short of one of the ritual conditions. Those who push methodological concern to the point of obsession are like Freud's patient who spent all his time cleaning his spectacles and never put them on.

To take seriously the project of methodically transmitting an *ars inveniendi* requires one to see that it implies something more than and different from the *ars probandi* proposed by those who confuse the mechanical logic of validations and proofs, dismantled after the event, with the real processes of invention. It also requires one to see, with equal clarity, that the paths, or rather short cuts, that a reflection on research can now trace are a far cry from the unwavering, unrepentant course that would be marked out by a genuine discourse on sociological method.

In contrast to the tradition which draws the line at the logic of proof, refusing on principle to enter into the arcana of invention, thereby condemning itself to oscillate between a rhetoric of formal exposition and a literary psychology of discovery, we try here to provide the means of acquiring a mental disposition which is the precondition for both invention and proof. If this reconciliation is not made, one must give up any hope of aiding the work of discovery, and one is reduced, along with so many methodologists, to invoking the miracles of creative insight, as purveyed by the hagiography of scientific discovery, or the mysteries of depth psychology.[6]

Though it goes without saying that acquired automatic behaviours can reduce the need for permanent invention, it should not be supposed that the subject of scientific invention is an *automaton spirituale* guided by the built-in mechanisms of a methodological programming, set up once and for all. This would lock the researcher into a blind submission to the programme which rules out reflexive re-examination of the programme, the precondition for the invention of new programmes.[7] Methodology, said Weber, "is no more the precondition of fruitful intellectual work than the knowledge of anatomy is the precondition for 'correct' walking".[8] But, while it is futile to hope to discover a science of the way to do science or to expect logic to provide more than a way of controlling science in progress or of validating science that has been done, the fact remains that, as J. S. Mill observed, "invention can be cultivated". It follows that even a partial spelling-out of the logic of invention can help to rationalize the teaching of the capacity to invent.

Epistemology of the social sciences and epistemology of the natural sciences

Most of the errors that tend to arise both in sociological practice and in reflection on it have their roots in a misconceived view of the epistemology of

---

[6] When defining the object of scientific logic, the methodological literature always takes care explicitly to "leave aside... the question of *ways of discovery*": "For our purposes it will suffice to consider the scientific *ways of validation*" (C. Hempel, *Aspects of Scientific Explanation and Other Essays in the Philosophy of Science*, New York: Free Press; London: Collier–Macmillan, 1965, p. 83). Popper often returns to this dichotomy, which for him seems to correspond to the distinction between public and private life: "The question, 'How did you first *find* your theory?' relates, as it were, to an entirely private matter, as opposed to the question, 'How did you *test* your theory?'" (K. R. Popper, *The Poverty of Historicism*, London: Routledge & Kegan Paul, 2nd ed. 1960, p. 135). Or again: "There is no such thing as a logical method of having new ideas, or a logical reconstruction of this process. My view may be expressed by saying that every discovery contains 'an irrational element', or 'a creative intuition', in Bergson's sense" (K. R. Popper, *The Logic of Scientific Discovery*, London: Hutchinson, 1959, p. 32). By contrast, as soon as, exceptionally, one explicitly considers the "context of discovery" (as opposed to the "context of justification"), one is forced to break with a number of routine conceptions of the epistemological and methodological tradition, in particular with the image of the process of research as a succession of distinct, predetermined stages (see P. E. Hammond [ed.], *Sociologists at Work: Essays on the Craft of Social Research*, New York: Basic Books, 1964).

[7] Consider, for example, the ease with which research can reproduce itself without producing anything, in accordance with the logic of "pump-handle research".

[8] M. Weber, "Critical Studies in the Logic of the Cultural Sciences", in *The Methodology of the Social Sciences*, trans. and ed. E. A. Shils and H. A. Finch, New York: Free Press, 1949, p. 115.

the natural sciences and its relationship to the epistemology of the social sciences. Epistemologies as different in their manifest assertions as Diltheyan dualism, which is able to posit the specificity of the method of the social sciences only by contrasting it with an image of the natural sciences that springs from a pure concern for distinction, and positivism, which endeavours to mimic an image of the natural sciences that is devised for the purposes of imitation, are unequally unaware of the exact philosophy of the exact sciences. This misperception has led some people to invent artificial distinctions between the two methods in order to indulge humanistic nostalgia or pious wishes; led others to herald discoveries that are mere rediscoveries; and still others into a positivism that naively copies a reductive image of experience as a copy of the real.

But it is all too obvious that positivism only takes over a caricature of the method of the exact sciences, without *ipso facto* achieving an exact epistemology of the social sciences. Indeed, it is a constant feature of the history of ideas that the critique of mechanical positivism serves to strengthen the subjective character of social facts and their irreducibility to the rigorous methods of science. Thus, having observed that "the methods which scientists or men fascinated by the natural sciences have so often tried to force upon the social sciences were not always necessarily those which the scientists followed in their own field, but rather those which they believed that they employed",[9] Hayek immediately concludes that the facts of the social sciences "differ from the facts of the physical sciences in being beliefs or opinions held by particular people", and therefore "must not be defined in terms of what we might find out about them by the objective methods of science, but in terms of what the person acting thinks about them".[10] Any questioning of automatic imitation of the natural sciences is so automatically associated with the subjectivist critique of the objectivity of social facts that every effort to deal with the specific problems raised by transposing the epistemological heritage of the natural sciences to the social sciences is always liable to be seen as a reaffirmation of the imprescriptible rights of subjectivity.[11]

[9] F. A. Hayek, *The Counter-Revolution of Science: Studies on the Abuse of Reason*, Glencoe (Ill.): Free Press, 1952, p. 14.
[10] *ibid.*, pp. 28 and 30.
[11] And yet Durkheim's whole enterprise would be sufficient to show that it is possible to escape from the dilemma of blind imitation and the equally blind refusal to imitate: "Sociology had its origin in the shadow of the natural sciences, and in intimate contact with them... . To be sure, some of the first sociologists made the mistake of exaggerating this close connection to the point that they ignored the originality of the social sciences and the autonomy which they must enjoy vis-à-vis the sciences that preceded them. But such excesses must not make us forget how much there is that is fruitful in the natural sciences, those principal forges of scientific thought" (É. Durkheim, "Sociology and its Scientific Field", in *Émile Durkheim, 1858–1917*, ed. K. H. Wolff, Columbus (Ohio): Ohio State University Press, 1960, p. 373).

Methodology and the displacement of vigilance

The way to move beyond these academic debates, and beyond the academic way of moving beyond them, is to subject scientific practice to a reflection which, unlike the classical philosophy of knowledge, is applied not to science that has been done—*true* science, for which one has to establish the conditions of possibility and coherence or the claims to legitimacy—but to science in progress. This specifically epistemological task consists in discovering, within scientific practice itself, which is constantly confronted with error, the conditions in which one can extract the true from the false, moving from a less true to a more true knowledge, or rather, as Bachelard puts it, an "approximated, that is to say, rectified, knowledge". Transposed to the social sciences, this philosophy of scientific work as the "unceasing polemical action of reason" can yield the principles of a reflection capable of inspiring and controlling the concrete acts of a truly scientific practice, by defining the specificity of the principles of the "regional rationalism" characteristic of sociological science. The fixist rationalism that inspired the inquiries of the classical philosophy of knowledge is more often expressed nowadays in the endeavours of some sociologists who tend to reduce reflection on method to a formal logic of the sciences. However, as Paul Feyerabend points out, "any form of meaning invariance is bound to lead to difficulties when the task arises... to give a proper account of the growth of knowledge, and of discoveries contributing to this growth".[12] More precisely, an exclusive concern with the atemporal relationships between abstract propositions, at the expense of the processes through which each proposition or concept has been established and has given rise to others, can be of no help to those who are involved in the drama of scientific work, because all the action takes place behind the scenes and only the denouement is brought on to the stage. Entirely occupied with the search for an ideal logic of research, the methodologists can only address themselves to a researcher abstractly defined by the capacity to achieve these standards of perfection—an impeccable, i.e. impossible or infertile, researcher. Unconditional obedience to an *organon* of logical rules tends to produce an effect of "premature closure" by removing, as Freud puts it, "the elasticity of definitions" or what Carl Hempel calls the "openness of meaning" of scientific terms[13]—which, at least in certain phases in the history of a science or the unfolding of research, is one of the conditions of invention.

This is not to deny that logical formalization, treated as a means of testing the ongoing logic of research and the coherence of its results, is one of the

---

[12] P. K. Feyerabend, "Explanation, Reduction and Empiricism", in H. Feigl and G. Maxwell (eds.), *Scientific Explanation, Space, and Time*, (Minnesota Studies in the Philosophy of Science, Vol. III,) Minneapolis: University of Minnesota Press, 1962, p. 31.

[13] C. G. Hempel, *Fundamentals of Concept Formation in Empirical Science*, Chicago and London: Chicago University Press, 1952, p. 29.

most effective instruments of epistemological control. But this legitimate usage of logical instruments is too often exploited to justify the perverse passion for methodological exercises which have no discernible purpose beyond that of displaying the arsenal of available means. Faced with some research designed for the sake of the logical or methodological cause, one is reminded of Abraham Kaplan's story of the "drunkard searching under a street lamp for his house key, which he had dropped some distance away. Asked why he didn't look where he had dropped it, he replied 'It's lighter here!'"[14] [*Kaplan, text no. 3*].

The cult of technological rigour, based on faith in a rigour defined once and for all and for all situations, i.e. on a fixist representation of truth or, equally, of error as the transgression of unconditional norms, is diametrically opposed to the search for *specific rigours*, which is based on a theory of truth as rectified error. "The knowing," says Bachelard, "has to evolve with the known." It is therefore futile to seek a logic prior to and external to the history of science in progress. To understand the processes of research, one has to examine how it proceeds, instead of enclosing it in the observance of a decalogue of procedures that may appear to be in advance of real practice only because they are defined in advance.[15] "Fascinated by the fact that in mathematics the avoidance of error is a matter of technique, some people claim to define truth as the product of an intellectual activity that complies with certain norms; they want to treat experimental data as mathematicians treat the axioms of geometry; they hope to define rules of thought that would fulfil the same role that logic fulfils in mathematics. Starting from a limited experiment, they want to define its theory in a single operation. Calculus was very slowly established, the idea of number took two and a half millennia to be clarified. The procedures that establish rigour arise as answers to questions which cannot be posed *a priori* and which only the development of science brings to light. Naïveté is lost very slowly. This is true in mathematics and it is true *a fortiori* in sciences based on observation, in which every disproved theory suggests new demands of rigour. It is therefore futile to seek to lay down *a priori* the conditions for truly scientific thought."[16]

At a deeper level, the insistent calls for methodological perfection are likely to lead to a *displacement* of epistemological vigilance. Instead, for example, of questioning the object of measurement and asking whether it is worth measuring, and how much accuracy is desirable and legitimate in view of the particu-

---

[14] A. Kaplan, *op. cit.*, p. 11.

[15] The authors of a long study of the functions of the statistical method in sociology eventually admit that their "suggestions regarding the possibility of applying statistical theory to empirical research only characterize the present state of methodological discussion, *with practice lagging behind*" (E. K. Scheuch and D. Rüschemeyer, "Soziologie und Statistik. Über den Einfluß der modernen Wissenschaftslehre auf ihr gegenseitiges Verhältnis", *Kölner Zeitschrift für Soziologie und Sozialpsychologie*, Vol. 8, pp. 272–291, 1956).

[16] A. Régnier, *Les infortunes de la raison*, Paris: Seuil, 1966, pp. 37–38.

lar conditions of measurement, or even, more simply, examining whether the
instruments measure what they are supposed to measure, one may be carried
away by the wish to translate the pure idea of methodological rigour into
realizable tasks and, obsessed by the decimal, pursue the contradictory ideal of
an intrinsically indefinable accuracy. This would be to forget that, as A. D.
Ritchie points out, "it is really just as bad technique to make a measurement
more accurately than is necessary as it is to make it not accurately enough",[17]
or that, as N. R. Campbell observes, when it is established that all propositions contained within certain limits are equivalent and that the proposition,
defined approximately, lies within these limits, "approximation is completely
justified".[18] It is clear that, by generating a casuistry of technical errors, the
ethic of methodological duty can lead, indirectly at least, to a procedural
ritualism which may be the caricature of methodological rigour but which is
certainly the exact opposite of epistemological vigilance.[19] It is particularly
significant that statistics, the science of error and of approximated knowledge,
which, in such standard procedures as calculating error or the limits of reli-
ability, implements a philosophy of critical vigilance, is so frequently used as a
scientific alibi for blind submission to technical instruments.

Similarly, whenever theoreticians summon empirical research and its conceptual tools to the bar of a theory whose constructions they refuse to measure
against the heritage of the science it claims to theorize and rule over, it is only
the prestige indiscriminately attached to any theoretical undertaking that wins
them the forced and purely verbal homage of the practitioners. And whenever
the intellectual climate enables the pure theoreticians to foist on scientists their
own logical or semantic ideal of complete, universal coherence of the system of
concepts, they can even paralyse research, inasmuch as they manage to instil
the obsession of conceptualizing everything, in every way, and in all respects
at once. In the real situations of scientific practice, the construction of new
problematics or theories requires one to renounce the impossible ambition of
saying everything about everything, in the right order.[20]

[17] A. D. Ritchie, *Scientific Method: An Inquiry into the Character and Validity of Natural Laws*,
London: Kegan Paul, Trench, Trubner, 1923, p. 113. Analysing this pursuit of "ill-founded
precision", which consists in believing that "the quality of the solution is measured by the
number of decimal places", Bachelard points out that "when accuracy in a result is greater than
the accuracy of the experimental data, it is quite precisely the determination of nothing... . As
Dulong said ironically of an experimenter, 'He is quite sure of the third figure after the decimal
point, it's the first one that worries him'" (G. Bachelard, *La formation de l'esprit scientifique*,
4th edn., Paris: Vrin, 1965, p. 214).

[18] N. R. Campbell, *An Account of the Principles of Measurement and Calculation*, London &
New York: Longmans Green, 1928, p. 186.

[19] Anxious interest in diseases of the scientific mind can have as depressive an effect as hypochon-
driac addiction to reading medical dictionaries.

[20] Some theoretical dissertations on everything that is known or knowable no doubt perform a
function of pre-emptive annexation similar to that of astrological prophecies, which always
manage to subsume events retrospectively. As Claude Bernard put it: "There are some people
who, on any given question, say all that can be said in order to be able to stake a claim when an

The epistemological order of reasons

But these sociological or psychological analyses of the methodological perversion or the speculative diversion are no substitute for the specifically epistemological critique to which they point. The warnings issued by the methodologists have to be strongly warned against, because, by focusing attention exclusively on formal controls of experimental procedures and operational concepts, they are likely to divert vigilance from more serious dangers. The sometimes powerful instruments and assistance that methodological reflection provides for vigilance turn against vigilance whenever the preconditions for their use are not fulfilled. The science of the formal conditions of rigour in scientific operations, presenting itself in the guise of an "operational" version of epistemological vigilance, may seem to be grounded in the claim to provide automatic implementation of the principles and precepts that define methodological vigilance, so that additional vigilance is required in order to prevent it from automatically producing this displacement effect.

As Saussure put it, "the linguist needs to be shown what he is doing."[21] To ask what it means to practise science, or rather, to try to know what the scientist does (whether or not he knows what he is doing) is not only to inquire into the efficacy and formal rigour of the available theories and methods but also to question the methods and theories at the very moment at which they are implemented, in order to determine what they do to objects and what objects they make. The order in which this inquiry has to be conducted is imposed as much by epistemological analysis of the obstacles to knowledge as by sociological analysis of the epistemological implications of present-day sociology, which define the hierarchy of epistemological dangers and therefore the order of priorities.

Bachelard's premise that *the scientific fact is won, constructed, and confirmed* calls into question both the empiricism which reduces the scientific act to one of validation and the conventionalism which sets against it only the preliminary of construction. By so much emphasizing the imperative of validation, in opposition to the whole speculative tradition of the social philosophy from which it seeks to break away, the sociological community is now tending to forget the epistemological hierarchy of scientific acts which subordinates validation to construction and construction to the break with self-evident appearances. In an experimental science, a simple appeal to experimental proof is a mere tautology if one does not, at the same time, explicate the theoretical

experiment is subsequently carried out on it. They are like astronomers who plot planets all over the sky so as to claim that any new one was the planet they had predicted" (*Principes de médecine expérimentale*, Paris: P.U.F., 1947, p. 255).

21 É. Benveniste, "Lettres de Ferdinand de Saussure à Antoine Meillet", *Cahiers Ferdinand de Saussure*, Vol. 21, pp. 92–135, 1964.

principles which are the basis of genuine experimentation; and this explication itself has no heuristic value if one does not, at the same time, make explicit the epistemological obstacles which present themselves in a specific form in each scientific practice.

Simulation too!

Part One
The break

1 The social fact is won against the illusion of immediate knowledge

Epistemological vigilance is particularly necessary in the social sciences, where the separation between everyday opinion and scientific discourse is more blurred than elsewhere. Though it is readily acknowledged that their concern for political and moral reform of society may have led the 19th century sociologists to fall short of scientific neutrality, and even that 20th century sociology may have renounced the ambitions of social philosophy without thereby escaping ideological contaminations of another sort, the very critics who are so quick to point this out all too often fail to recognize and realize the full implications of the fact that, for the sociologist, familiarity with his social universe is the epistemological obstacle *par excellence*, because it continuously produces fictitious conceptions or systematizations and, at the same time, the conditions of their credibility. The sociologist's struggle with spontaneous sociology is never finally won, and he must conduct unending polemics against the blinding self-evidences which all too easily provide the illusion of immediate knowledge and its insuperable wealth. The separation between perception and science, which is expressed for the physicist in the opposition between the laboratory and daily life, is even harder for the sociologist to make, because his theoretical heritage does not provide him with the tools that would make it possible to radically challenge ordinary language and everyday notions.

1.1 Prenotions and techniques for breaking with them

Because they have the function of reconciling everyday consciousness with itself at all costs by offering explanations (even if they are mutually exclusive) of the same fact, spontaneous opinions on social facts present themselves as a spuriously systematized collection of judgements for alternating use. These preconceptions or "prenotions" — "schematic, summary representations" that are "formed by and for experience" — derive their self-evidence and their "authority", as Durkheim observes, from the social functions that they fulfil [*Durkheim, text no. 4*].

Everyday notions are so tenacious that all the techniques of objectification have to be applied in order to achieve a break that is more often proclaimed than performed. Thus, the results of statistical measurement may have at least the negative virtue of disconcerting the first impressions. Similarly, insufficient attention has been paid to the break-inducing function that Durkheim ascribed to the preliminary definition of the object as a "provisional" theoretical construct intended, above all, to "substitute an initial scientific notion for common-sense notions"[1] [*Mauss, text no. 5*]. In fact, to the extent that ordinary language and certain scholarly uses of ordinary words constitute the main vehicle for common representations of society, it is clear that the most indispensable preliminary for the controlled development of scientific notions is a logical and lexicological critique of ordinary language [*Goldthorpe and Lockwood, text no. 6*].

In observation and experimentation, the sociologist enters a relationship with his object which, being a social relationship, is never one of pure knowledge. The data therefore appear to him as living, singular, "all-too-human" configurations that tend to impose themselves as object structures. By taking apart the patent, concrete totalities that are presented to intuition and replacing them with the set of abstract criteria which define them sociologically—occupation, income, educational level, etc.—by forbidding the spontaneous inductions which, by a halo effect, lead one to extend the salient features of the apparently most "typical" individuals to a whole class, in short, by tearing apart the network of relationships which is constantly woven in experience, statistical analysis helps to make it possible to construct new relationships that are capable, by virtue of their unusual character, of forcing one to search for the higher-order relationships that would account for them.

In short, invention can never be reduced to a simple reading-off of the real, however disconcerting the "real" may be, because it always presupposes a break with the real and with the configurations that it offers to perception. Those who have an exaggerated view of the role of chance in scientific discovery, like Robert K. Merton with his analysis of the "serendipity pattern",[2] run the risk of reviving the most naive representations of invention, summed up in the paradigm of Newton's apple. Apprehending an unexpected fact presupposes at least the decision to devote methodical attention to the unexpected, and its heuristic value depends on the pertinence and cohesion of the system of questions that it calls into question. Everyone knows that the act of invention which leads to the solution of a sensorimotor or abstract problem has to break the relationships that are most apparent because most familiar, in order to bring out the new system of relations among the elements. In soci-

---

[1] P. Fauconnet and M. Mauss, article "Sociologie", *Grande Encyclopédie Française*, Vol. XXX, Paris, 1901, p. 173. It is no accident that those who try to find the origin and justification of "operationism" in Durkheim, and more precisely in his theory of the definition and the indicator (see for example R. K. Merton, *Social Theory and Social Structure*, Glencoe: Free Press, 1957), ignore the break function that Durkheim gave to definition. In fact, a number of so-called "operational" definitions are nothing more than a logically controlled or formalized version of common-sense ideas.

[2] R. K. Merton, *Social Theory and Social Structure*, Glencoe: Free Press, 1957, pp. 103–108.

ology as elsewhere, "serious research leads one to unite what is ordinarily separated or to distinguish what is ordinarily confused".[3]

1.2 The illusion of transparency and the principle of non-consciousness

All the techniques for performing breaks—logical critique of ideas, statistical testing of spurious self-evidences, radical and methodical challenging of appearances—remain powerless, however, until one has overthrown the very principle of spontaneous sociology, i.e. the philosophy of knowledge of the social and of human action on which it is based. Sociology cannot constitute itself as a science truly separated from common-sense notions unless it combats the systematic pretensions of spontaneous sociology with the organized resistance of a theory of knowledge of the social whose principles contradict, point by point, the presuppositions of the naive philosophy of the social. In the absence of such a theory, the sociologist can ostentatiously reject preconceptions while still building up the semblance of a scientific discourse on the foundations of the unconsciously accepted presuppositions on the basis of which spontaneous sociology generated these preconceptions. Artificialism, the illusory representation of the genesis of social facts according to which the social scientist can understand and explain these facts merely through "his own private reflection" rests, in the last analysis, on the presupposition of innate wisdom which, being rooted in the sense of familiarity, is also the basis of the spontaneous philosophy of knowledge of the social world. Durkheim's polemic against artificialism, psychologism, or moralism is simply the counterpart of the postulate that social facts "have a constant mode of being, a nature that does not depend on individual arbitrariness and from which there derive necesary relationships" [Durkheim, text no. 7]. Marx was saying the same thing when he posited that "in the social production of their life, men enter into determinate relations that are necessary and independent of their will"; and so was Weber, when he refused to reduce the cultural meaning of actions to the subjective intentions of the actors. Durkheim, who insists that the sociologist must enter the social world as one enters an unknown world, gives Marx credit for having broken with the illusion of transparency: "We think it a fertile idea that social life must be explained, not by the conception of it created by those who participate in it, but by profound causes which escape awareness."[4] [Durkheim, text no. 8].

---

[3] "For example, the science of religions has brought together impurity taboos and purity taboos in the same genus because they are all taboos; by contrast, it has carefully distinguished funeral rites from the cult of ancestors" (P. Fauconnet and M. Mauss, loc. cit., p. 173).

[4] É. Durkheim, review of Antonio Labriola, Essais sur la conception matérialiste de l'histoire [1897], in Émile Durkheim on Institutional Analysis, ed. M. Traugott, Chicago and London: University of Chicago Press, 1978, p. 127.

Such a convergence is easily explained.[5] What might be called the principle of non-consciousness, conceived as the *sine qua non* for the constitution of sociological science, is nothing other than the reformulation in the logic of that science of the principle of methodological determinism which no science can reject without disowning itself as a science.[6] This is what is obscured when the principle of non-consciousness is expressed in the vocabulary of the unconscious. Those who do so thereby transform a methodological postulate into an anthropological thesis, either by inferring a substance from the substantive, or by exploiting the polysemy of the term "unconscious" in order to reconcile attachment to the mysteries of internality with the imperatives of distanciation.[7] In fact, the principle of non-consciousness has no other function than to dispel the illusion that anthropology can constitute itself as a reflexive science and, by the same token, to define the methodological conditions on which it can be an experimental science[8] [*Durkheim, text no. 9; Simiand, text no. 10*].

[5] The charge of syncretism which might be provoked by the juxtaposition of texts by Marx, Weber, and Durkheim would be based on a confusion between the theory of knowledge of the social as the condition of possibility of a truly scientific sociological discourse and the theory of the social system (on this point, see pp. 4–5 and 29–31 and *Bachelard, text no. 2*). If this distinction is not granted, one would still have to examine whether the apparent disparateness does not derive from a continuing attachment to the traditional representation of a plurality of theoretical traditions. This representation is precisely what the theory of sociological knowledge challenges when, on the basis of experience of sociological practice, it questions certain oppositions which have become ritual institutions in another practice, that of the teaching of philosophy.

[6] As Claude Bernard puts it, "If a phenomenon were to present itself in an experiment with such a contradictory appearance that it were not attached in a necessary way to determinate conditions of existence, reason would have to *reject that fact* as non-scientific... since the admission of a fact without a cause, i.e. one whose conditions of existence are undetermined, is nothing more or less than the negation of science" (C. Bernard, *Introduction à l'étude de la médecine expérimentale*, Paris: Baillère, 1865, Ch. II, section 7).

[7] Although he remained trapped in the problematic of the "collective consciousness" by the conceptual instruments available to the social sciences of his time, Durkheim was careful to distinguish the principle on which the sociologist establishes the existence of non-conscious regularities from the assertion of an "unconscious" endowed with specific characteristics. Discussing the relationship between individual and collective representations, he writes: "All that we wish to say is that certain phenomena occur in us which are of a psychic order and which are nevertheless not known by our conscious selves. Whether they are known to some other unknown 'self' or whether they are outside the realm of all apprehension is not for us a matter of primary importance. All we wish to be conceded is that representational life extends beyond our present consciousness." Durkheim had already spelt out the difference between the methodological affirmation that there are non-conscious regularities in behaviours, and the affirmation of an "unconscious" as a specific psychic level. He thus suggests the role of language in the tendency to "realize" levels of consciousness that are distinguished in analysis. There are terms that call for a complement, verbs that call for a subject, etymologies that call for lateral meanings: "The idea of an unconscious representation and that of a consciousness without an ego that apprehends are basically equivalent. When we say that a mental fact is unconscious we mean simply that it is not apprehended. The question is merely which is the more suitable expression. From the point of view of the imagination both are equally difficult. It is no easier for us to imagine a representation without the thinking subject than to imagine a representation without consciousness" (É. Durkheim, "Individual and Collective Representations", in *Sociology and Philosophy*, trans. D. Pocock, London: Cohen & West, 1953, p. 23).

[8] This is what Lévi-Strauss suggests when he distinguishes Mauss's use of the idea of the

If spontaneous sociology reappears so insistently and in such different guises in would-be scientific sociology, this is probably because sociologists who seek to reconcile the scientific project with affirmation of the rights of the person—the right to free action and the right to full consciousness of action—or who simply fail to subject their practice to the fundamental principles of the theory of sociological knowledge, inevitably return to the naive philosophy of action and of the subject's relation to his action which is applied in their spontaneous sociology by subjects concerned to defend the lived truth of their experience of social action. The resistance that sociology arouses when it endeavours to dispossess immediate experience of its gnoseological privilege is inspired by the same humanistic philosophy of human action as a certain type of sociology which, by employing, for example, concepts such as "motivation", or preferring to address questions of "decision-making", fulfils, in its own way, the naive wish of every social subject. Seeking to remain the master and possessor of himself and of his own truth, wishing to know no other determinism than that of his own determinations (even if he grants them unconsciousness), the naive humanist who lurks inside every man resents as a "sociologistic" or "materialist" reduction every attempt to establish that the meaning of the most personal and "transparent" actions does not belong to the subject who performs them but to the complete system of relations in which and through which they are enacted. The spurious depths offered by the language of "motivations" (ostentatiously distinguished from simple "motives") perhaps have the function of safeguarding the philosophy of choice by draping it in the scientific prestige that is attached to the search for unconscious choices. Superficial prospecting for psychological functions as they are experienced—"reasons" or "gratifications"—often stands in the way of the search for the social functions that the "reasons" disguise and the fulfilment of which provides, as a by-product, the directly experienced gratifications.[9]

In opposition to this ambiguous method which serves to justify the endless exchange of services between common common-sense and scientific common-

unconscious from the Jungian idea of a collective unconscious "full of symbols and even filled with symbolized things which form a kind of substrate to it" and credits Mauss with having "referred constantly to the unconscious as providing the common and specific character of social facts" (C. Lévi-Strauss, Introduction to the Work of Marcel Mauss, trans. F. Baker, London: Routledge & Kegan Paul, 1987, p. 34, 36). It is also in this sense that he recognizes in Tyler's work the affirmation, "though still obscure and ambiguous", of "the principle that anthropology draws its originality from the unconscious nature of collective phenomena": "Even when interpretations are offered, they always have the character of rationalizations or secondary elaborations. There is rarely any doubt that the unconscious reasons for practising a custom or sharing a belief are remote from the reasons given to justify them" (Structural Anthropology, New York & London: Basic Books, 1963, p. 18).

[9] This is the meaning of Durkheim's critique of Spencer: "Social facts are not the simple development of individual natures, but the second are in large part only the prolongation of the first within consciousnesses. This proposition is very important, for the contrary point of view exposes the sociologist, at every moment, to mistaking the cause for the effect, and conversely." (On the Division of Labor in Society, trans. G. Simpson, New York: Macmillan, 1933, p. 349.)

E-state structuralism?

sense, a second principle of the theory of knowledge of the social has to be posited. It is simply the positive form of the principle of non-consciousness: social relations cannot be reduced to relationships between subjectivities driven by intentions or "motivations", because they are established between social conditions and positions and therefore have more reality than the subjects whom they link. Marx's criticisms of Stirner equally apply to the psychologists and sociologists who reduce social relationships to the representations which subjects form of them, and who suppose, on the basis of a practical artificialism, that one can transform objective relations by transforming the representations that subjects have of them: "Sancho does not want, for example, two individuals to be 'in contradiction' with each other, as bourgeois and proletarian ... he would like to have them enter into a purely personal relation, to associate with one another merely as individuals. He does not take into consideration that in the framework of the division of labour personal relations necessarily and inevitably develop into class relations and become fixed as such and that, therefore, all his talk amounts simply to a pious wish, which he expects to realize by exhorting the individuals of these classes to get out of their heads the idea of their 'contradiction' and their 'special' 'privilege' ... 'Contradiction' and the 'special' are abolished by a change of *opinion* and *wanting*."[10] Because of their implicit epistemology, and independently of the ideologies of "participation" and "communication" that they often serve, the classical techniques of social psychology incline one to privilege the representations of individuals at the expense of the objective relations in which they are engaged and which define the "satisfaction" or "dissatisfaction" they feel, the conflicts they experience, and the ambitions they express. By contrast, the principle of non-consciousness requires one to construct the system of objective relations in which individuals are located, which are expressed more adequately in the economy or morphology of groups than in the subjects' opinions and declared intentions. Far from the description of individual attitudes, opinions, and aspirations being able to provide the explanatory principle of the functioning of an organization, it is an understanding of the objective logic of organization that leads to the principle capable of additionally explaining individual attitudes, opinions, and aspirations.[11] This provisional objectivism, which is the precondition for grasping the objectified truth of the subjects, is also the precondition for a complete understanding of the experiential relationship that the subjects have with their truth as objectified in a system of objective relations.[12]

[10] K. Marx and F. Engels, *The German Ideology*, *Collected Works*, Vol. 5, London: Lawrence & Wishart, 1976, pp. 436–7.

[11] This reduction to psychology finds one of its preferred models in the study of small groups, sub-systems of action and interaction abstracted from the larger society. In innumerable surveys, isolated study of psychological conflicts between cliques takes the place of analysis of the objective relations between social forces.

[12] While for pedagogic reasons it was necessary to stress the preliminary of objectification that

E-state analysis is veductive, but... is it explanatory?

1.3 Nature and culture: substance and system of relations

If the principle of non-consciousness is only the reverse side of the principle of the primacy of relations, the latter principle must itself lead one to reject all attempts to define the truth of a cultural phenomenon independently of the system of historical and social relations in which it is located. The concept of human nature, the simplest and most natural of simple natures, though so often condemned, still circulates in the small change of concepts such as the "tendencies" or "motivations" appealed to by some economists, the "motivations" of social psychology, or the "needs" and "prerequisites" of functionalist analysis. The essentialist philosophy that was bound up with the notion of nature is still at work in some naive uses of criteria of analysis such as sex, age, race, or intellectual capacities, when these characteristics are conceived as natural, necessary, and eternal realities, whose efficacy can be grasped independently of the historical and social conditions that constitute them in their specificity for a given society and a given moment in time.

In fact, the concept of human nature is at work whenever sociologists transgress Marx's precept that a product of history should not be treated as an eternal nature, or Durkheim's precept that the social should be explained by the social and only by the social [*Marx, text no. 11; Durkheim, text no. 12*]. Durkheim's formula retains all its value so long as it expresses neither the demand for a "real object", really distinct from that of the other sciences of man, nor the sociologistic pretension to give a sociological account of all aspects of human reality, but serves only as a reminder of the methodological decision not to prematurely abdicate the right to sociological explanation, in other words, not to resort to an explanatory principle borrowed from another science (biology, psychology, etc.) until the efficacy of specifically sociological methods of explanation has been fully tested. By appealing to factors that are by definition trans-historical and trans-cultural, one is not only liable to

any sociological inquiry must perform in order to break with spontaneous sociology, there can be no question of reducing sociological explanation to the scale of an objectivism: "Sociology presupposes, by its very existence, the supersession of the fictitious opposition arbitrarily raised by subjectivism and objectivism. If sociology as an objective science is possible, this is because there are external, necessary relationships, independent of individual wills and, as it were, unconscious (in the sense that they are not available to simple reflection) which can only be grasped by means of a detour through objective observation and experimentation... . But, in contrast to the natural sciences, a total anthropology cannot be satisfied with constructing objective relationships because the experience of meanings is part of the total meaning of experience: even the sociology least suspected of subjectivism resorts to intermediate concepts that mediate between the subjective and the objective, such as alienation, attitude, or ethos. Sociology has to construct the system of relationships which encompasses both the objective meaning of behaviours organized in accordance with measurable regularities and the individual relations that subjects have with the objective conditions of their existence and with the objective meaning of their behaviours, a meaning that possesses them because they are dispossessed of it. In other words, description of objectified subjectivity sends one back to the description of the internalization of objectivity." (P. Bourdieu, *Un art moyen*, Paris: Editions de Minuit, 1970 [1st edn. 1965], pp. 18–20.)

give as an explanation precisely that which has to be explained, but one is condemned, at best, simply to give an account of the ways in which institutions resemble one another, while missing everything that makes their historical specificity or their cultural originality. As Lévi-Strauss puts it: "A discipline whose main, if not sole, aim is to analyse and interpret differences evades all problems when it takes into account only similarities. But at the same time it loses all means of distinguishing between the general truths to which it aspires and the trivialities with which it must be satisfied."[13] [*Weber, text no. 13*].

But even when the characteristics assigned to social man in his universality present themselves as "residues" or invariants yielded by an analysis of concrete societies, one has not seen the last of this essentialist philosophy, which owes the greater part of its seductiveness to the scheme of thought that "there is nothing new under the sun". From Pareto to Ludwig von Mises, there has been no lack of apparently historical analyses which merely give a sociological name to explanatory principles as unsociologized as "the inclination to create associations", "the need to manifest emotions through external acts", resentment, the pursuit of prestige, the insatiability of need, or the will to power.[14] It would be hard to understand why sociologists should so often deny themselves as sociologists by offering, with no further explanation, explanations that they should only accept as a last resort, if the temptation to explain in terms of the agents' declared opinions were not reinforced by the generic seduction of explanation by simple causes, which Bachelard tirelessly denounced as "epistemologically ineffectual".

1.4   Spontaneous sociology and the powers of language

If sociology is a science like others except that it encounters particular difficulty in being a science like others, this is fundamentally because of the particular relationship that is set up between scientific experience and naive experience of the social world and between the naive and scientific expressions of these experiences. It is not sufficient to denounce the illusion of transparency and to acquire the principles capable of breaking with the pre-

---

[13] C. Lévi-Strauss, *Structural Anthropology*, op. cit., p. 14.

[14] To establish that hostility to capitalism can only be inspired by the resentment of individuals whose social ambitions are frustrated, von Mises has to assume—independently of any sociological specification—a propensity to self-justification combined with an aspiration towards social ascension. Because some natural inferiority has lost them their chance of rising in society ("the biological equipment of a man rigidly restricts the field in which he can serve") and frustrated their ambitions, a number of people supposedly turn their resentment against capitalism. In short, as, according to Leibniz, it is inscribed in Caesar's destiny that he will cross the Rubicon, so the destiny of each social subject is contained in his nature (defined psychologically and sometimes biologically). Essentialism logically leads to a "sociodicy" (L. von Mises, *The Anti-Capitalistic Mentality*, Princeton, Toronto, London, New York: Van Nostrand, 1956, p. 143).

"status"?

suppositions of spontaneous sociology, in order to be free of the illusory constructs that it proposes. Ordinary language—"A legacy of words, a legacy of ideas", as Brunschvicg's title puts it—passes unnoticed, because it *is* so ordinary, but it carries in its vocabulary and syntax a petrified philosophy of the social, always ready to spring out of the common words, or complex expressions made up of common words, that the sociologist inevitably uses. When they come in the guise of erudite elaboration, prenotions are able to insinuate themselves into sociological discourse without thereby losing the credibility they derive from their origin. Warnings against the contamination of sociology by spontaneous sociology would be no more than verbal exorcisms if they were not accompanied by an effort to provide epistemological vigilance with the tools it needs to prevent the contamination of concepts by preconceptions. Because it is often premature, the ambition of simply rejecting ordinary language in favour of a perfect language, constructed and formalized by the sociologist, is liable to divert efforts away from the more urgent task of analysing the logic of ordinary language. Only such an analysis can provide the sociologist with the means of redefining common words within a system of expressly defined and methodologically clarified concepts, while critically examining the categories, problems, and schemes which scientific language borrows from ordinary language and which always threaten to reappear in the guise of the most formalized language. "The scrutiny of the grammar of a word," writes Wittgenstein, "weakens the position of certain fixed standards of our expression which had prevented us from seeing facts with unbiased eyes. Our investigation tried to remove this bias, which forces us to think that the facts *must* conform to certain pictures embedded in our language."[15] Failure to subject ordinary language, the primary instrument of the "construction of the world of objects",[16] to a methodological critique entails the risk of mistaking objects pre-constructed in and by ordinary language for data. The concern for rigorous definition remains inert and misleading until the unifying principle of the objects subjected to definition has been subjected to critical examination.[17] Like philosophers who allow the search for an essential defini-

[15] L. Wittgenstein, *The Blue and Brown Books*, Oxford: Basil Blackwell, 2nd ed., 1969, p. 43.

[16] See E. Cassirer, "Le langage et la construction du monde des objets", *Journal de psychologie normale et pathologique*, Vol. 30, pp. 18–44, 1933, and "The Influence of Language upon the Development of Scientific Thought", *The Journal of Philosophy*, Vol. 33, pp. 309–327, 1936.

[17] Maxime Chastaing extends Wittgenstein's critique of the conceptual games arising from play on the word "play": "People do not 'play' as either their woodwork or their institutions 'play'. They do not play on words as they play on a stage; or play the violin as they play the baton; play with money as they do with misfortune; play a waltz as they do [with] an opponent; they do not play with a ball as they 'play' a rod or play football. They may say that play in one situation is not play in another. They should say: 'playing is not playing'" (M. Chastaing, "Jouer n'est pas jouer", *Journal de psychologie normale et pathologique*, no. 3, pp. 303–326, juillet–septembre 1959). Chastaing's logical and linguistic critique of the word "play" would apply almost entirely to the notion of leisure, the uses ordinarily made of it, and the "essential" definitions that some sociologists give of it: "Substitute for the old word 'play' the neologism 'leisure'. Then, in some classic definitions of games, replace 'the will to play' or 'free activity'

tion of "games" to be foisted on them, on the grounds that ordinary language
has a single ordinary name for "children's games, the Olympic Games, mathematical games, and playing on words", sociologists who organize their scientific problematic around terms purely and simply borrowed from everyday
vocabulary are complying with the language that gives them their objects at the
very moment when they imagine they are simply submitting to the "given".
The divisions performed by ordinary vocabulary are not the only unconscious
and uncontrolled preconstructions that may find their way into sociological
discourse; and the technique for breaking with appearances that is offered by
the logical critique of spontaneous sociology would no doubt find an invalu-
able instrument in the nosography of ordinary language that is at least
sketched in the work of Wittgenstein [*Chastaing, text no. 14*].

Such a critique would give the sociologist the means of dispelling the semantic halo (the "fringe of meaning", as William James called it) that surrounds
the most common words, and of controlling the fluctuating meanings of all the
metaphors, even the seemingly most dead ones, which threaten to situate the
coherence of his discourse in an order other than that in which he seeks to set
his formulations. Here are a few of these images, which could be classified
according to the biological or mechanical realm to which they relate or the
implicit philosophies of the social that they suggest: equilibrium, pressure,
force, tension, reflection, root, body, cell, secretion, growth, regulation, ges-
tation, withering-away, etc. Under the cover of metaphor or homonymy,
these interpretative schemes, generally borrowed from the language of physics
or biology, are liable to smuggle in an inadequate philosophy of social life and,
above all, to discourage the search for specific explanation by supplying too
easily the appearance of explanation[18] [*Canguilhem, text no. 15*]. Thus a
psychoanalysis of the sociological mind would no doubt find a barely
transposed mechanical scheme in the many descriptions of the revolutionary
process as an explosion following oppression. Similarly, more often
unconsciously than consciously, studies of cultural diffusion resort to the
metaphor of the patch of oil to explain the extent and rate of dispersion of a
cultural feature. It would be a contribution to the clarification of the scientific
mind to concretely analyse the logic and functions of schemes such as "change
of scale", which is used to justify transferring observations or propositions
valid at the level of small groups to national or world society; or the idea of
"manipulation" or the "plot", which, being ultimately based on the illusion of

---

by a leisure defined as *voluntary* or *individual choice*, without worrying about directed leisure
and paid holidays or the ancient opposition *licet–libet*. Replace the 'pleasure of playing' with
the *hedonistic aim* of leisure, taking care not to sing *Rainy Sunday* followed by *I hate Sundays*.
Finally, replace a few gratuitous games by leisure *unfolding outside of any utilitarian purpose*, if
you can forget working-class or lower-middle-class gardening, or home decorating" (*ibid.*).

[18] This is only fair exchange: if sociology has suffered from the uncontrolled importation of
biological schemes and images, biology, in its time, had to strip concepts like "cell" and
"tissue" of their moral and political connotations (see below, G. *Canguilhem, text no. 15*).

transparency, has the spurious depth of explanation by reference to something hidden and gives the emotional satisfaction of denouncing cryptocracy; or, again, the idea of "action at a distance" which leads to the effects of the modern media being conceived in terms of the categories of magical thought.[19]

It can be seen that most of these metaphorical schemes are common to naïve utterances and erudite discourse, and indeed they derive their pseudo-explanatory force from this double life. As Yvon Belaval says, "if they convince us, it is because they make us switch and slide unwittingly between image and thought, concrete and abstract. Allied to imagination, this language surreptitiously transposes the certainty of sensory self-evidence into the certainty of logical self-evidence".[20] Hiding their common origin in the garb of scientific jargon, these mixed schemes escape refutation—either because they immediately offer a blanket explanation and awaken the most familiar experiences (for example, the concept of "mass society" may derive its resonance from experience of urban congestion, and the term "mutation" often evokes nothing more than banal experience of the extraordinary); or because they imply a spontaneous philosophy of history, like the scheme of cyclical return when it simply evokes the succession of the seasons, or the functionalist scheme when it has no content beyond the "it's designed to..." of naïve teleology; or because they encounter already popularized erudite schemes (e.g. understanding of a sociogram may rely on the buried image of hooked atoms). Pierre Duhem observed apropros of physics that in the self-evidences of common sense the scientist is always liable to find the dross of earlier theories which science has abandoned there. Given that everything predisposes the concepts and theories of sociology to enter the public domain, the sociologist is more likely than any other scientist to "withdraw from the fund of common-sense knowledge the money that theoretical science had itself deposited in that treasury, in order to return it to theoretical science".[21]

Scientific rigour by no means obliges one to forswear all use of analogical schemes for explanation or understanding, as is shown by the use that modern physics can make of paradigms—even mechanical ones—for didactic or heuristic purposes. But they still have to be used scientifically and methodically. Just as the physical sciences had to make a categorical break with animist representations of matter and action on matter, so the social sciences have to perform the epistemological break that can separate scientific interpretation from all artificialist or anthropomorphic interpretations of the functioning of society. The schemes used by sociological explanation have to be tested by being made completely explicit in order to avoid the contamination to which

[19] Chomsky shows that the language of Skinner, which makes a purely metaphorical use of technical terms, reveals its inconsistency as soon as it is subjected to logical and linguistic critique (N. Chomsky, review of B. F. Skinner, *Verbal Behavior*, *Language*, Vol. 35, pp. 16–58, 1959).

[20] Y. Belaval, *Les philosophes et leur langage*, Paris: Gallimard, 1952, p. 13.

[21] P. Duhem, *The Aim and Structure of Physical Theory*, New York: Atheneum, 1974, p. 261.

even the most purified schemes are exposed whenever they have a structural affinity with ordinary-language schemes.[22] Bachelard shows that the sewing machine could not be invented until designers stopped aping the actions of sewing by hand; and sociology would perhaps draw the best lesson from a correct representation of the epistemology of the natural sciences if it strove to verify at every moment that it is really constructing its own sewing machines, instead of transposing, with varying success, the spontaneous movements of naive practice.

1.5   The temptation to prophesy

Skvovetz & Fararo

Because it has more difficulty than any other science in shedding the illusion of transparency and making an irreversible break with prenotions, and because it is often called upon, willingly or not, to answer ultimate questions about the future of civilization, sociology is now predisposed to maintain an ill-defined relationship with an audience that is never merely a peer group. This relationship is always liable to return to the logic of the relationship between a successful author and his readers or even sometimes the prophet and his followers. More than any other specialist, the sociologist is exposed to the ambiguous, ambivalent verdict of non-specialists who feel themselves entitled to give credence to the analyses that are put forward, to the extent that they awaken the presuppositions of their spontaneous sociology, but who are equally disposed to contest the validity of a science that they approve only insofar as it is interchangeable with plain common sense. And indeed, when the sociologist does no more than take over common-sense objects of thought and common-sense thought on those objects, he has no arguments left to contest the common certainty that it is a human right to talk about everything that is human and to judge every discourse, albeit scientific, about what is human. And how could anyone fail to see himself as a bit of sociologist when the "sociologist"'s analyses so completely concur with the themes of everyday chatter and when the analyst's discourse and the discourses analysed are separated only by the fragile barrier of quotation marks? It is no accident that the banner of "humanism", which brings together those who believe that it is sufficient to be human to be a sociologist and those who come to sociology in order to satisfy an all-too-human passion for the "human", should serve as a rallying-point for all resistances to objective sociology, whether they are inspired by the illusion of reflexivity or the assertion of the imprescriptible rights of the free creative subject.

Yea, verily

A sociologist who communes with his object is never far from succumbing to indulgent complicity with the eschatological expectations that the wider

D!

[22] In this task of semantic control, sociology can arm itself not only with what Bachelard called the psychoanalysis of knowledge or with a purely logical and linguistic critique, but also with a sociology of the social use of schemes of interpretation of the social.

Contrast large N-studies of small vs groups versus large small-N studies of small groups.

intellectual audience is now tending to transfer to the "human sciences", which should rather be called sciences of man. As soon as he agrees to define his object and the functions of his discourse in accordance with the demands of his audience and presents anthropology as a system of total answers to the ultimate questions about man and his destiny, the sociologist makes himself a prophet, even if the style and themes of his message vary depending on whether, as a "minor State-accredited prophet", he speaks as a master of wisdom to a student audience's anxieties about intellectual, cultural, or political salvation; or whether he pursues the theoretical politics that Wright Mills ascribes to the "statesmen" of science and strives to unify the little kingdom of concepts over which he means to reign; or whether, as a marginal minor prophet, he offers a larger audience the illusion of gaining access to the last secrets of the sciences of man [*Weber, text no. 16; Berger, text no. 17*].

Sociological language, which, even in its most controlled uses, always draws on words from the common lexicon but uses them in rigorous and systematic senses, and which therefore always becomes equivocal as soon as it is spoken outside the circle of specialists, lends itself, more than other language, to fraudulent usages. The plays on polysemy made possible by the subterranean affinity of the most purified concepts with common schemes of thought encourage the *double-entendres* and knowing misunderstandings which give the prophetic double game its multiple and sometimes contradictory audiences. If, as Bachelard says, "every chemist has to struggle with the alchemist within himself", then every sociologist has to fight the social prophet that his audience wants him to be. The seemingly scientific elaboration of the self-evidences that are most likely to find a public because they are public self-evidences, and the use of a language with several registers, which juxtaposes common words and technical words intended to serve as their guarantee, provide the sociologist with his best mask when he seeks, despite everything, to disconcert those whose expectations he fulfils by giving a grandiose orchestration to their favourite themes and by offering a discourse whose esoteric appearance in fact serves the exoteric functions of a prophetic undertaking. Prophetic sociology naturally rediscovers the logic through which common sense constructs its explanations, when it is content to give a spuriously systematic character to the answers that spontaneous sociology gives to the existential questions that common experience encounters in scattered order. Of all simple explanations, explanations in terms of simple causes and simple natures are the ones most frequently invoked by prophetic sociologies, which find in such familiar phenomena as television the explanatory principle of "global mutations". "'Every truth'," says Nietzsche, "'is simple': is this not a double lie? Reducing something unknown to something known calms the mind and also gives a sense of power. First principle: any explanation is better than no explanation. As it is really just a matter of freeing oneself from distressing representations, one does not look too closely at the

part taken for the whole

means used; the first representation through which the unknown declares itself known does so much good that it is held to be true."[23]

Whether it has the function of reassuring or alarming, whether it works through *pars pro toto* fallacies, allusive and elliptical systematization or the powers of spontaneous analogy, this recourse to simple explanations always draws its explanatory power from its deep affinities with spontaneous sociology. As Marx puts it:

> "Such belletristic phrases, which relate everything to everything else by means of some analogy, may even appear profound the first time they are expressed, all the more so if they identify the most disparate things. Repeated, however, and then repeated with outright complacency as statements of scientific value, they are purely and simply ridiculous. Good only for belletristic sophomores and empty chatterboxes who defile all the sciences with their liquorice-sweet filth."[24]

1.6   Theory and the theoretical tradition

Running through Bachelard's epistemology is the question "why not?"; and for him the whole history of scientific reason is one of discontinuity, or rather of continuous breaks. He thereby denies science the certainties of a definitive heritage and reminds us that it can only progress by perpetually calling into question the very principles of its own constructs. But in order for an experiment like that of Michelson and Morley to be able to lead to a radical questioning of the fundamental postulates of theory, there has to be a theory capable of giving rise to such an experiment and of bringing out a disagreement as subtle as the one which emerges from that experiment. The situation of sociology is hardly conducive to the kind of dramatic demonstrations which carried negation to the very heart of an apparently perfected theory and made it possible to conceive non-Euclidean geometries or non-Newtonian physics. The sociologist is limited to the obscure efforts that are required by the endlessly renewed rejection of the entreaties of naive or erudite common sense. When he turns to review the theoretic past of his discipline, he finds not a constituted scientific theory but a *tradition*. Such a situation favours the division of the epistemological field into two camps that are opposed only by the opposing relations they maintain with one and the same representation of theory. Both are equally incapable of countering the traditional image of theory with a truly scientific theory, or at least a scientific theory of scientific theory, but while one group plunges recklessly into a practice that claims to find its own theoretical basis within itself, the others continue to maintain the traditionalist relationship to tradition which communities of *literati* customarily maintain

large # of groups

[23] F. Nietzsche, *Götzen-Dämmerung. Kritische Studienausgabe*, Vol. 6, ed. G. Colli and M. Montinari. Munich: Deutscher Taschenbuch Verlag, and Berlin & New York: de Gruyter, 1988, pp. 59.

[24] K. Marx, *Grundrisse: Foundations of the Critique of Political Economy*, translated with a foreword by M. Nicolaus, Harmondsworth: Penguin, 1973, p. 293.

with a corpus in which the declared principles mask unconscious essential presuppositions and whose semantic or logical coherence may be no more than the manifest expression of ultimate choices based on a philosophy of man and history rather than a consciously constructed set of axioms. — Estates — paper

Those who strive to compile a summa of the theoretical contributions bequeathed by the "founding fathers" of sociology are taking on a task comparable to that of the theologians and canonists of the Middle Ages, who brought together the totality of the arguments and questions bequeathed by the "authorities", whether canonical texts or Fathers of the Church.[25] The modern-day "theoreticians" of sociology might well agree with Whitehead that "a science has to forget its founders", but their syntheses may differ less than they seem from mediaeval compilations. The demand for "cumulativeness" to which they ostentatiously subscribe is in many cases perhaps nothing more than the Scholastic demand for reconciliation of contraries, reinterpreted by reference to another intellectual tradition. As Erwin Panofsky observes, for the Scholastics "it could not escape notice that the authorities, and even passages of Scripture itself, often conflicted with one another. There was no way out then but to accept them just the same and to reinterpret them over and over again until they could be reconciled".[26] This is indeed the essential logic of a "theory" which, like that of Talcott Parsons, is never more than the endless reworking of theoretical elements artificially extracted from a select body of authorities,[27] or, equally, the logic of a doctrinal corpus like the œuvre of Georges Gurvitch, which, both in its topics and its organization, presents all the features of the mediaeval canonists' collections, vast confrontations of contradictory authorities crowned by the concordantiae violentes of the final syntheses.[28] Nothing is more opposed to the architectonic reason of sociological grand theories, which can digest all theories, all theoretical critiques, and even all empirical phenomena, than the polemical reason which,

[25] This traditional relation to a tradition is always observed in the early stages of the history of a science. Bachelard shows that, in the scientific works of the 18th century, there is a parasitic erudition that reveals the unorganized state of the "scientific city" and its dependence on worldly society. If "Baron de Marivetz and Goussier, dealing with fire in their famous *Physique du Monde* (Paris, 1870), saw it as a duty and a credit to themselves to examine forty-six different theories before proposing the correct one, their own", this was because their science "had not yet broken with even its most primitive past; and also because, lacking its own organization and autonomous rules, scientific discussion was always modelled on polite conversation" (G. Bachelard, *La formation de l'esprit scientifique*, 4th edn, Vrin: Paris, 1965, p. 27). See below, *Bachelard, text no. 42*, p. 233.

[26] E. Panofsky, *Gothic Architecture and Scholasticism*, Latrobe (Penn.): Archabbey Press, 1951, p. 65.

[27] One of the most artificial features of Talcott Parsons' *The Structure of Social Action* is the contortions it forces on the classic doctrines to make them acknowledge their cumulativeness.

[28] Theoretical traditionalism perhaps survives through the opposition it encounters from the most positivist practitioners and even *in* what they oppose to it. Does it have to be pointed out that, as Politzer puts it, "however sincere one's intention, however great the desire for precision, one cannot turn Aristotle's physics into experimental physics"? (G. Politzer, *Critique des fondements de la psychologie*, Paris: Rieder, 1928, p. 6.)

"through its dialectics and its critiques", has led to the modern theories of physics; and consequently, there is every difference in the world between the "super-object", "the result of an objectivity that only retains from an object that which it has criticized", and the sub-object, born of the concessions and compromises through which the great empires of would-be universal theories are established [*Bachelard, text no. 18*].

Given the nature of the works that the sociological community recognizes as theoretical, and more especially the form of relationship to these theories that is encouraged by the logic of their transmission (which is often inseparable from the logic of their production), the break with the traditional theories and the traditional relation with these theories is simply a particular case of the break with spontaneous sociology. Every sociologist has to reckon with erudite presuppositions that threaten to force their problematics, themes, and schemes of thought on him. For example, there are problems that sociologists fail to pose because the tradition of the discipline does not recognize them as worthy of being posed or does not offer the conceptual tools or the techniques that would make it possible to treat them in canonical fashion; and conversely, there are questions they feel bound to pose because they rank high in the consecrated hierarchy of research subjects. Likewise, even the ritual denunciation of common prenotions is liable to degenerate into an academic prenotion tending to discourage any challenging of erudite prenotions.

If traditional theory has to be fought with the same weapons as are needed against spontaneous sociology, this is because the most erudite constructs borrow not only their schemes of thought but also their fundamental project from the logic of common sense. They have not made the "break" with the "simple spirit of order and classification" which, as Bachelard observes, characterizes the "true modern scientific mind". When Whitehead observes that classificatory logic, a half-way house between the immediate concreteness of the individual thing and the complete abstraction of mathematical notions, is always "lifted from incomplete abstractions",[29] he accurately characterizes those would-be universal theories of social action which, like that of Parsons, succeed in presenting the appearances of generality and exhaustiveness only insofar as they use "concrete–abstract" schemes entirely analogous in their function and functioning to the genera and species of an Aristotelian classification. And Robert K. Merton, with his theory of "theories of the middle range", is able to renounce the now untenable ambitions of a general theory of the social system, without however calling into question the logical presuppositions of these concept-classifying and clarifying undertakings inspired by pedagogic rather than scientific purposes. The cross-tabulation procedure—also known by its more dignified name of "substruction of an attribute space to a typology"—no doubt owes its recurrence in academic

[29] A. N. Whitehead, *Science and the Modern World*, New York: Mentor, 1925, p. 34.

sociology (one thinks of Merton's typology of anomie, or the multiple typologies, and their multiple dimensions, in Gurvitch's work) to the fact that it favours the indefinite inter-fertilization of a finite batch of lineages of academic concepts. To seek to add together all the concepts bequeathed by the tradition and all the consecrated theories, or to seek to incorporate everything that exists into a kind of casuistry of the real, by means of the didactic exercises in universal taxonomy which, as Jevons observes, are characteristic of the Aristotelian age of social science and "will be found to break down as the deeper similarities of the objects come to be detected",[30] is to ignore the fact that true cumulation presupposes breaks, that theoretical progress presupposes the integration of new data at the cost of a critical challenging of the bases of the theory that the new data put to the test. In other words, if it is true that every scientific theory clings to the "given" as a historically constituted, provisional code which, for the space of an epoch, constitutes the sovereign principle of an unequivocal distinction between the true and the false, the history of a science is always discontinuous because the refining of the interpretative grid never goes on forever but always culminates in the substitution of one grid for another.

1.7   Theory of sociological knowledge and theory of the social system

A theory is neither the highest common denominator of all the grand theories of the past nor, *a fortiori*, is it that part of sociological discourse which opposes empiricism simply by escaping experimental control. Neither is it the gallery of canonical theories in which theory is reduced to the history of theory; nor a system of concepts that recognizes no other criterion of scientificity than that of semantic coherence and refers to itself instead of measuring itself against the facts; nor, on the other hand, is it the compilation of minor true facts or fragmentarily demonstrated relationships, which is merely the positivists' reinterpretation of the traditional ideal of the sociological *Summa*.[31] Both the traditional representation of theory and the positivist representation, which assigns theory no other function than that of representing a set of experimental laws as fully, as simply, and as exactly as possible, dispossess theory of its primordial function, which is to secure the epistemo-

---

[30] W. S. Jevons, *The Principles of Science*, London: Methuen, 1892, p. 691.

[31] An inventory of the propositions regarded as established is clearly useful as a convenient way of mobilizing acquired information (see B. Berelson and G. A. Steiner, *Human Behavior: An Inventory of Scientific Findings*, New York: Harcourt, Brace & World, 1964). But this kind of "mechanically empirical" compilation of decontextualized data cannot seriously be presented as a theory, or as a fragment of a future theory, the realization of which is in fact left to future research. Similarly, the theoretical work that consists in testing the coherence of a system of concepts, even without reference to empirical research, has a positive function — so long as it does not present itself as the construction of scientific theory.

logical break and to lead to the principle capable of accounting for the contradictions, incoherences, and lacunae that this principle alone can bring to light in the system of established laws.

But warnings against the theoretic abdication of empiricism can never legitimate the terroristic admonitions of the theoreticians, who, by excluding the possibility of regional theories, trap research in an all-or-nothing dilemma in which it has to choose between pointillist hyper-empiricism and a universal general theory of the social system. Reminders of the urgent need for a sociological theory may express either the untenable demand for a general, universal theory of social formations or the ineluctable demand for a theory of sociological knowledge. This confusion, which is encouraged by the sociological doctrines of the 19th century, has to be cleared away, in order to make it possible to avoid the eclecticism or syncretism of the theoretical tradition while recognizing the convergence of the great classical theories on the fundamental principles that define the theory of knowledge as the basis of *partial theories*, limited to a definite order of facts. In the first sentences of his introduction to the *Cambridge Economic Handbooks*, Keynes wrote: "The theory of economics does not furnish a body of settled conclusions immediately applicable to policy. It is a method rather than a doctrine, an apparatus of the mind, a technique of thinking, which helps its possessor to draw correct conclusions."[32] The theory of sociological knowledge, understood as a system of rules governing the production of all possible sociological acts and discourses, and only those, is the generative principle of the various partial theories of the social (such as the theory of matrimonial exchanges or the theory of cultural diffusion), and as such it is the unifying principle of specifically sociological discourse, which is not to be confused with a unitary theory of the social.[33] As Michael Polanyi observes: "Natural science is regarded as a knowledge of things, while knowledge *about* science is held to be quite distinct from science, and is called 'meta-science'. We have then three logical levels: a first floor for the objects of science, a second for science itself and a third for meta-science, which includes the logic and epistemology of science."[34] To confuse the theory of sociological knowledge, which is at the level of meta-science, with the partial theories of the social that implement the principles of sociological meta-science in the systematic organization of a set of relations and principles explaining those relations, is to condemn oneself either to renounce the practice of science by expecting a science of meta-science to stand in for

[32] *The Collected Writings of J. M. Keynes*, Vol. XII, London: Macmillan, 1983, p. 856.
[33] The social definition of the relationship between theory and practice, which is homologous with the traditional opposition between the noble tasks of the scholar and the painstaking labours of the craftsman and, in France at least, with the academic opposition between the brilliant and the solid, is revealed as much in the reluctance to recognize theory when it is embodied in partial research as in the difficulty of actualizing it in research.
[34] M. Polanyi, *Personal Knowledge: Towards a Critical Philosophy*, London: Routledge & Kegan Paul, 1958, p. 344.

science, or to treat a necessarily empty synthesis of general theories (or even partial theories) of the social as the meta-science that is the precondition for any possible scientific knowledge.

Part Two
Constructing the object

2 The social fact is constructed: the forms of empiricist surrender

(handwritten: E-state structuralism)

"The point of view," says Saussure, "creates the object." In other words, a science cannot be defined by a domain of reality that is distinctively its own. As Marx observes, "the concrete totality is a totality of thoughts, concrete in thought, in fact a product of thinking and comprehending... . The totality as it appears in the head, as a totality of thoughts, is a product of the thinking head, which appropriates the world in the only way it can, a way different from the artistic, religious, and practical appropriation of this world. The real subject retains its autonomous existence outside the head just as before... ."[1] [*Marx, text no. 19*]. The same epistemological principle, an instrument for breaking with naive realism, is formulated by Max Weber: "It is not the 'actual' interconnections of 'things' but the *conceptual* interconnections of *problems* which define the scope of the various sciences. A new 'science' emerges where new problems are pursued by new methods, and truths are thereby discovered which open up significant new points of view"[2] [*Weber, text no. 20*].

(handwritten: Final paper)

Even if the physical sciences can sometimes be divided into sub-units defined, like selenography or oceanography, by the juxtaposition of diverse disciplines applied to one domain of reality, this is only for pragmatic purposes. Scientific research is in fact organized around constructed objects that no longer have anything in common with the units divided up by naive perception. *(handwritten: ← !.)* The links that still exist between scientific sociology and the categories of spontaneous sociology might be seen in the fact that it often conforms to classifications by apparent domains—sociology of the family or sociology of leisure, rural sociology or urban sociology, sociology of youth or sociology of old age. More generally, empiricist epistemology conceives the relations between neighbouring sciences—psychology and sociology, for example—as border conflicts, because it sees the scientific division of labour as a real division of reality.

Durkheim's principle that "social facts should be treated as things" (with the emphasis on "treated as") can legitimately be seen as the specific equivalent of the theoretic *coup d'état* through which Galileo constituted the object of modern physics as a system of quantifiable relationships, or the methodic

[1] K. Marx, *Grundrisse: Foundations of the Critique of Political Economy*, trans. M. Nicolaus, Harmondsworth: Penguin, 1973, p. 101.
[2] M. Weber, *The Methodology of the Social Sciences*, trans. and ed. E. A. Shils and H. A. Finch, New York: Free Press, 1949, p. 68.

decision whereby Saussure gave linguistics its existence and its object by distinguishing *langue* and *parole*. Durkheim does indeed formulate a similar distinction when, making completely explicit the epistemological significance of the cardinal rule of his method, he asserts that none of the implicit rules which constrain social subjects "are to be found wholly in the application made of them by individuals, since they can exist without being applied at the time".[3] In the Preface to the second edition of the *Rules*, he makes it quite clear that it is a question of defining a mental attitude and not of assigning an ontological status to the object [*Durkheim, text no. 21*]. And if the quasi-tautology whereby science constitutes itself by constructing its object in opposition to common sense does not impose itself by its sheer self-evidence, that is because nothing is more opposed to the self-evidences of common sense than the distinction between the "real" object, preconstructed by perception, and the object of science as a system of expressly constructed relations.[4]

The task of constructing the object cannot be avoided without abandoning research to preconstructed objects—social facts demarcated, perceived, and named by spontaneous sociology[5] or "social problems" whose claim to exist as sociological problems rises with the degree of social reality they have for the sociological community.[6] It is not sufficient to increase the intersection of criteria borrowed from common experience (as in the innumerable research projects of the type "leisure activities of adolescents in a high-rise estate in the eastern suburbs of Paris") and to construct an object which, being the product of a series of real divisions, remains a common object and does not attain the status of a scientific object simply because it lends itself to the application of scientific techniques. Allen H. Barton and Paul F. Lazarsfeld are no doubt right to point out that expressions such as "conspicuous consumption" or "white-collar crime" construct specific objects, irreducible to common objects, by drawing attention to known facts which, by the simple effect of

---

[3] É. Durkheim, *The Rules of Sociological Method*, trans. W. D. Halls, London: Macmillan, 1982, p. 55.

[4] A beginning, or a new beginning, is one of the most favourable situations for making explicit the principles of construction that characterize a science. It is probably for this reason that the polemical arguments with which the Durkheimians put forward the principle of the "specificity of social facts" retain even today a value that is not merely archaeological.

[5] Many beginners in sociology proceed as if they only had to find an object endowed with social reality in order to possess an object endowed with sociological reality. Quite apart from the countless village monographs, one could point to all the research subjects which have no other problematic than simple *designation* of social groups or problems perceived by the common consciousness at a given moment.

[6] It is no accident that domains of sociology such as study of the modern media or leisure are those most permeable to the problematics and schemes of thought of spontaneous sociology. Not only do these objects already exist as obligatory themes of common conversation on modern society, but they derive their ideological force from the fact that when the intellectual studies the relation of the working class to culture he is still concerned with his relation to himself. The intellectual's relation to culture contains the whole question of the intellectual's relation to the intellectual condition, which is never more dramatically raised than in the question of his relation to the working class as a class dispossessed of culture.

juxtaposition, take on a new meaning.[7] But the need to construct specific labels which, even if they are composed of words from everyday vocabulary, construct new objects by constructing new relationships between aspects of things, is little more than an index of the first degree of the epistemological break with the preconstructed objects of spontaneous sociology. The concepts most capable of disconcerting common notions do not possess, in their isolated state, the power to offer systematic resistance to the systematic logic of ideology: the analytical and formal rigour of so-called "operational" concepts is quite different from the synthetic and real rigour of what have been called "systemic" concepts because their use presupposes permanent reference to the complete system of their interrelationships.[8] An object of research, however minor or partial, can only be defined and constructed in terms of a *theoretical problematic* which makes it possible to conduct a systematic questioning of the aspects of reality that are brought into relationship by the question that is put to them.

2.1   "The abdications of empiricism"

It is only too readily acknowledged nowadays that, as all traditional thinking on science has maintained, there can be no observation or experimentation that does not involve hypotheses. The definition of the process of science as a dialogue between hypothesis and experience can, however, easily degenerate into the anthropomorphic image of an exchange in which the two partners take perfectly symmetrical and interchangeable roles. But it should not be forgot-

---

[7] A. H. Barton and P. F. Lazarsfeld, "Some Functions of Qualitative Analysis in Social Research", in S. M. Lipset and N. J. Smelser (eds.), *Sociology: The Progress of a Decade*, Englewood Cliffs (N.J.): Prentice-Hall, 1961, pp. 95–122.

[8] Concepts and propositions exclusively defined by their "operational" character may be no more than a logically irreproachable formulation of prenotions and as such, they are to systematic concepts and theoretical propositions as the pre-constructed object is to the constructed object. If emphasis is placed exclusively on the operational character of definitions, one is liable to present a simple classificatory terminology as a genuine theory, leaving it to future research to deal with the question of the systematicity of the concepts proposed and even their theoretical fruitfulness, as S. C. Dodd does (*Dimensions of Society*, New York, 1942, or "Operational Definitions Operationally Defined", *American Journal of Sociology*, Vol. 48, pp. 482–489, 1942–43). As Hempel puts it: "In the contemporary methodological literature of psychology and the social sciences, the need for 'operational definitions' is often emphasized to the neglect of the requirement of systematic import, and occasionally the impression is given that the most promising way of furthering the growth of sociology as a scientific discipline is to create a large supply of 'operationally defined' terms of high determinacy and uniformity of usage, leaving it to subsequent research to discover whether these terms lend themselves to the formulation of fruitful principles. But concept formation in science cannot be separated from theoretical considerations; indeed, it is precisely the discovery of concept systems with theoretical import which advances scientific understanding; and such discovery requires scientific inventiveness and cannot be replaced by the—certainly indispensable, but also definitely insufficient—operationist or empiricist requirement of empirical import alone" (C. J. Hempel, *Fundamentals of Concept Formation in Empirical Research*, Chicago and London: University of Chicago Press, 1952, p. 47).

ten that reality never has the initiative in this exchange, since it cannot reply unless it is questioned. Bachelard put it another way when he postulated that "the epistemological vector... points from the rational to the real and not, as all philosophers from Aristotle to Bacon professed, from the real to the general" [*Bachelard, text no. 22*].

If it has to be recalled that "theory dominates the experimental work from its initial planning up to the finishing touches in the laboratory",[9] or again, that "without theory, it is impossible to regulate a single instrument or to interpret a single reading",[10] this is because the representation of the experiment as the protocol of an observation free of any theoretical implication shows through in countless ways, for example in the still widespread conviction that there are facts which can exist as such after the demise of the theory for which and by which they were made. Yet the sad fate of the notion of totemism (which Lévi-Strauss himself compares to that of hysteria) would be sufficient to destroy belief in the scientific immortality of facts. Once the theory that held them together was abandoned, the "facts" of totemism fell back into the dust of amorphous data from which a theory had briefly raised them and from which any new theory cannot resurrect them without giving them another meaning.[11]

Anyone who has ever tried to carry out secondary analysis of material collected in relation to another problematic, however neutral-seeming, knows that even the richest of data can never fully and adequately answer questions for which, and by which, they were not constructed. It is not a question of challenging on principle the validity of using second-hand material, but rather of recalling the epistemological conditions of this work of *retranslation*, which always deals with (well or badly) constructed facts and not with data. Such an effort of interpretation, of which Durkheim gave an early example in *Suicide*, might even constitute the best training in epistemological vigilance, since it requires one to make explicit, in a methodical way, the problematics and the principles of object construction that are implied both in the material and in the new treatment applied to it. Those who expect miracles from the mythical triad, *archives*, *data*, and *computers*, do not understand the difference between the constructed objects which are scientific facts (collected by questionnaire or in an ethnographic inventory), and the real objects which are conserved in museums and which, through their "concrete surplus", offer unlimited possibilities for new constructions as new questions are put to them. If these epistemological preliminaries are ignored, there is a great risk of treating identical things differently and different things identically, of comparing the incomparable and failing to compare the comparable, because in sociology even the most objective "data" are obtained by applying grids (age groups,

[9] K. R. Popper, *The Logic of Scientific Discovery*, London: Hutchinson, 1959, p. 107.
[10] P. Duhem, *The Aim and Structure of Physical Theory*, New York: Atheneum, 1974, p. 182.
[11] C. Lévi-Strauss, *Totemism*, London: Merlin Press, 1964, p. 1.

income brackets, etc.) which involve theoretical presuppositions and therefore overlook information which another construction of the facts might have grasped.[12] The positivism which treats facts as data is condemned either to unrecognized and therefore fallacious reinterpretations, or to simple confirmations obtained in technical conditions that are as similar as possible. In either case it uses methodological reflection on the conditions of replication as a substitute for epistemological reflection on secondary reinterpretation.

Only an impoverished image of the experimental process can make "submission to the facts" the sole imperative. As the exponent of a contested science, the sociologist is particularly tempted to reassure himself as to the scientific character of his discipline by trying to outdo the demands he attributes to the natural sciences. Reinterpreted in accordance with a logic that is none other than that of cultural borrowing, the scientific imperative of submission to the fact leads to pure and simple surrender to the given. Those practitioners of the social sciences who have an outdated faith in what Nietzsche called "the dogma of immaculate perception" need to be reminded that, as Alexandre Koyré put it, "direct experience played no part, other than as an obstacle, in the birth of classical science".[13]

Indeed, everything takes place as if the ideal which radical empiricism offers to the sociologist were that of his own disappearance as such. Sociologists would be less prone to the temptations of empiricism if it were sufficient to remind them, in Poincaré's words, that "facts do not speak". It is perhaps the curse of the human sciences that they deal with a *speaking object*. When the sociologist counts on the facts to supply the problematic and the theoretical concepts that will enable him to construct and analyse the facts, there is always a danger that these will be supplied from the informants' mouths. It is not sufficient for the sociologist to listen to the subjects, faithfully recording their statements and their reasons, in order to account for their conduct and even for the reasons they offer; in doing so, he is liable to replace his own preconceptions with the preconceptions of those whom he studies, or with a spuriously scientific and spuriously objective blend of the spontaneous sociology of the "scientist" and the spontaneous sociology of his object.

Those who choose to restrict their means of interrogating the real (and of interrogating their methods for doing so) to elements that are in fact created by an interrogation that refuses to admit it *is* an interrogation, and who thereby deny that observation presupposes construction, inevitably end up observing a void that they have unwittingly constructed. Countless examples could be cited of cases in which a sociologist who imagines he is opting for neutrality by

---

[12] See P. Bourdieu and J.-C. Passeron, "La comparabilité des systèmes d'éducation", in R. Castel and J.-C. Passeron (eds.), *Education, démocratie et développement*, Cahiers du Centre de sociologie européenne, no. 4, Paris–The Hague: Mouton, 1967, pp. 20–58.

[13] A. Koyré, *Etudes galiléennes*, Vol. I, *A l'aube de la science classique*, Paris: Hermann, 1940, p. 7. And he adds: "The 'experiments' which Galileo claimed then or later, even those he really conducted, were not and could never be more than mental experiments" (*ibid.*, p. 72).

deriving the elements of his questionnaire exclusively from his subjects' discourse, invites his subjects to judge judgements formulated by other subjects, with the result that he either tries to situate his subjects in relation to judgements that he cannot himself situate, or sees the expression of a deep-rooted attitude in superficial judgements provoked by the necessity of responding to unnecessary questions. This is not all: the sociologist who refuses the controlled, conscious construction of his distance from the real and his action on reality may not only impose questions on his subjects that their experience does not pose them and omit the questions that it does pose them, but he may also naively pose them the questions he poses himself about them, through a positivist confusion between the questions that objectively arise for them and the questions they consciously pose themselves. Thus the sociologist is spoilt for choice when, led astray by a false philosophy of objectivity, he undertakes to nullify himself as a sociologist.

It is not surprising that hyperempiricism, which abdicates the right and duty of theoretical construction in favour of spontaneous sociology, rediscovers the spontaneous philosophy of human action which sees it as the self-transparent expression of a conscious, willed deliberation. Many studies of motivations (especially retrospective ones) presuppose that subjects can momentarily possess the objective truth of their behaviour (and that they continuously preserve an adequate memory of it), as if the representation they formed of their decisions or actions owed nothing to retrospective rationalization.[14] No doubt one can and should collect the most unreal discourses—but only so long as they are seen not as the explanation of behaviour but as an aspect of the behaviour to be explained. Whenever he believes he can avoid the task of constructing the facts in relation to a theoretical problematic, the sociologist submits himself to a construction of which he is unaware; in extreme cases he will collect nothing more than the fictitious discourses that the subjects devise to cope with the situation of inquiry and to answer artificial questions, or even with the supreme artifice of a lack of questions. In short, whenever the sociologist renounces his epistemological privilege, he sanctions a spontaneous sociology.

2.2   Hypotheses or presuppositions

It could very easily be shown that all scientific practice, even and especially when it blindly claims allegiance to the blindest empiricism, involves theoretical presuppositions and that the sociologist's only choice is between

[14] The notion of opinion surely owes its practical and theoretical success to the fact that it combines all the illusions of the atomistic philosophy of thought and the spontaneous philosophy of the relationship between thought and action, starting with the illusion of the privileged role of verbal expression as an indicator of dispositions towards action. It is not surprising that sociologists who have a blind faith in "opinion polls" constantly confuse declarations of action, or worse, declarations of intention, with the probabilities of action.

unconscious, and therefore unchecked and incoherent, hypotheses and a body
of hypotheses methodically constructed with a view to experimental proof. To
refuse the explicit formulation of a body of hypotheses based on a theory
amounts to accepting presuppositions that are nothing other than the prenotions of spontaneous sociology and ideology, i.e. the questions and concepts that one has as a social subject when one wants to have none as a
sociologist. Thus Elihu Katz shows how the authors of the study published as
The People's Choice, whose research was based on the prenotion of the
"mass", an amorphous, atomized audience of receivers, were consequently
unable to grasp empirically what is in fact the most important phenomenon in
cultural diffusion, namely "two-step flow"[15] [*Katz, text no. 23*].

Even if it were to break free of the presuppositions of spontaneous sociology, sociological practice could never achieve the empiricist ideal of presuppositionless recording, if only because it uses recording techniques and tools.
"To set up apparatus to make a measurement is in itself to ask nature a
question," said Max Planck. Measurement and measuring instruments and,
more generally, all the operations of sociological practice, from drawing up
questionnaires and coding to statistical analysis, are so many theories in
action, inasmuch as they are conscious or unconscious procedures for constructing facts and relations between facts. The less conscious the theory
engaged in a practice—the theory of knowledge of the object and the theory of
the object—the less controlled it will be, and the less well adapted to the
specific object. When, as often happens, the term "methodology" is used to
dignify what is never more than the decalogue of technological precepts, one
evades the real methodological question, which is that of the choice among
techniques (metrical or not) by reference to the epistemological significance of
the effects that the chosen techniques have on the object and the theoretical
significance of the questions that one wants to put to the object to which they
are applied.

For example, a technique as apparently irreproachable and inevitable as
random sampling may completely destroy the object of research, whenever
this object owes something to the structure of the groups which random

[15] E. Katz, "The Two-Step Flow of Communication: An Up-to-Date Report on an Hypothesis",
Public Opinion Quarterly, Vol. 21, pp. 61–78, Spring 1957: "Of all the ideas in *The People's
choice*, [...] the two-step flow hypothesis is probably the one that was least well documented by
empirical data. And the reason for this is clear: the design of the study did not anticipate the
importance which interpersonal relations would assume in the analysis of the data. Given the
image of the atomized audience which characterized so much of mass media research, the
surprising thing is that interpersonal influences attracted the attention of the researchers at all."
It can be seen how strongly a technique can exclude an aspect of a phenomenon, when one
knows that rural sociologists and ethnologists, working with other problematics and other
techniques, had much earlier grasped the logic of two-step flow. There are countless examples
of such discoveries which have to be rediscovered; for example, A. H. Barton and P. F.
Lazarsfeld point out that the problem of "informal groups", which other sociologists had long
been aware of, emerged as a belated and "surprising discovery" for the Western Electric
researchers (see "Some Functions of Qualitative Analysis", *loc. cit.*).

sampling precisely has the effect of annihilating. Thus, Katz also observes that "for studying that part of the flow of influence which had to do with contacts among people, the study design fell short, since it called for a random sample of individuals abstracted from their social environments [... .] Because every man in a random sample can speak only for himself, opinion leaders in the 1940 voting study had to be located by self-designation". And he further notes that this technique "does not permit a comparison of leaders with their respective followers, but only of leaders and non-leaders in general".[16] It can be seen how the seemingly most neutral technique brings in an implicit theory of the social, that of the public conceived as an "atomized mass", i.e., as it so happens, the theory consciously or unconsciously engaged in the research project which, by a kind of pre-established harmony, armed itself with this technique.[17] Another theory of the object and, by the same token, another definition of the techniques would have called for the use of another sampling technique, such as cluster sampling. By taking the totality of the members of social units that are themselves chosen at random (an industrial plant, a family, a village, etc.), it becomes possible to study the complete network of the relations of communication that may be set up within these groups, it being understood that this method, which is particularly adequate in this particular case, becomes less and less effective as the cluster becomes more homogeneous and as the phenomenon whose variations are to be studied depends more on the criterion by which the cluster is defined. Every statistical operation needs to be subjected to epistemological questioning. As Simiand puts it: "The best statistics (not to mention the less good) must only be asked and should only be made to say what they do say, and only in the way and in the conditions in which they say it."[18] It follows that in each case one has to consider what they do and can say, within what limits and in what conditions [*Simiand, text no. 24*].

2.3 The spurious neutrality of techniques: constructed object or artefact

The imperative of "ethical neutrality" which Max Weber counterposed to the moralizing naïveté of social philosophy is now tending to turn into a

---

[16] E. Katz, *loc. cit.*, p. 64.

[17] C. Kerr and L. H. Fisher demonstrate similar affinities between technique and presuppositions in the research of E. Mayo and his school: daily observation of face-to-face contacts and interpersonal relations within the plant implies the diffuse conviction that "the small work team is the essential cell in the organization of the firm and this group and its members essentially respond to determinations... . Mayo's system flows automatically from two fundamental choices. Once these choices had been made, everything was given—the methods, the field of interest, the practical prescriptions, the problems selected for research [and in particular] indifference to problems of class, ideology and power" ("Plant Sociology: The Elite and the Aborigines", in M. Komarovsky [ed.], *Common Frontiers of the Social Sciences*, New York: Free Press, 1957, pp. 281–309).

[18] F. Simiand, *Statistique et expérience: remarques de méthode*, Paris: Rivière, 1922, p. 24.

routinized commandment of the sociological catechism. If the most trivialized readings of Weber's precept are to be believed, one only has to avoid affective partiality and ideological prompting in order to dispense with any epistemo-logical consideration of the significance of one's concepts or the appropriate-ness of one's techniques. The illusion that "value-neutral" operations are also "epistemologically neutral" limits the critique of one's own or anyone else's sociological work to an always easy and generally sterile examination of its ideological presuppositions and ultimate values. The endless debate about "ethical neutrality" often serves as a substitute for a genuinely epistemological discussion of the "methodological neutrality" of techniques, and, as such, it provides further support for the positivist illusion. By a *displacement* effect, interest in ethical presuppositions and ultimate values or ends diverts attention from critical examination of the theory of sociological knowledge that is engaged in the most elementary acts of practice.

Why, for example, is the non-directive interview so frequently exalted at the expense, for example, of ethnographic observation—which, when armed with the constraining rules of its tradition, more fully achieves the ideal of a system-atic inventory performed in a real situation—if not because it presents itself as the paradigmatic realization of neutrality in observation? There are grounds for suspecting the reasons for the popularity of this technique, given that neither the "theoreticians", nor the methodologists, nor the users of the technique, though normally so generous with their advice and warnings, have ever undertaken a methodical consideration of the specific distortions induced by such a profoundly artificial social relationship. When one does not control its implicit presuppositions and consequently provides oneself with social subjects equally predisposed to speak freely on all matters, not least of them-selves, and equally capable of adopting a restrictive yet intemperate relation to language, the non-directive interview which breaks the reciprocity of ordinary exchanges (itself variable according to milieu and situation) encourages sub-jects to produce a verbal *artefact*, the artificiality of which moreover varies according to the distance between the relation to language favoured by their social class and the artificial relation to language that is demanded of them. Those who forget to question the neutrality of the most formally neutral techniques have failed to notice, among other things, that survey techniques are socially qualified techniques of social intercourse [*Schatzman and Strauss, text no. 25*]. Ethnographic observation, which is to social experimentation as observation of animals in their natural habitat is to laboratory experimenta-tion, brings home the fictitious, forced character of most of the social situa-tions created by a routine exercise of sociology that induces neglect of the "laboratory reaction" precisely because it knows nothing but the laboratory and laboratory instruments, in the form of tests or questionnaires.

Just as there is no neutral recording, so there is no neutral question. A sociologist who does not subject his own questioning to sociological question-ing will be incapable of making a truly neutral sociological analysis of the answers it receives. Take a question as seemingly self-evident as "Have you worked today?". Statistical analysis shows that it produces different responses from peasants in Kabylia and in south Algeria, whereas, if they were thinking of an "objective" definition of work, i.e. the one which the modern economy tends to inculcate in its economic agents, the two groups would be expected to give similar answers. Only if he questions the meaning of his own question, instead of precipitately concluding that the answers are absurd or in bad faith, will the sociologist have some chance of discovering that the definition of work that is implied in his question is variably distant from the one that the two categories of agents imply in their answers.[19] It can be seen that a question which is not transparent for the person who asks it can obscure the object that it inevitably constructs, even if it has not been deliberately designed to construct it [*Goldthorpe and Lockwood, text no. 26*]. Given that one can ask anything of anyone and that almost anyone always has enough good will to give some sort of answer to any question, however unreal, a questioner who, for lack of a theory of the questionnaire, does not ask himself the question of the specific meaning of its questions is all too likely to find a confirmation of the realism of his questions in the reality of the answers they receive.[20] If, like Daniel Lerner, one questions sub-proletarians in under-developed countries about their capacity to identify with their favourite film stars, not to mention their reading of the press, one is obviously likely to collect a *flatus vocis* that has no other meaning than the one the sociologist gives it by treating it as a meaningful discourse.[21] Whenever the sociologist is unaware of the problematic he puts into his questions, he has no chance of understanding the problematic that the subjects put into their answers. The conditions are then fulfilled for him to fail to notice the blunder whereby realities that are masked by the very instrument of observation and by the socially conditioned intention of the user of the instrument are described in terms of absence.

[19] See P. Bourdieu, *Algeria 1960*, Cambridge: Cambridge University Press; Paris: Editions de la Maison des Sciences de l'Homme, 1979, p. 57.

[20] If secondary analysis of the documents yielded by even the most naïve inquiry remains almost always possible, and legitimate, this is because it is rare for the respondents to reply entirely at random and to reveal nothing of themselves in their answers. For example, "Don't knows" and refusals to answer can themselves be interpreted. However, recovering the meaning that they supply despite everything implies an effort of rectification, if only to work out what question they have really answered, which is not necessarily the one they were asked.

[21] D. Lerner, *The Passing of Traditional Society*, New York: Free Press, 1958. Without entering into a systematic critique of the ideological presuppositions underpinning a questionnaire which, among its 117 questions, has only two on work and socio-economic status (as against 87 on the "mass media" — cinema, newspapers, radio, and television), it may be pointed out that a theory which really took account of the objective conditions of existence of the sub-proletarian, and in particular the generalized instability that characterizes them, would be able to account for the sub-proletarian's capacity to imagine himself as a grocer or a journalist, and even the particular modality of these "projections", whereas Lerner's "modernization theory" is incapable of accounting for the sub-proletarian's relation to work or the future. This rough-and-ready criterion seems to make it possible to distinguish an ideological instrument, which can only produce an artefact, from a scientific instrument.

Even the most closed questionnaire does not necessarily guarantee the univocity of the responses merely because it subjects all the subjects to formally identical questions. To suppose that the same question has the same meaning for social subjects separated by differences of culture associated with their class membership, is to ignore the fact that the different class languages differ not only in their lexical range or their degree of abstraction but also in the themes and problematics that they articulate. Maxime Chastaing's critique of the "psychologist's sophism" is valid whenever the sociologist ignores the question of the differential meaning that the questions and answers really take on according to the social condition and position of the persons questioned: "The student who confuses his perspective with that of the children studied receives back his own perspective in the study in which he imagines he is collecting that of the children... . When he asks 'Are work and play the same thing? What's the difference between work and play?', he imposes, with his substantives, the adult difference that he seems to call into question... . When the interviewer classifies the responses, not according to the words which constitute them, but according to the meaning he would give them if he uttered them himself, in the three categories of 'Play = easy', 'Play = pointless' and 'Play = freedom', he is forcing children's thoughts into his own philosophical pigeon-holes."[22] To escape from this linguistic ethnocentrism, it is not sufficient to carry out content analysis of the utterances collected by the non-directive interview, at the risk of having the notions and categories of the language used by the subjects imposed on oneself. The only way to break free of the preconstructions of language, whether it be the language of the scientist or that of his subject, is to set up the dialectic which leads to adequate constructions by methodically confronting the two systems of preconstructions[23] [*Lévi-Strauss, text no. 27; Mauss, text no. 28; Malinowski, text no. 29*].

Sociologists have not drawn out all the methodological implications of the fact that the most classic techniques of empirical sociology are condemned by their very nature to create situations of fictitious experimentation essentially different from the social experimentations that are constantly produced in the unfolding of social life. The more closely the behaviour and attitudes studied depend on the immediate context, the more likely it is that, within the particular context which authorizes the survey situation, research will only capture attitudes and opinions that are not valid beyond the limits of that situation. Thus, surveys on class relations, and more precisely on the political aspect of these relations, are almost inevitably condemned to conclude that class conflicts are in decline, because the technical demands to which they have to

[22] M. Chastaing, "Jouer n'est pas jouer", *Journal de psychologie normale et pathologique*, no. 3, pp. 303–326, juillet-septembre 1959.

[23] Thus, non-directive interviewing and content analysis cannot be used as a kind of absolute standard but should provide a means of continuously controlling both the meaning of the questions asked and the categories according to which the responses are analysed and interpreted.

submit lead them to exclude crisis situations and consequently make it difficult for them to grasp or predict the behaviour that would arise from a conflict situation. As Marcel Maget observes, one has to "look to history to discover the constant features, if any, of reactions to new situations. Historical novelty acts as a 'reagent' revealing latent potentialities. Hence the interest of following the groups one is studying in their encounters with new situations; evoking these situations is never more than a second-best, since one cannot pose questions *ad infinitum*".[24]

Whereas the restrictive definition of data-collecting techniques gives undisputed pre-eminence to the questionnaire and sees only approximate substitutes for this royal technique in the well-codified and well-tested methods of ethnographic research (with its specific techniques—morphological description, technology, cartography, lexicology, biography, genealogy, etc.), epistemological primacy should properly be given to methodical and systematic observation.[25] Far from constituting the most neutral and most controlled way of establishing data, the questionnaire presupposes a whole set of exclusions, the most pernicious of which are unconscious. To know how to establish a questionnaire and what to do with the facts it produces, one has to know what the questionnaire does, i.e., among other things, what it cannot do. Not only are there some questions that the social norms governing the survey situation forbid one to ask; not only are there questions that the sociologist fails to ask when he accepts a social definition of sociology which is simply a transposition of the public image of sociology as a referendum; but even the most objective questions, those that deal with behaviour, can never yield more than the result of the subject's own observation of his behaviour. The interpretation is therefore only valid if it is guided by the express intention of methodically distinguishing actions from declarations of intention and declarations of action whose relationship to action can range from self-aggrandizing exaggeration or discreet omission to distortion, reinterpretation, and even "selective amnesia". Such an intention presupposes that one gives oneself the means to perform this distinction scientifically, either through the questionnaire itself, or through a particular use of this technique (as in surveys on budgets or time-management conducted as quasi-observation), or through direct observation. One is thus led to reverse the relationship that some methodologists establish between the questionnaire, a simple inventory of utterances, and ethnographic observation understood as a systematic inventory of cultural acts and objects.[26] The ques-

---

[24] M. Maget, *Guide d'étude directe des comportements culturels*, Paris: C.N.R.S., 1950, p. xxxi.

[25] For a systematic presentation of this methodology, see M. Maget, *op. cit.*

[26] By placing all ethnographic techniques in the disparaged category of "qualitative analysis", those who give absolute pre-eminence to "quantitative analysis" are led to see them as no more than an expedient, by a kind of methodological ethnocentrism. "Qualitative" information is related to statistics as if to its own true essence, it itself being no more than "quasi-statistics" yielding "quasi-distributions", "quasi-correlations", and "quasi-empirical data": "The gathering and analysis of 'quasi-statistical data' can probably be made more systematic than it has been in the past, if the logical structure of quantitative research is kept in mind to give general

tionnaire is only one of the instruments of observation, one whose methodological advantages, such as the capacity to collect homogeneous data equally amenable to statistical handling, must not conceal its epistemological limits. Thus, not only is it not the most economical technique for apprehending normalized behaviours, whose rigorously "regulated" patterns are highly predictable and which can therefore be apprehended through observation or by alert questioning of a few informants, but also, in its most ritualized uses, it is likely to lead one to ignore this aspect of behaviours and so, through a *displacement* effect, to devalue the very project of grasping them.[27]

Methodologists will occasionally recommend use of the classic techniques of ethnology but, because they make measurement the measure of all things and measurement techniques the measure of all technique, they can only see them as marginal aids or expedients for "finding ideas" in the early phases of research;[28] and in so doing they exclude the specifically epistemological question of the relationship between the methods of ethnology and those of sociology. This reciprocal ignorance is just as detrimental to each discipline as the modish enthusiasm which induces uncontrolled borrowings (not that the attitudes are mutually exclusive). Restoring the unity of social anthropology —in the full sense and not simply as a synonym of ethnology—presupposes an epistemological reflection that would tend to determine what the two methodologies owe in each case to the traditions of each of the disciplines and to the actual characteristics of the societies they study. While the uncontrolled importation of methods and concepts that have been developed in the study of non-literate societies which lack historical traditions, are socially little differentiated and have been little exposed to contact with other societies, can undoubtedly lead to absurdities (as in some "culturalist" analyses of stratified societies), it is clear that conditional limitations should not be regarded as limits of validity inherent in the methods of ethnology.[29] Nothing forbids one to apply ethnological methods to modern societies, so long as in each case the implicit presuppositions of these methods regarding the structure of the society and the logic of its transformations are subjected to epistemological reflection.

Even the most elementary and seemingly most automatic information-processing operations involve epistemological choices and even a theory of the object. It is all too clear, for example, that a whole conscious or unconscious

warnings and directions to the qualitative observer" (A. H. Barton and P. F. Lazarsfeld, *loc. cit.*, pp. 112–113).

[27] Conversely, ethnologists' overriding concern with the most regulated aspects of behaviour is often accompanied by indifference to the use of statistics, which would alone be able to measure the discrepancy between the norms and the real behaviour.

[28] See, for example, A. Barton and P. F. Lazarsfeld, *loc. cit.*. C. Selltiz, M. Deutsch, and S. W. Cook undertake to define the conditions on which techniques originating in ethnology can usefully be transferred to sociology (*Research Methods in Social Relations*, revised one-vol. ed., London: Methuen, 1959, pp. 59–65).

[29] R. Bierstedt performs this kind of substantification in his article "The Limitation of Anthropological Method in Sociology", *American Journal of Sociology*, Vol. 54, pp. 23–30, 1948–49.

theory of social stratification is brought into play in the coding of the indicators of social position or the definition of categories (consider, for example, the various indices that can be chosen in order to define degrees of "status crystallization"). Those who carelessly or recklessly fail to draw out all the implications of this obvious point lay themselves open to the criticism often made of scholastic descriptions which tend to suggest that the experimental method serves to discover relations among "data" or pre-established properties of these "data". "There is nothing more deceptive," wrote Dewey, "than the seeming simplicity of scientific procedure as it is reported in logical treatises. This specious simplicity is at its height when letters of the alphabet are used [to represent the articulation of the object—given ABCD in one case, BCFG in another, and CDEH in a third, it is quickly concluded that C is what determines the phenomenon]. They are an effective device for obscuring the fact that the materials in question are always highly *standardized*, thus concealing from view that the whole burden of inductive-deductive inquiry is actually borne by the operations through which materials are standardized."[30] If methodologists are more attentive to the rules that should govern the manipulation of already constituted categories than to the operations that enable them to be constituted, this is because the problem of constructing the object can never be resolved in advance, once and for all, whether it be a question of dividing the population into social categories, income bands, or age groups. Because every taxonomy implies a theory, a distribution that is unaware of its own choices is necessarily made on the basis of an unconscious theory, which almost always means an ideology. For example, given that incomes vary in a continuous way, the division of a population into income bands necessarily involves a theory of stratification: "One cannot draw a line which absolutely separates rich and poor, property owners and workers. A number of authors claim to conclude from this fact that in our society one cannot speak of a capitalist class, or oppose the bourgeois to the workers."[31] One might as well say, Pareto adds, that there are no old people, on the grounds that one cannot say at what age, what stage of life, old age begins.

Finally one needs to ask whether the method of data analysis that seems most applicable to all types of quantifiable relations, i.e. multivariate analysis, should not be subjected each time to epistemological scrutiny. For, by postulating that one can successively isolate the action of the different variables from the complete system of relations within which they act, in order to identify the intrinsic efficacy of each of them, this technique makes it impossible to identify the efficacy that a factor may derive from its insertion in a structure and even the specifically structural efficacy of the system of factors.

[30] J. Dewey, *Logic: The Theory of Inquiry*, London: Allen & Unwin, 1939, p. 431, n. 1.

[31] V. Pareto, *Cours d'économie politique*, Vol. II, Geneva: Droz, 1964. The most abstract techniques for dividing up material have precisely the effect of cancelling out concrete units such as generation, biography, and career.

Moreover, when one uses a synchronic cross-section to produce a system defined by a momentary equilibrium, one is liable to fail to grasp all that the system owes to its past and, for example, the different meanings that two elements, similar in the order of simultaneities, may derive from their membership of systems that differ in the order of succession, i.e. different biographical trajectories.[32] More generally, an informed use of all the forms of calculation that make it possible to analyse a set of relations would presuppose perfectly clear knowledge and awareness of the theory of the social fact that is implied in the procedures through which each form of calculation selects and constructs the type of relations among variables which defines its object.

Whereas the technical rules for the use of techniques readily lend themselves to codification, the principles that can define a use of each technique that would consciously take account of the logical or sociological presuppositions of its operations are hard to define and even harder to put into practice. As for the principles of the principles, those which govern the correct use of the experimental method in sociology and which, as such, constitute the basis of the theory of sociological knowledge, they are so contrary to spontaneous epistemology that they can be constantly transgressed in the very name of the precepts or rules of thumb into which some claim to translate them. Thus, the methodological intention not to be content with conscious expressions can lead one to credit constructions such as the hierarchical analysis of opinions with the power to trace the path from even the most superficial declarations to the attitudes from which they arise, i.e. magically to transmute the conscious into the unconscious. Or, with an identical procedure, but one which fails for the opposite reasons, it can lead one to seek the unconscious structure of a media message through a structural analysis that can, at best, only laboriously rediscover a few basic truths consciously possessed by the producers of the message.

Similarly, the principle of ethical neutrality, a commonplace of all the methodological traditions, can, in its routine form, paradoxically induce the epistemological error that it claims to prevent. It is precisely a simplistic conception of cultural relativism that leads some sociologists of "popular culture" and the modern media to give themselves the illusion of complying with the golden rule of ethnological science by treating all cultural behaviours—folk songs, Bach cantatas, or pop songs—as if the value that the different groups assign to them were not part of their reality, and as if it were not always necessary to refer cultural behaviours to the values to which they objectively refer, in order to restore to them their specifically cultural meaning. The sociologist who insists on ignoring the value differences that social subjects establish between cultural products in fact performs an uncontrolled

[32] See P. Bourdieu, J.-C. Passeron, and M. de Saint-Martin, *Rapport pédagogique et communication*, Cahiers du centre de sociologie européenne, no. 2, Paris–The Hague: Mouton, 1965, pp. 43–57.

and therefore illegitimate transposition of the relativism that the ethnologist must observe when he considers cultures belonging to different societies. The different "cultures" that coexist in a single stratified society are objectively situated in relation to one another, because the different groups situate themselves in relation to one another, especially when they make reference to their cultures. By contrast, the relationship between cultures belonging to different societies may exist only in and through the comparison performed by the ethnologist. Thorough-going, mechanical relativism leads to the same result as ethical ethnocentrism; in either case the observer substitutes his own relation to the values of those whom he observes (and therefore to their own value) for the relation that these groups objectively have to their values.

"Would any physicist," asks Bachelard, "be willing to spend his grant on assembling apparatus that had no theoretical purpose?" Many sociological surveys would not stand up to such scrutiny. The pure and simple surrender before the "given" by practice that reduces the body of hypotheses to a series of fragmentary, passive anticipations condemns the researcher to the blind manipulations of a technique automatically generating *artefacts*, involuntary constructions which are a caricature of the methodically and consciously, i.e. scientifically, constructed fact. In refusing to be the scientific subject of his sociology, the positivistic sociologist condemns himself (barring a miracle of the unconscious) to conduct a sociology without a scientific object.

A scientific "fact" that is constructed by procedures that are formally irreproachable but unaware of what they are and do, may well be no more than an *artefact*: to forget this amounts to the arbitrary conclusion that because techniques can be applied, the object to which they are applied must be real. It is not surprising that those who profess that an object which cannot be grasped or measured with the available techniques has no scientific existence, should be led, in their practice, to regard only what is measurable as worthy of being known, or even worse, to confer scientific existence on everything that can be measured. Those who proceed as if all objects were amenable to a single technique, or indifferently to all techniques, forget that the various techniques may, to varying extents and with varying effectiveness, contribute to knowledge of the object, so long as their use is controlled by methodological reflection on the conditions and limits of their validity, which depends in each case on their adequacy to the object, i.e. to the theory of the object.[33] Furthermore, only this reflection can make possible the creative reinvention that is ideally required by the application of a technique, a "lifeless intelligence that intelligence has to resurrect", and, *a fortiori* the invention and implementation of new techniques.

[33] Monomaniac use of a particular technique is the most frequent and also the most frequently denounced: "Give a small boy a hammer," says Kaplan, "and he will find that everything he encounters needs pounding" (*The Conduct of Inquiry: Methodology of Behavioral Science*, Chandler: San Francisco, 1964, p. 28).

[handwritten: ⁴₄[ ] — "A relation on members of groups of 4 is distribution of outcomes 49 different from 'chance'?"]

2.4 Analogy and the construction of hypotheses

One has to be aware that every distinctively scientific object is consciously and methodically constructed, in order to know how to construct the object and to know what it is that one has constructed; and all this has to be known in order to reflect on the techniques for constructing the questions to be put to the object. A methodology that never asks itself the question of the invention of the hypotheses to be tested cannot, as Claude Bernard observes, "give new and fertile ideas to those who have none; it can only serve to direct the ideas of those who have some and to develop them so as to draw the best possible results from them... . Method by itself brings forth nothing".[34]

In contrast to positivism, which tends to see the hypothesis as the product of spontaneous generation in a sterile environment and which naively hopes that knowledge of the facts or, at best, induction from the facts, will automatically lead to the formulation of hypotheses, both Husserl's eidetic analysis and Koyré's historical analysis show, with reference to Galileo's paradigmatic processes of reasoning, that winning and constructing a hypothesis like that of inertia required a theoretical *"coup d'état"* that found no support in the suggestions of experience and could only be legitimated by the coherence of the imaginative challenge to the facts and to naive or erudite images of the facts.[35]

[handwritten: ∧ {⁴₄[ ]}?]

This kind of exploration of lateral possibles, which presupposes a deliberate self-distancing from the facts, remains vulnerable to the temptations of intuitionism, formalism, or pure speculation, and at the same time can only achieve an illusory escape from the constraints of language or the controls of ideology. As R. B. Braithwaite points out, "thinking of scientific theories by means of models is always *as-if thinking*... . The price of the employment is eternal vigilance".[36] In distinguishing the *ideal type* from the generic concept obtained by induction, Max Weber was simply trying to make explicit the rules of

[handwritten: E-state structuralism?]

---

[34] C. Bernard, *Introduction à l'étude de la médecine expérimentale*, Paris: Baillère, 1865, Ch. II, section 2.

[35] E. Husserl, *Die Krisis der europäischen Wissenschaften und die transzendentale Phänomenologie: Eine Einleitung in die phänomenologische Philosophie*, Hamburg: Meiner, 1977. Koyré, though as sensitive as any other historian of science to Galileo's experimental ingenuity, does not hesitate to see the determination to construct an Archimedean physics as the driving principle of the scientific revolution begun by Galileo. It is theory, i.e., in this case the theoretical intuition of the principle of inertia, that precedes experiment and makes it possible by making conceivable the experiments that are capable of validating the theory (see A. Koyré, *Études galiléennes, op. cit.*, Vol. III, *Galilée et la loi d'inertie*, 1966, pp. 226–227).

[36] R. B. Braithwaite, *Scientific Explanation*, Cambridge: Cambridge University Press, 1963, p. 93. It is no accident that there is greater awareness of the dangers of the "immunization" against experience inherent in any formalist, i.e. simplifying, approach in sciences which, like econometrics, have long resorted to the construction of models, than in sociology. H. Albert has pointed out the "unlimited alibi" provided by the habit of reasoning *ceteris paribus*: a hypothesis becomes irrefutable as soon as every observation seeming to contradict it can be attributed to variation in the factors that the hypothesis neutralizes by assuming them constant (H. Albert, "Modell-Platonismus", in E. Topitsch [ed.], *Logik der Sozialwissenschaften*, Cologne & Berlin: Kiepenheuer und Witsch, 1965, pp. 406–434).

functioning and the conditions of validity of a procedure which even the most positivist thinker uses, consciously or unconsciously, but which cannot be mastered unless it is used with full awareness of what one is doing. In contrast to the speculative constructions of social philosophy, whose logical refinements have no other purpose than to construct a well-ordered deductive system and which are irrefutable because they are unprovable, the ideal type, used as "a guide to the construction of hypotheses", as Weber puts it, is a coherent fiction "with which the real situation is compared or surveyed", an *approximated* (*approchée*)—and not approximate—construct designed to be measured against the real, deviating from it by a distance which can then be measured and reduced. The ideal type makes it possible to measure reality because it measures itself against it and specifies itself by specifying the gap that separates it from the real [*Weber, text no. 30*].

So long as one removes the ambiguities that Weber leaves unresolved when he identifies the ideal type with the model, in the sense of an exemplary or limiting case (whether constructed or observed), reasoning by "moving to the limit" is an irreplaceable technique for inventing hypotheses. The ideal type can equally well mean a theoretically privileged case in a constructed group of transformations (as with the role Bouligand gives to the right-angled triangle as a privileged instance of "Pythagoreanism");[37] or a paradigmatic case, which in turn may be either a pure fiction obtained by moving to the limit and "one-sidedly accentuating" the pertinent properties; or a really observable object exhibiting in the highest degree the greatest number of properties of the constructed object. To avoid the dangers inherent in this procedure, the ideal type has to be treated, not in itself and for itself—as if it were a revealing sample that one only has to copy in order to know the whole collection—, but as an element in a group of transformations, by relating it to all the cases of the family of which it is a privileged case. Thus, by using a methodological fiction to construct the system of behaviours that would apply the most rational means in pursuit of rationally calculated ends, Weber provides himself with a privileged means of understanding the range of real behaviours that the ideal type enables him to objectify by objectifying their differential distance from the pure type. Even the ideal type in the sense of a revealing sample or "ostensive instance", which exhibits what one is looking for, as Bacon puts it, "bare and substantial, and in its exaltation, or the height of its power",[38] can be put to rigorous use. It is possible to avoid what has been called "the fallacy of the dramatic example", a variant of the "French redhead fallacy", so long as the extreme case which presents itself for observation is seen as revealing the structure of the system of the whole set of isomorphic cases.[39] This is the logic

---

[37] See G. Bachelard, *Le rationalisme appliqué*, 1st edn., Paris: P.U.F., 1949, pp. 91–97.

[38] F. Bacon, *Novum Organum*, trans. G. W. Kitchin, Oxford: Oxford University Press, 1855, pp. 168–169.

[39] Thus, Goffman makes sense of the psychiatric hospital by re-placing it in the series of "total

that leads Mauss to privilege *potlatch* as the "extreme form" of the family of total, competitive exchanges, or that entitles one to see the Paris humanities student, of bourgeois origin, and his inclination to dilettantism, as a privileged point of departure for constructing the model of possible relations between the sociological truth of the student condition and its ideological transfiguration.[40]

The *ars inveniendi* therefore has to aim to provide the techniques of thought that make it possible to perform the work of hypothesis construction in a methodical fashion while minimizing its inherent risks through an awareness of the dangers of this undertaking. The reasoning by analogy which many epistemologists regard as the first principle of scientific invention is called upon to play a specific role in sociological science, the specificity of which is that it can only constitute its object by the *comparative approach*.[41] To escape from idiographic consideration of cases that do not contain their own reason, the sociologist has to multiply the hypotheses of possible analogies until he constructs the family of cases that gives an adequate account of the case in question. And to construct these analogies themselves, he can legitimately make use of the hypothesis of structural analogies between social phenomena and phenomena already given form by other sciences, starting with the closest ones: linguistics, ethnology, and even biology. "It is always interesting," Durkheim observes, "to see whether a law established for one order of facts may not, *mutatis mutandis*, be found to apply elsewhere. This comparison may even serve to confirm it and give a greater understanding of its implications. In fact, analogy is a legitimate form of comparison, and comparison is the only practical means we have for the understanding of things."[42] In short, comparison guided by the hypothesis of analogies is not only the privileged instrument for breaking with pre-constructed data, which insistently demand

institutions", along with barracks and boarding schools. The privileged case in the constructed series may then be the one which, taken in isolation, best disguises the logic of the system of isomorphic cases by its officially humanitarian functions (see E. Goffman, *Asylums*, New York: Doubleday, 1961).

[40] See P. Bourdieu and J.-C. Passeron, *The Inheritors*, Chicago: Chicago University Press, 1979 (translator's note).

[41] See, for example, G. Polya, *Induction and Analogy in Mathematics*, Princeton (N.J.): Princeton University Press, 1954. Durkheim himself suggested the principles for reflection on the correct use of analogy: "The fault of the biological scientists was not that they used analogy but that they used it wrongly. Instead of trying to control their studies of society by their knowledge of biology, they tried to infer the laws of the first from the laws of the second. Such inferences are worthless. If the laws governing natural life are found also in society, they are found in different forms and with specific characteristics which do not permit of conjecture by analogy and can only be understood by direct observation. However, if one had already by the use of sociological methods begun to determine certain qualities of social organization, it would be perfectly legitimate to inquire afterwards whether these qualities did not show some partial similarities with the animal organism as established by the biologist. It might be assumed that all organisms must have certain characteristics in common which are worthwhile studying" (É. Durkheim, "Individual and Collective Representations", in *Sociology and Philosophy*, trans. D. Pocock, London: Cohen & West, 1953, p. 1).

[42] É. Durkheim, *ibid*.

to be treated in and for themselves, but also the principle of the hypothetical construction of relations between relations.

2.5 Model and theory

The "model" may be granted the properties and functions commonly granted to the theory,[43] only on condition that one refuses the definition given of the term by the positivists, who make so much use of it. There is no harm in using the term "model" to refer to any system of relations among selected, abstracted, and simplified properties which is deliberately constructed for purposes of description, exposition and prediction and which is therefore kept under full control; but only so long as one refuses to play on the connotations of the word and to suggest that the model can in this case be anything more than a copy which replicates the real and which, when it is obtained by a simple procedure of adjustment and extrapolation, in no way leads to the principle of the reality that it mimics. Duhem complained that Lord Kelvin's "mechanical models" had only a superficial resemblance to the facts. These devices, designed simply to "expound", speak only to the imagination and cannot guide invention, because, at best, they are no more than a presentation of existing knowledge and tend to impose their own logic, discouraging the search for the objective logic that has to be constructed in order to give a theoretical account of what they merely represent.[44] Some erudite reformulations of common-sense prenotions are reminiscent of the automata constructed by Vaucanson and Le Cat, which, for lack of knowledge of the real principles of functioning, resorted to mechanisms based on other principles to produce a simple reproduction of the most (phenomenal) properties. As Georges Canguilhem observes, the use of models became fruitful in biology only when mechanical models, conceived in terms of the production and transmission of energy, were replaced by cybernetic models based on the transmission of information which thus linked up with the logic of the functioning of neural circuits.[45] It is no accident that indifference to principles condemns one to an operationism which limits its ambitions to "saving appearances", even if this means putting forward as many models as there are phenomena or offering several models for a single phenomenon that are not even contradictory, because, being produced by ingenious improvisation, they

[43] In this whole section, the word "theory" will be used in the sense of a partial theory of the social (see above, section 1.7, pp. 29–31).

[44] Among the uncontrolled metaphors that stand in the way of grasping deep analogies, one should include those which language carries in its metaphors, even the most dead ones (see above, section 1.4, pp. 20–24).

[45] G. Canguilhem, "The Role of Analogies and Models in Biological Discovery", in A. C. Crombie (ed.), *Scientific Change: Historical Studies in the Intellectual, Social and Technical Conditions for Scientific Discovery and Technical Invention, from Antiquity to the Present*, Symposium on the History of Science, London: Heinemann, 1963, pp. 507–520.

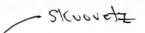

are all equally unprincipled. Applied research may well content itself with such "40 per cent possibilities", as Boas put it, but anyone who confuses an approximate (and not *approximated*) reconstruction of the phenomenon with the theory of the phenomena will fail inevitably, but inexplicably, so long as an *ad hoc* explanatory power remains unexplained.

Playing on the confusion between simple *resemblance* and *analogy*—a relation between relations that has to be won against appearances and constructed by means of abstraction and conscious comparison—, *mimetic models, which grasp only the external similarities, are opposed to analogical models* aimed at apprehending the hidden principles of the realities they interpret. "To reason by analogy," says the Académie Française, "is to construct a reasoning based on the resemblances or relations between one thing and another," or rather—Cournot corrects—"based on relations or resemblances insofar as they indicate relations. For, in analogical judgement, the mind attends only to the *reason* of resemblances; resemblances are worthless if they do not indicate relations in the order of facts to which the analogy applies."[46]

The various procedures for constructing hypotheses may achieve greater effectiveness by resorting to formalization, which, in addition to the clarifying function of a rigorous shorthand for concepts and the critical function of a logical test of the rigour of definitions and the coherence of the system of propositions, may also, in certain conditions, fulfil a heuristic function by allowing a systematic exploration of the possible and a controlled construction of a systematic body of hypotheses as a complete table of possible experiments. But if the mechanical and at the same time methodical efficacy of the symbols and operators of logic or mathematics, "the comparative instruments par excellence", in Marc Barbut's phrase, enables imaginary variation to be taken to its limits, analogical reason can, even in the absence of any formal refinement, also fulfil its function as an instrument of discovery, albeit more laboriously and less surely. In its most common use, the model provides the substitute for experimentation that is often impossible in practice and supplies the means of comparing against reality the consequences that this mental experiment makes it possible to identify fictitiously and therefore more fully: "Marx followed Rousseau in saying—and saying once and for all, as far as I can see—" Claude Lévi-Strauss observes, "that social science is no more based upon events than physics is based upon sense-perception. Our object is to construct a model, examine its properties and the way it reacts to laboratory tests, and then apply our observations to the interpretation of empirical happenings."[47]

Models derive their explanatory value from their principles of construction

[46] A. Cournot, *Essai sur les fondements de nos connaissances et sur les caractères de la critique philosophique*, Paris: Hachette, 1912, p. 68.
[47] C. Lévi-Strauss, *A World on the Wane* [*Tristes Tropiques*, 1956], trans. J. Russell, London: Hutchinson, 1961, p. 61.

and not from their degree of formalization. It is true that, as many philosophers, from Leibniz to Russell, have shown, recourse to the "blind self-evidence" of symbols is an excellent protection against the blinding self-evidence of intuition: "Symbolism is useful because it makes things difficult... . What we wish to know is, what can be deduced from what. Now, in the beginnings, everything is self-evident; and it is very hard to see whether one self-evident proposition follows from another or not. Obviousness is always the enemy to correctness. Hence we invent some new and difficult symbolism, in which nothing seems obvious. Then we set up certain rules for operating on the symbols, and the whole thing becomes mechanical."[48] But mathematicians have had fewer reasons than sociologists to point out that formalization can consecrate the self-evidence of common sense rather than condemn it. As Leibniz said, one can devise an equation for the curve that runs through all the points of a face. The perceived object does not become a constructed object by a simple wave of a mathematical wand. Indeed, insofar as it symbolizes the break with appearances, symbolism gives the preconstructed object a usurped respectability that protects it from theoretical criticism. If a warning is needed against the spurious prestige and prodigies of formalization conducted without epistemological control, this is because, by giving the appearance of abstraction to propositions that may be blindly borrowed from spontaneous sociology or ideology, it is liable to suggest that one can dispense with the effort of abstraction, which alone can dispel the apparent similarities and construct the hidden analogies.

The pursuit of structural homologies does not always have to resort to formalism in order to provide its own basis and prove its rigour. One only has to follow the steps that lead Panofsky to compare Aquinas's *Summa* with the Gothic cathedral to observe the conditions that make such an operation possible, legitimate, and fruitful. To uncover the hidden analogy while escaping the curious blend of dogmatism and empiricism, mysticism and positivism that characterizes intuitionism, one has to refrain from seeking the unifying principle of the data of sense experience in those data themselves, and instead subject the compared realities to a treatment that makes them equally available for comparison. The analogy is not established between the *Summa* and the cathedral taken, so to speak, at face value, but between two systems of intelligible relations; not between "things" available to immediate perception but between objects won against the immediate appearances and constructed by a methodical elaboration [*Panofsky, text no. 31*].

Thus the *theoretical model* is characterized by its capacity for breaking with appearances and its capacity for generalization, these two qualities being inseparable. It is a formal outline of the relations among relations that define constructed objects, which can be transposed to phenomenally very different

---

[48] B. Russell, *Mysticism and Logic, and Other Essays*, London: Allen and Unwin, 1963, p. 61 (first publ. as *Philosophical Essays*, London: Allen & Unwin, 1910).

orders of reality and suggest, by analogy, new analogies that can give rise to new object constructions [*Duhem, text no. 32; Campbell, text no. 33*]. Just as the mathematician can find the principle of a general theory of curves in the definition of the straight line as a curve with zero curvature, because the curved line is a better generalizer than the straight line, so the construction of a pure model makes it possible to treat different social forms as realizations of a single group of transformations and to bring out hidden properties which only emerge through the interrelating of each of the realizations with all the others, i.e. by reference to the complete system of relations, in which the principle of their structural affinity is expressed.[49] It is this procedure that gives their fruitfulness, i.e. their generalizing power, to comparisons between different societies or sub-systems of the same society, as opposed to simple parallels suggested by similarity of content. Insofar as these "scientific metaphors" lead to the underlying principles of the structural homologies that were blurred by phenomenal differences, they are, as it has been said, "miniature theories", since, by formulating the generative and unifying principles of systems of relations, they fully satisfy the demands of rigour with respect to proof and fruitfulness with respect to invention which define a theoretical construction. As generative grammars of transposable schemas, they supply the principle of infinitely renewable questions and questionings; as systematic realizations of a system of relations either verified or to be verified, they call for a verification procedure which itself is necessarily systematic; as conscious products of a self-distancing from reality, they always bring one back to reality and make it possible to measure against reality properties whose unreality alone entitles one to extract them fully, by deduction.[50]

[49] This same procedure, of conceiving the particular case and even the whole set of real cases as particular cases of an ideal system of logical compossibles, may lead one, in the most concrete operations of sociological practice such as interpreting a statistical relation, to invert the significance of the notion of statistical significance. Just as mathematics sometimes regards the absence of properties as a property, so an absence of statistical relationship between two variables may be highly significant when one considers this relationship within the complete system of relations of which it is part.

[50] A whole education of the scientific mind would be needed, in the social sciences, in order for sociologists, when reporting on surveys for example, to break more often with the inductive procedure which leads, at best, to a recapitulatory account (see below, section 3.2, pp. 63–64), and instead to reorganize the set of empirically discovered relations on the basis of one (or several) unifying principles, so as to account for them systematically, i.e. to comply with the requirements of theory in their practice, if only at the level of a regional problematic.

Part Three
Applied rationalism

3   The social fact is won, constructed, and confirmed: the hierarchy of epistemological acts

this is the hierarchy. per PB

The principle of the empiricist, formalist, or intuitionist error lies in the dissociation of the epistemological acts and in an impoverished representation of technical operations, each of which presupposes the acts of breaking with appearances, construction, and confirmation. The debate over the intrinsic virtues of theory or measurement, intuition, or formalism is necessarily fictitious, because it is based on the autonomizing of operations that derive all their meaning and fertility from their necessary insertion in a unitary process.

3.1   The implication of operations and the hierarchy of epistemological acts

The most usual representation of the process of research as a cycle of successive phases (observation, hypothesis, experimentation, theory, observation, etc.) may have some pedagogic usefulness, if only because it substitutes the image of a sequence of epistemologically qualified operations for a list of tasks parcelled out according to the logic of the bureaucratic division of labour. It is nonetheless doubly misleading. First, by projecting the phases of the "experimental cycle" into space as a set of mutually external stages, it gives an inadequate picture of the real unfolding of operations, since in reality the whole cycle is present in each of them. Secondly, and more importantly, this image fails to capture the logical order of epistemological acts—break, construction, testing against the facts—which is never reducible to the chronological order of the concrete operations of research. To say that scientific facts are won, constructed, and confirmed does not imply that for each of these epistemological acts there are corresponding and successive operations, each armed with a specific instrument.[1] Thus, as we have seen, the theoretical model is simultaneously a construction and a break, since one needs to have broken free from the phenomenal resemblances in order to construct the deep analogies, and this break with apparent relations presupposes the construction of new relations among the appearances.

[1] By automatically associating a given epistemological act with a particular technique—e.g. the break with the distancing power of ethnological vocabulary, construction with the specific effect of formalism, or verification with the most standardized forms of the questionnaire—, one may give oneself the illusion of having met all the epistemological demands simply by using the appropriate instrument.

The distinction between the different epistemological acts appears most clearly in erroneous practice, which, as has been seen, is defined precisely by its omission of one or another of the acts whose hierarchical integration defines sound practice. By showing what it costs to miss out one of the epistemological acts, analysis of error and the conditions of error makes it possible to define the hierarchy of epistemological dangers, which flows from the order in which the epistemological acts imply one another: break, construction, confirmation. Experimentation is only as good as the construct that it tests, and the heuristic value and proof value of a construct depends on the extent to which it has made it possible to break with appearances and, thereby, to understand appearances by understanding them as appearances. It follows that it is neither contradictory nor eclectic to insist simultaneously on the dangers and the value of an operation such as formalization or even intuition. The value of a formal model is a function of the degree to which the *epistemological preliminaries* of breaking and constructing have been fulfilled. While symbolism is, as we have seen, liable to authorize and mask a pure and simple submission to spontaneous sociology, it can also help to prevent relapses into common-sense understanding when it exerts its controlling power over relations constructed against the apparent relations.

Even intuition can be endowed with a scientific function when, subject to proper control, it suggests hypotheses and even contributes to the epistemological control of the other operations. Intuitionism is certainly to be condemned when, guided by the conviction that a social system expresses the action of one and the same principle in each of its parts, it imagines it can grasp the unique, unitary logic of a culture in a kind of "central intuition", and when, as a number of culturalist descriptions tend to do, it thereby avoids methodical study of the different sub-systems and investigation of their real interrelations. However, when an intuitive apprehension, *uno intuitu*, of the immediately perceptible unity of a situation, a life-style or a pattern of behaviour leads one to examine the significant relations among properties or relations that present themselves successively only in the work of analysis, it constitutes a safeguard against the atomization of the object that results, for example, from resorting to indicators which cannot objectify the manifestations of an attitude or an *ethos* without fragmenting them.[2] Intuition then

---

[2] It could be useful to reintroduce the whole set of experiences, attitudes, and rules of observation summed up in the ethnological imperative of "fieldwork" into a sociological practice which, as it becomes more bureaucratized, tends to interpose the layer of executant interviewers and the apparatus of mechanical analysis between the designer of the survey and those whom he studies. Direct experience of the individuals and the concrete situations in which they live (domestic interiors, landscape, body language, intonations, etc.) is indeed not in itself knowledge, but it can provide the intuitive link that sometimes suggests the hypothesis of unusual but systematic relations between data. More than the sociologist, who, if anything, is threatened by a distance from his object that is not always an epistemological distanciation, the ethnologist, like all those who resort to participant observation, is liable to take "human contact" for a means of knowledge. Sensitive to the appeals and seductions of his object, which

contributes not only to invention but also to epistemological control, inasmuch as, when itself subject to control, it reminds sociological research of the ambition of reconstituting the interrelationships that define the constructed totalities. Thus, epistemological reflection shows that one cannot ignore the hierarchy of epistemological acts without falling into the real dissociation of research operations which defines intuitionism, formalism, or positivism.

Applied rationalism breaks with spontaneous sociology above all by reversing the relationship between theory and experiment. The most elementary of operations, observation, which positivism describes as a recording that will be faithful insofar as it eschews theoretical presuppositions, is in fact scientific only insofar as the theoretical principles with which it is armed are conscious and systematic. Noting that "the lowest level of success is achieved if the grammar presents the observed data correctly", Noam Chomsky adds that: "What data is relevant is determined in part by the possibility for a systematic theory, and one might therefore hold that the lowest level of success is no easier to achieve than the others... . The problem of determining what data is valuable and to the point is not an easy one. What is observed is often neither relevant nor significant, and what is relevant and significant is often very difficult to observe, in linguistics no less than in the freshman physics laboratory, or, for that matter, anywhere in science."[3] And Freud observes that: "Even at the stage of description, it is not possible to avoid applying certain abstract ideas to the material in hand, ideas derived from somewhere or other but certainly not from the new observations alone."[4] A proof of the immanence of theory in relevant observation would be found in the fact that every undertaking of systematic deciphering, such as the structural analysis of a corpus of myths, necessarily discovers lacunae in any documentation that has been assembled blindly, even if, in the interests of presuppositionless recording, the first observers had aimed at exhaustive collection. Indeed, it sometimes happens that a reading armed with a theory will bring out "facts" which had remained imperceptible even to those who reported them. Thus Panofsky was able to pick up the phrase *inter se disputando* on the groundplan of a cathedral chevet, which had been read a thousand times before him and is

emerge in nostalgic evocations of people and places, he has to make a particular effort to construct a problematic capable of breaking the singular configurations offered to him by concrete objects.

[3] N. Chomsky, *Current Issues in Linguistic Theory*, The Hague & Paris: Mouton, 1964, p. 28.

[4] Quoted in K. M. Colby, *An Introduction to Psychoanalytic Research*, New York: Basic Books, 1960, p. 65. Comte himself did not have the positivistic theory of the role of theory that his opponents complacently ascribe to him: "If, on the one hand, every theory must necessarily be founded upon observations, it is, on the other hand, no less true that, in order to observe, our mind has need of some theory or other. If in contemplating phenomena we did not immediately connect them with some principles, not only would it be impossible for us to combine these isolated observations and, therefore, to derive any profit from them, but we should even be entirely incapable of remembering the facts, which would for the most part remain unnoted by us" (A. Comte, *Introduction to Positive Philosophy*, ed. with introdn. and revd. transln. by F. Ferré, Indianapolis: Bobbs-Merrill, 1970, pp. 4–5).

typical of Scholastic dialectics, only because he constituted it as a fact by questioning it on the basis of the theoretical hypothesis that the same dialectically minded *habitus* might be expressed both in Gothic architecture and in the Scholastic codification of *disputationes*.[5]

What is true of observation is also true of experimentation, although the classic accounts of the experimental cycle present these two operations as the starting point and point of arrival of a process divided into distinct stages. All experimentation, as we have seen, involves principles or presuppositions: "An experiment," writes Max Planck, "is nothing other than a question addressed to nature; measurement, the record of the answer. But before performing the experiment, one has to think it through, i.e. formulate the question to be put to nature; and before drawing any conclusion from the measurement, one has to interpret it, i.e. understand nature's answer. These two tasks are for the theoretician."[6] For its part, only successful experimentation, "reason confirmed", can demonstrate the explanatory value and deductive power of a theory, i.e. establish its capacity to generate a systematic body of propositions amenable to confirmation or invalidation by the test of facts.[7] But the theoretic value of experimentation is not grounded in the pure and simple fact of accordance with the facts: as Canguilhem observes, one has to be able "to establish that the agreement or disagreement between a supposition and an experimental observation that is sought on the basis of the supposition taken as a principle is not due to coincidence, even repeated coincidence, but that one has indeed been led to the observed fact by the methods that the hypothesis implies,"[8] [*Canguilhem, text no. 34*]. In other words, the facts that validate the theory are only as good as the theory they validate. The best way to be told by the facts what one wants to make them say is of course to question them on the basis of a "theory" that calls forth facts which no longer mean anything worth saying. This is true of the spuriously scientific elaborations of preconceptions

[5] E. Panofsky, *Gothic Architecture and Scholasticism*, Latrobe (Pennsylvania): Archabbey Press, 1951, p. 87.

[6] Max Planck, "Sinn und Grenzen der exakten Wissenschaft", in *Vorträge und Erinnerungen*, 5th edn., Stuttgart: Hirzel 1949, p. 376.

[7] Though it is characteristic of positivist epistemology that it separates the test of facts from the theoretical construct from which the facts derive their meaning, it goes without saying that Comte's rule requiring one "only to imagine hypotheses amenable, by their nature, to positive verification, more or less distant but always clearly inevitable" (A. Comte, *Cours de philosophie positive*, Vol. II, Paris: Bachelier, 1835, Leçon 28) distinguishes scientific discourse from all others, negatively at least. Schuster, who declared that "a theory is worthless when it cannot be demonstrated that it is false" (quoted by L. Brunschvicg, *L'expérience humaine et la causalité physique*, Paris: P.U.F., 1949, 3rd edn., p. 432), and especially Popper, who makes the "falsifiability" of theory the "criterion of demarcation" of science, can provide the logical argument that leads one to prefer falsification to confirmation as a form of experimental control (see K. R. Popper, *The Logic of Scientific Discovery*, London: Hutchinson, 1959, pp. 40–42 and 86–87).

[8] G. Canguilhem, "Leçons sur la méthode", lectures at the Strasbourg Faculté des Lettres evacuated to Clermont Ferrand, 1941–42 (unpublished). Quoted by kind permission of the author.

It is Not the initial objects that object, it is what they, as a collection, lead to. *E.G.?* *My plan to run all* *4LJ* *"groups"?*

which can only encounter facts that are in a sense made to measure; of some methodological exercises which create data made to be measured; and of the type of theoretical work which can only ground the parthenogenesis of its own theoretical facts in what one has to call, paraphrasing Nietzsche, the "dogma of the immaculate conception".[9] The object, it has been said, is what objects. Experiment only fulfils its function insofar as it sets up a permanent reminder of the reality principle against the temptation to yield to the pleasure principle which inspires the gratuitous fantasies of some types of formalism, the self-indulgent fictions of intuitionism or the academic exercises of pure theory.

the initial ☐ is not the object.

One has not finished with theory, nor even with the construction of hypotheses, once one has subjected the hypothesis to verification, and not even when it is verified or belied. Every well-constructed experiment has the effect of intensifying the dialectic between reason and experiment, but only on condition that one has an adequate understanding of the results, even negative ones, that it produces, and asks oneself what reasons make the facts right to say no. When Brunschvicg reminds us that "points of contradiction are points of reflection",[10] he does not mean to suggest that the "incontrovertible impact of experience" can suffice to stimulate reflection automatically in the absence of the decision to reflect and to reflect on oneself reflecting. As Bertrand Russell puts it, "one of the merits of a proof is that it instils a certain doubt as to the result proved; and when what is obvious can be proved in some cases, but not in others, it becomes possible to suppose that in these other cases it is false."[11] Evidence of failure is as decisive as a confirmation, but only on condition that it coincides with reconstruction of the systematic body of theoretical propositions in which it takes on positive meaning. "It is quite exceptional," says Norman Campbell, "for a new law to be discovered or suggested by experimentation, observation and the examination of results; most advances in the formulation of new laws result from the invention of theories capable of explaining old laws."[12] In short, the dialectic of scientific procedure cannot be reduced to an alternation, however often repeated, between independent operations, with verification following hypothesis and bearing no relation to it beyond confrontation.

Might happen.

---

[9] While it has to be recalled that every system of propositions claiming scientific validity has to be amenable to the test of reality, one also has to warn against the tendency to identify this epistemological imperative with the technological imperative that seeks to subordinate every theoretical formulation to the actual existence of techniques with which it can be verified at the time when it is expressed. Equally, as Hempel says, "no scientific hypothesis is ever proved completely and definitively; there is always at least the theoretical possibility that new evidence will be discovered which conflicts with some of the observational statements inferred from the hypothesis, and which thus leads to its rejection" (C. G. Hempel, *Aspects of Scientific Explanation*, New York: Free Press; London: Collier-Macmillan, 1965, p. 84).

[10] L. Brunschvicg, *Les étapes de la philosophie mathématique*, Paris: Alcan, 1912.

[11] B. Russell, *Mysticism and Logic, and Other Essays*, London: Allen & Unwin, 1963, p. 61.

[12] N. Campbell, *What is Science*, London: Methuen, 1921, p. 88. See also J. B. Conant, *Modern Science and Modern Man*, New York: Columbia University Press, 1952, p. 53.

There is no operation, however partial, that does not involve the dialectic between theory and verification. When designing a code, for example, the hypotheses that were set to work in the questionnaire have to be reviewed, specified, and modified in the light of the facts to be analysed, in order to be subjected to the experimental test of coding and statistical analysis. The technological formula of establishing the code at the same time as the questionnaire (at the risk of reducing what is worthy of being coded to what is encodable, which often means pre-codable), contains an implicit fixist ideology since it eliminates one of the opportunities for adapting, in the light of the data, the categories through which the data are apprehended. Similarly, the formally most irreproachable survey procedures may lose all sociological significance if the choice of sampling method is not made in relation to the specific hypotheses and objectives of the research. More generally, the illusion that there are all-purpose tools encourages the researcher to dispense with examining the validity of his techniques in the particular case in which he has to use them. Technological controls turn against their own intention when they lead to the illusion that one can dispense with controlling these controls. As well as threatening to induce paralysis and even error, the mania for methodology also makes it possible not so much to achieve the economy of thought that all method permits, but rather to economize on thought about method [*Bachelard, text no. 2*].

Routine meticulousness not only brings the risk of failing to look at objects that would not show off the excellence of the instrument; it is also liable to make researchers forget that, in order to observe certain facts, they should not so much refine the observing and measuring instruments as question the routine use that is made of the instruments. If Uvarov had let his tidy-minded laboratory assistant have his own way and put back in their proper place every morning the grey *locusta migratoria* which had been mislaid among the green *locusta danica*, he would never have noticed the *fact* that these were not two species but one and that *locusta danica* turned grey when it ceased to be solitary. One is inclined to think that a number of traditional techniques, when used without epistemological control, destroy the scientific fact in the same way as Uvarov's assistant's tidying principle. The fascination exerted by scientific equipment may stand in the way of the right relationship to facts and to proof by the facts, just as effectively as the prestige of theoretical apparatus. Submission to automatic thought processes is as dangerous as the illusion of creation without support or control. If the refinement of techniques of verification and proof is not accompanied by a redoubling of theoretical vigilance, it can lead one to see more and more in less and less, or even to miss the essential point through one of the oversights that form a functional couple with the blind use of techniques intended to sharpen and control one's sight [*Mills, text no. 35*].

3.2 The system of propositions and systematic verification

The operations of practice are only as good as the theory in which they are grounded, because theory owes its position in the hierarchy of operations to the fact that it actualizes the epistemological primacy of reason over experi- ✻ ence. It is not surprising, therefore, that theory constitutes the fundamental precondition for breaking with appearances, object construction, and experimentation, and that it does so by virtue of the systematicity that defines it. Only a scientific theory can resist the promptings of spontaneous sociology and the spurious systematizations of ideology, setting against them the organized resistance of a systematic body of concepts and relationships defined as much by the coherence of what it excludes as by the coherence of what it establishes;[13] it alone can construct the system of facts among which it sets up a systematic relationship [*Hjelmslev, text no. 36*]; and it alone can give experimentation its full power to invalidate by presenting it with a body of hypotheses so systematic that it is entirely exposed in each of them.

One would like to be able to say of sociology what Bachelard said of experimental physics: "The time of disconnected, mobile hypotheses is past, as is that of isolated, curious experiments. Henceforward, the hypothesis is a synthesis."[14] The pointillist verification which subjects a discontinuous series of fragmentary hypotheses to partial experimentations can indeed never derive more from experiments than denials that are of little consequence. Consider for example how the sociologist analysing the results of a survey facilitates his task by taking the statistical table as the unit of interpretation. By failing to address the question of the articulation of the propositions extracted from each table or of the strings of tables each duly accompanied by its made-to-measure commentary, he avoids the challenge of exposing a whole systematic body of propositions to the denial that each of the tables could provide. Nothing is better designed to preserve the easy conscience of positivism than the procedure that consists of moving from one observation to another with no other idea than the idea that an idea might spring up, since the test of overall denial that a theoretical model, for example, would be exposed to is constantly pushed aside, and the facts taken one by one can offer no resistance to the discontinuous, tentative questioning of those twilight states of the epistemo-

---

[13] Because prenotions, whether popular or erudite, derive their power from the systematic character of the intelligibility that they provide, there can be no hope of refuting them one by one. Historically, only systematic theories have been able to overcome systematic illusions, as has been shown, for the physical sciences, by T. S. Kuhn ("The Function of Dogma in Scientific Research", in A. C. Crombie [ed.], *Scientific Change: Historical Studies in the Intellectual, Social and Technical Conditions for Scientific Discovery and Technical Invention, from Antiquity to the Present*, Symposium on the History of Science, London: Heinemann, 1963, pp. 347 ff.) and N. R. Hanson (*Patterns of Discovery*, Cambridge: Cambridge University Press, 1965).

[14] G. Bachelard, *The New Scientific Spirit*, Boston (Mass.): Beacon Press, 1984, p. 6.

logical consciousness which generate propositions that are "not even wrong". The apparent rigour of the techniques of proof has in this case no other function than that of masking an evasion: like Horatius, the researcher wins an easy victory over the facts by backing away and confronting them one by one.

By contrast, when the hypothesis involves a systematic theory of the real, experimentation—which should then be called theoretical experimentation —can systematically exert its full power of denial. As Duhem observed, "an experiment can never condemn an isolated hypothesis but only a whole theoretical group".[15] As opposed to a discontinuous series of *ad hoc* hypotheses, a system of hypotheses derives its epistemological value from the coherence that makes it so vulnerable. On the one hand, one single fact can call it into question as a whole; and, on the other hand, having been constructed by means of a break with phenomenal appearances, it cannot expect the immediate, easy confirmation that would be provided by facts taken at face value or documents taken literally. Opting to risk losing everything in order to win everything, the scientist at all times invites the facts that he questions to test everything that he puts into his questioning of the facts. If it is true that in their most complete form, scientific propositions are won against the phenomenal appearances and that they presuppose the theoretic act which has the function, as Kant puts it, of "spelling out the phenomena so as to be able to read them as experiments", then it follows that they no longer find their proof anywhere except in the full coherence of the whole system of facts created by—and not for—the theoretical hypotheses that are to be validated.

Such a method of proof, in which the coherence of the constructed system of intelligible facts is itself its own proof, as well as being the principle of the proof-value of the partial proofs that the positivist manipulates one by one, clearly presupposes the systematic decision to question the facts as to the relations that make them a system. Thus, when Erwin Panofsky presents as "a scrap of evidence" the *inter se disputando* of the "Album" of Villard de Honnecourt, he knows full well that this inscription does not answer a question of fact—e.g. that of the influence of the Scholastics on the architects—as would be assumed by positivist historiographers, for whom an inquiry is a simple questionnaire to which reality replies, question by question, with straight yes or no answers. In reality, this little fact derives its proof-value from its relations with other facts, insignificant in themselves so long as they are constituted independently of the relations that the system of hypotheses sets up among them, but which take on their full value as the organized terms of a series: "Whether we deal with historical or natural phenomena, the individual observation assumes the character of a 'fact' only when it can be related to other, analogous observations in such a way that the whole series

[15] P. Duhem, *The Aim and Structure of Physical Theory*, New York: Atheneum, 1974, p. 183.

'makes sense'. This 'sense' is, therefore, fully capable of being applied, as a control, to the interpretation of a new individual observation within the same range of phenomena. If, however, this new individual observation definitely refuses to be interpreted according to the 'sense' of the series, and if an error proves to be impossible, the 'sense' of the series will have to be reformulated to include the new individual observation"[16] [*Wind, text no. 37*]. The sociologist anxious not to impose his own presuppositions on the given performs the same circular movement when, analysing a survey, he examines the whole set of answers to his questionnaire in order to decipher the meaning of each of the questions through which he has elicited and constructed these answers, while reformulating the meaning of the whole on the basis of what he learns from each of them. Duhem describes in very similar terms the logic of the progress of physics, "a symbolic painting in which continual retouching gives greater comprehensiveness and unity... whereas each detail of this picture, cut off and isolated from the whole, loses all meaning and no longer represents anything" and in which the uninitiated would only see "a monstrous confusion of fallacy, reasoning in circles and begging the question".[17]

Proof by the coherence of the system of proofs commits one to the *methodic circle*, which it would be too easy to write off as a vicious circle. Reinterpreting this logic of proof by reference to an analytic definition of verification, the positivist can only see this systematic construction of the facts as the result of a manipulation of the data inspired by system-building for its own sake. The same blindness leads some people to see the structural analysis of a myth as a projection of the researcher's own categories of thought or even as the schedule of a projective test, and to see an effect of bias in the methodological decision to interpret each of the statistical relations established by multivariate analysis on the basis of the system of relations among relations from which each relation derives its significance. The strength of the proof provided by an empirically recorded relation does not depend solely on the strength of the statistical link: the compound probability of the hypothesis being tested is a function of the complete system of already established relations (whether statistical or any other type of regularities), i.e. of the "concatenations of evidence", in Reichenbach's phrase, "a chain of probable inference [which] may very well be stronger than its weakest link, stronger even than its strongest link",[18] because the validity of such a system of proofs is measured not only by the simplicity and coherence of the principles at work in it, but also by the extension and diversity of the facts taken into account, and finally

---

[16] E. Panofsky, "Iconography and Iconology", *Meaning in the Visual Arts*, Harmondsworth: Penguin, 1970, p. 61 n. 3.

[17] P. Duhem, *The Aim and Structure of Physical Theory, op. cit.*, p. 204–205.

[18] A. Kaplan, *The Conduct of Inquiry: Methodology for Behavioral Science*, San Francisco: Chandler, 1964, p. 245.

the multiplicity of the unexpected consequences to which it leads [*Darwin, text no. 38*].

3.3 Epistemological couples

Bachelard shows that philosophies of the natural sciences naturally distribute themselves as a spectrum in which idealism and realism constitute the two extremes. The central point is "applied rationalism", which alone can yield the full truth of scientific practice by closely associating the "values of coherence" and "fidelity to the real": "And so the epistemologist must indeed stand at the crossroads, between realism and rationalism. That is where he can grasp the new dynamism of these opposing philosophies, the twofold movement through which science complicates the real and simplifies reason" [*Bachelard, text no. 39; Canguilhem, text no. 40*].

The fictitious or fertile forms of dialogue between symmetrical philosophies that Bachelard describes in the case of physics could easily be shown to have their equivalents in the implicit philosophies of the human sciences. These too are organized as couples of epistemological positions, and the further they are from the "central position", i.e. from the scientific practice in which the most intense dialectic is set up between reason and experiment, the more easily they can serve as each other's alibi, and the more sterile, albeit vehement, the dialogue they can conduct. It would then be seen that the positions which clash in the most passionate scientific polemics are in reality complementary: debate with the adversary dispenses one from setting up the argument with him, i.e. with oneself, within scientific practice. Thus the academic or prophetic rhetoric of social philosophy is able to see the disorderly proliferation of monographs and partial investigations, with all the renunciations they imply, as the justification for its planetary ambitions and its disdain for proof, while blind hyper-empiricism finds a justification on the opposite grounds in denunciation of the empty syntheses of ideology. Similarly, positivism uses the ritual condemnation of intuitionism as a pretext for handing itself over to the automatic use of techniques and even, paradoxically, to intuition, while intuitionism is able to use the dryness and pointillism of the bureaucratic research of positivism as an argument for the most impressionistic literary variations on ill-defined totalities[19] [*Durkheim, text no. 41*].

The linkage between the terms of these couples is so strong, in spite of appearances, that it is not uncommon for the researchers most strongly attached to one or other of these polar positions to betray, in their nostalgia or

---

[19] Between the Wars, Georges Politzer pointed out the relations of complementarity and complicity that united the technomaniac use of laboratory methods and attachment to theoretic traditionalism. This infernal cycle of introspection and experimentation is not without analogies with the couple formed in sociology by loyalty to the intuitions of spontaneous sociology and recourse to terrifying magic of ill-understood symbolism.

their (epistemologically significant) slips of the pen, that epistemological choices, good or bad, conscious or unconscious, form a system, so that the autonomizing of one of the operations of scientific practice obliges one to resort to the unconscious or covert substitute for the operations that are refused. Thus, because it restricts control of its practice to technical control of its instruments, positivism hunts out intuitionism in the phases of research that best lend themselves to technological refinement, without seeing that, having deprived itself of the resources of theory, it is forced to draw on spontaneous sociology for the notions that it translates into refined indices and also for the concepts in which it wraps the most subtle results of its manipulations (liberalism, empathy, satisfaction, participation, etc.).[20] Methodology manuals abound in precepts and guidelines for the design and administration of a questionnaire but open the door to intuition, sometimes of the riskiest sort, when it comes to formulating the principles for conceiving hypotheses or grids for the interpretation of quantitative results. Their proclaimed opposition must not be allowed to hide the deep solidarity between positivism and intuitionism, which often draw the basis of their explanations from the same source and only diverge in their techniques of verification. One only has to read some classics of positivist sociology to see that intuitionism is the real face of positivism, inasmuch as it exhibits what positivism tends to disguise under technological refinement.[21] Intuitionism, for its part, which thinks it can short-cut the laborious paths of scientific analysis and directly grasp real totalities by using models of thought borrowed from popular or middle-brow sociology, has a penchant for the "significant little fact" and—vice paying homage to virtue—sometimes seeks in a caricature of experimental proof a proof of its capacity to provide proofs.

In contrast to spontaneous sociology, where positivism and intuitionism have their roots and which traps all intellectual activity in the dilemma of

---

[20] In a very general way, operations that are excluded on principle manage to reappear, uncontrolled, in scientific procedure. Simiand showed that economists who explicitly limit themselves to deducing formal properties from a model will sometimes appeal to "conscious or unconscious" observation, in order, for example, to choose between several eventualities, with the result that "recourse to the experimental method is in this case surrounded by none of the precautions and guarantees that are required as a basis for its judicious and convincing use" (F. Simiand, "La méthode positiviste en science économique", *Revue de Métaphysique et de Morale*, Vol. 16, no. 6, pp. 889–904, 1908).

[21] It can even happen that the most methodical adversaries of intuition grant the supreme consecration of methodological christening to the most risky enterprises of intuitionism, such as Ruth Benedict's way of encapsulating a number of impressionistic observations on the general style of a culture in an "Apollonian pattern": "Such a formula capable of summing up in a single descriptive concept a great wealth of particular observations may be called a matrix formulation. This definition covers the notion of a 'Basic pattern' of a culture, a 'theme', an 'ethos', a 'zeitgeist' or 'mentality of the time', a 'national character', and on the level of the individual person a 'personality type'" (A. H. Barton and P. F. Lazarsfeld, "Some Functions of Qualitative Analysis in Social Research", in S. M. Lipset and N. J. Smelser [eds.], *Sociology: The Progress of a Decade*, Englewood Cliffs (N.J.): Prentice-Hall, 1961, p. 116).

boldness without rigour or rigour without boldness, the truly scientific project situates itself from the first in conditions in which every increase in the boldness of its theoretical ambitions calls for increased rigour in establishing the proofs to which it submits itself. Nothing, therefore, condemns sociology to oscillate, as it too often does at present, between a "social theory" without empirical foundations and a theoretically rudderless empiricism, between the risk-free temerity of intuitionism and the undemanding meticulousness of positivism. Nothing—except an impoverished, caricatured, or exalted image of the natural sciences. Once it has outgrown its enthusiasms for the most superficial aspects of the experimental method or the wonders of the mathematical tool, sociology will perhaps be able to find, in the practical overcoming of the opposition between rationalism and empiricism, the means of progressing towards both greater theoretical coherence and greater fidelity to the real.

My FP is an "empirical" study of data generated via a "theoretical method" (Fararo?)

Conclusion
Sociology of knowledge and epistemology

All that has been said so far would lead one to deny sociology a special epistemological status. However, because in sociology the frontier between common knowledge and science is more blurred than elsewhere, the need for the epistemological break is particularly pressing. But since error is inseparable from the social conditions which make it possible and sometimes inevitable, one would have to have a naïve faith in the virtues of epistemological preaching if one neglected to consider the social conditions that would render the break with spontaneous sociology and ideology possible or even inevitable and would establish epistemological vigilance as an institution of the sociological field.

It is no accident that Bachelard borrows the language of the sociologist to describe the interpenetration of the scientific world and its worldly audience [*Bachelard, text no. 42*]. The sociologist of sociology would have no difficulty in finding the modern equivalent of the society entertainments to which the *curiosa* of physics gave rise in a past century — psychoanalysis, anthropology, and even sociology offer their own "electrical kisses" today. The sociology of sociological knowledge can provide the sociologist with the means of giving epistemological critique its full force and its specific form, when it is a matter of bringing to light the unconscious presuppositions and begged questions of a theoretical tradition, rather than of calling into question the principles of a constituted theory.

If, in sociology, here and now, empiricism ranks highest in the hierarchy of epistemological dangers, this is due not only to the particular nature of the sociological object as a subject who offers a verbal interpretation of his own behaviour, but also to the historical and social conditions in which sociology is practised. One must therefore take care not to confer a trans-historical reality on the structure of the epistemological field as a spectrum of philosophical positions opposed in couples. One reason for this is that the various sciences which emerge at different dates and in different historical and social conditions do not pass through the same stages of the same history of epistemological reason in accordance with some pre-established order.

What is the answer to my FP question?

Outline of a sociology of the positivist temptation
in sociology

In contemporary \French\ sociology, the attraction exerted by positivism is perhaps due not so much to the intrinsic seductions of this brief philosophy of scientific practice, or to the place occupied by sociology in a hypothetical evolutionary pattern valid for all sciences, but rather to a set of social and intellectual conditions. The latter are themselves inseparable from a specific history, with, in particular, the rise, routinization, and decline of Durkheimianism in the 1920s and 1930s. The intellectuals of the 1950s might have been less susceptible to the illusion of an absolute beginning and the utopia of a practice that provides its own epistemological foundation, were it not for the particular relationship they had to the intellectual generation of 1939. The outbreak of the Second World War had meant that French sociologists, who were linked to the philosophical tradition but cut off from empirical practice by a set of historically specific conditions, not the least of which was the inadequate institutional support for research, were obliged to put off the task of reconciling empirical research and theory. When French empirical sociology started up again after the War, it did so in an intellectual field dominated by philosophy, and more particularly by existentialism, and this led the sociologists to throw themselves blindly into the camp of the most empiricist American sociology, a commitment which implied a willing or forced renunciation of the theoretical past of European sociology.[1]

To show, in opposition to the evolutionist schema, how much the development of the various sciences owes to the structure of the field in which they coexist, one would only have to point out that, far from benefiting from the advantage that it might be expected to derive from its situation as the newcomer, able to leap forward by avoiding the misadventures of its forerunners and following a path already blazed for it, sociology paradoxically falls not only into epistemological errors that the natural sciences no longer commit, but also into specific errors that are suggested to it by the permanent confrontation with the daunting image of more perfected sciences. More precisely, one could show how much the relation that each sociologist has to the image of the scientificity of his own practice owes to the overall field within which he operates: a science that is anxious about its scientific recognition is led into endless self-questioning about the conditions of its own scientificity and, in this anguished quest for *reassurance*, uncritically adopts the most salient and often the most naive signs of scientific legitimacy. It is no accident that, as Poincaré put it, whereas the natural sciences talk of their results, the social sciences boast of their methods. The mania for methodology or the thirst for the latest refinements of componential analysis, graph theory, or matrix cal-

---

[1] Polemics on the philosophical presuppositions of the various orientations of sociological research are no substitute for philosophical reflection and often help to conceal its absence; one only has to consider, for example, the academic or trivial nature of the debate on the "philosophies of structuralism". The range of philosophical attitudes which the intellectual field offers sociologists to understand their practice does not express the epistemology that is really implied by scientific work. Bachelard saw the philosophical eclecticism of most scientists as a way of refusing the abstract purity of philosophical systems lagging behind science on the grounds of the "philosophical impurity" of science.

culus assume the same ostentatious function as recourse to prestigious labels or fascinated attachment to the instruments—questionnaires or computers—most likely to symbolize the specificity of the craft and its scientific quality.

Furthermore, the technical division of labour and the social organization of the profession entail a number of constraints capable of inclining the researcher towards bureaucratic automatisms, which are always associated with an empiricist philosophy of science. Some features of American sociological production, such as the redundant proliferation of small empirical monographs or the multiplication of "textbooks" and popularizing works, no doubt owe something to the characteristics of the American university system, where the university personnel is divided into specialized administrators and researchers and where the mechanisms of competition subject academic careers to the laws of the market. The professionalization of research, linked to the use of substantial grants, the growing number of research staff, and therefore the appearance of large research units, has led to a technical division of labour that owes its specificity to the ideology of the autonomy of operations which it has engendered. Thus, as has been seen, the parcelling-out of research operations, which serves at least as an unconscious paradigm for most researchers, is simply the projection into epistemological space of a bureaucratic organization chart.[2] Finally, when one adds that the popular representation of the miracle-working automaton overawes many researchers, who are inclined to hand over responsibility for operations to the machine, and that the generals of research tend to leave the greater part of the battle, i.e. contact with the facts (and, among other things, with the respondents), to their infantry, and to reserve for themselves the grand strategic decisions, such as the choice of the sample, design of the questionnaire, or the writing of the report, it can be seen that everything conspires to favour the dichotomy between blind empiricism and uncontrolled theory, formalistic magic and the ritual of the subaltern acts of the survey.

The taste for methodological prowess that is encouraged by an anxious relationship to the model of the exact sciences probably owes its most pathological characteristics to the split between humanities and science training and to the absence of specific and complete sociological training. Statistical tools, initially the monopoly of a few researchers who had taught themselves late in life how to manipulate them, were used in terroristic ways that presupposed the ill-surmounted terror of the fascinated novice, losing their protective function only as they became more widespread.

Thus, epistemological oppositions do not take on their full significance until they are seen in relation to the system of positions and oppositions established

[2] Cf. the "flow chart" of the phases of the survey as presented by most manuals, for example, A. A. Campbell and G. Katona, "The Sample Survey: A Technique for Social Science Research", in L. Festinger and D. Katz (eds.), *Research Methods in the Behavioral Sciences*, London: Staples, 1954, pp. 15–55.

between institutions, groups, or cliques differently situated within the intellectual field. The set of characteristics that define each researcher, namely his type of training (humanities or sciences, canonical or eclectic, complete or partial), his status in or relation to the university system, his affiliations of interest, and his membership of intellectual pressure groups (scientific or extra-scientific journals, panels and committees, etc.), combine to determine his chances of occupying this or that position, i.e. of espousing particular oppositions, within the epistemological field. One is an empiricist, a formalist, a theoretician, or none of these, much less by vocation than by destiny, inasmuch as the sense of one's own practice presents itself in the form of the system of possibilities and impossibilities defined by the social conditions of one's intellectual practice. It can be seen that it can be useful to take the methodic decision to treat epistemological professions of faith as professional ideologies aimed, in the last analysis, at justifying not so much the science as the scientist, not so much the real practice as the limits imposed on practice by the researcher's position and past. While the different forms of epistemological error and of the ideology that justifies them owe their generic strength to the theoretical conjuncture with its prevailing tone and its lacunae, they are not distributed randomly among sociologists. The system of ideological justifications that tend to transform *de facto* limitations into *de jure* limits might constitute the principle of resistances to epistemological lucidity. The sociology that each sociologist can perform of the social conditions of his sociological practice and his relation to sociology cannot, in itself, take the place of epistemological reflection, but it is the precondition for his making his unconscious presuppositions explicit and for a more complete internalization of a more adequate epistemology.

The sociologist in society

Perhaps the most fundamental presupposition that the sociologist owes to the fact that he is a social subject is the presupposition of the absence of presuppositions which defines ethnocentrism; the sociologist (more than the ethnologist) is vulnerable to the illusion of immediate self-evidence or the temptation to unconsciously universalize particular experience when he forgets that he is the cultivated subject of a particular culture and fails to subordinate his practice to a continuous questioning of this relationship.[3] But warnings against ethnocentrism count for little if they are not constantly revived and reinterpreted by epistemological vigilance. Within a given society, it is again the logic of ethnocentrism that governs the relations between groups. The code that the sociologist uses to decipher the behaviour of social subjects has been con-

---

[3] Cf. C. Lévi-Strauss's analysis of evolutionism as an intellectual ethnocentrism (*Race and History*, Paris: UNESCO, 1952, Ch. 3).

stituted through socially qualified learning-processes and always partakes of
the cultural codes of the different groups to which he belongs. Of all the
cultural presuppositions that the researcher is liable to involve in his interpretations, the one which operates most insidiously and most systematically is his
class *ethos*, the principle which in turn organizes the acquisition of his other
unconscious models. Because each social class derives the fundamental
principles of its ideology of the functioning and evolution of society from a
primary experience of social reality in which, among other things, determinisms are felt more or less directly, a sociologist who fails to perform the
sociology of the relation to society that is characteristic of his own social class
is likely to reintroduce into his scientific relation to the object the unconscious
presuppositions of his own primary experience of the social, or, more subtly,
the rationalizations that enable an intellectual to reinterpret his experience in
accordance with a logic which always owes something to the position he
occupies within the intellectual field. When one observes, for example, that
the working classes more readily use the language of destiny to express experience that is more directly subject to economic and social determinisms,
whereas any account of the determinisms that bear on the choices seemingly
most apt to symbolize the liberty of the person, e.g. in artistic taste or religious experience, encounters the horrified incredulity of the cultivated classes,
one has reason to question the sociological neutrality of a good many debates
on social determinisms and human freedom.

But epistemological vigilance has never finished with ethnocentrism: intellectual denunciation of class ethnocentrism can serve as an alibi for intellectual
or occupational ethnocentrism. As an intellectual, the sociologist belongs to a
group that is inclined to see as self-evident the interests, the schemes of
thought, the problematics, in short the system of presuppositions that is
linked to the intellectual class as a privileged reference group. It is no accident
that, when certain intellectuals denounce the contempt which the cultivated
classes or other intellectuals evince for "mass culture", they are led to credit
the working classes with a relation to this type of cultural goods which is none
other than their own or—which amounts to the same thing—its opposite.
What makes intellectual ethnocentrism particularly insidious is the fact that
the spontaneous or semi-intellectual sociology secreted by the intellectual class
and diffused by weekly magazines, journals, and intellectual conversations can
less easily be denounced as pre-scientific than the more popular formulations
of the same commonplaces, so that it is liable to supply researchers with
unexamined preconceptions and obligatory problems. Those who inhabit such
a strongly integrated milieu—and even more, perhaps, those who aspire to
enter it, such as students—receive from it a system of constraints that is made
all the more compelling by the fact that they present themselves as the implicit
rules of social grace or good taste. To be able to withstand the intellectual
insinuations and hidden persuasions of an intellectual consensus masquerading

as a dissensus, and to "systematically discard all prenotions"—which impress intellectuals rather more when they hear them on a café terrace in Saint-Germain-des-Prés than in some less chic suburban bar—and contrary to a naive representation of ethical neutrality as universal benevolence, one should not be afraid to encourage a systematic prejudice against all fashionable ideas and to make an allergy to modishness a rule for the direction of the sociological mind.

The "scientific city" and epistemological vigilance

Thus, the sociology of knowledge [connaissance], which has often been used to justify relativizing the validity of scientific knowledge [savoir], and more precisely the sociology of sociology—which has often been seen as merely a refutation per absurdum of the absurd pretensions of sociologism—can be a particularly effective means of epistemological control of sociological practice. If, in order to reflect on himself reflecting, each sociologist has to resort to the sociology of sociological knowledge, he cannot hope to escape from relativization by a necessarily fictitious effort to tear himself completely away from all the determinations that define his social situation and to attain the ethereal standpoint of true knowledge where Mannheim situated his "free-floating intellectuals". So we have to abandon the utopian hope that each individual can free himself from the ideologies that weigh on his research by the sheer strength of a self-imposed reform of a socially conditioned understanding or a "self-socio-analysis" which would serve no other purpose than to justify self-satisfaction in and by socio-analysis of others. The objectivity of science cannot be built on such shaky foundations as the objectivity of scientists. The gains from epistemological reflection cannot be really embodied in practice until the social conditions are established for epistemological control, i.e. for a generalized exchange of critiques armed with, among other things, the sociology of sociological practices [Maget, text no. 43].

Every scientific community is a social microcosm, furnished with institutions for control, constraint, and training—academic authorities, juries, critical forums, research councils, co-option panels, etc.—which define the norms of professional competence and tend to inculcate the values that they express.[4] Thus, the chances that scientific works will be produced do not depend solely on the strength of the resistance that the scientific community as such can put up against the most extrinsic demands, whether these be the expectations of

[4] As Duhem points out, "Contemplation of a set of experimental laws does not suffice to suggest to the physicist what hypotheses he should choose in order to give a theoretical representation of these laws; it is also necessary that the thoughts habitual with those among whom he lives and the tendencies impressed on his own mind by his previous studies come and guide him, and restrict the excessively great latitude left to his choice by the rules of logic" (*The Aim and Structure of Physical Theory, op. cit.*, p. 255).

the general intellectual audience, the diffuse or explicit pressures of users or sponsors, or the prompting of political or religious ideologies; they also depend on the degree of conformity to scientific norms that the very organization of the community manages to maintain. Sociologists of science who exclusively emphasize the inertia of the scientific world as an organized society are often simply transposing one of the commonplaces of scientific hagiography, that of the travails of the inventor. Reducing a specific problem to generalities on resistance to innovation, they fail to distinguish the opposing effects that the control of the scientific community may produce, depending on whether the formalistic constraints of erudite traditionalism confine research within conformity to a theoretical tradition or whether the institutionalization of a stimulating vigilance favours a continuous break with all traditions.[5] The question of whether sociology is or is not a science, and a science like others, therefore has to give way to the question of the type of organization and functioning of the "scientific city" most conducive to the appearance and development of research that is subject to strictly scientific controls. This new question can no longer be answered in all-or-nothing terms. In each case, one has to analyse the multiple effects of the multiple factors that combine to define the chances of emergence of a more or less scientific production and, more precisely, one has to distinguish the factors that help to increase the chances of scientificity of a scientific community as a whole and the chances each scientist has of benefiting from these chances on the basis of the position he occupies within the scientific community.[6]

It will readily be granted that everything that helps to intensify the exchange of information and critiques, to break down the epistemological isolation maintained by the barriers between institutions, and to reduce the obstacles to communication that derive from the hierarchy of reputation and status, from the diversity of types of training and career structures, and from the proliferation of chapels too inward-looking to engage in competition or overt conflict,

[5] An example of this kind of argument, in which the conservatism of scientific communities is attributed to such generic factors as *esprit de corps* or the inertia of academic organizations, can be found in the writings of B. Barber (e.g. "Resistance by Scientists to Scientific Discovery", *Science*, Vol. 34, no. 3479, pp. 596–602, 1 Sept. 1961).

[6] To show the extent to which individual chances of making discoveries depend on the collective chances of the community to which the scientist belongs, one only has to mention such well-known phenomena as premature inventions or simultaneous inventions. A number of discoveries have only been retrospectively discovered as such, by reference to a theoretical framework that did not exist when they first appeared. The frequency of simultaneous discoveries can only be explained by re-situating the invention in relation to a state of theory, which means, among other things, a state of the scientific community and its means of control and communication at a given time. T. S. Kuhn shows, apropos of the principle of the conservation of energy, that the convergence of discoveries can only appear *a posteriori*, when scattered elements have been integrated in and by a scientific theory which, when it is unanimously recognized, appears, by a retrospective quasi-illusion, as the necessary culmination of convergent inventions (T. S. Kuhn, "Energy Conservation as an Example of Simultaneous Discovery", in M. Clagett [ed.], *Critical Problems in the History of Science*, Madison: University of Wisconsin Press, 1959, pp. 321–358).

will help to bring the scientific community, subjected to the inertia of the institutions it needs to have in order to exist, closer to the ideal city of scientists, in which, ideally, all the scientific communications required by science and the progress of science, and only those, would be able to take place. It is clear how far the community of sociologists remains from that ideal situation: a good many polemics reveal oppositions that are rooted in external affinities more often than they express divergences implying recognition of the same scientific values. Moreover, the scientific value of criticism depends on the form and structure of the exchanges within which it takes place. There is every reason to think that the generalized exchange of judgements in which, as in the matrimonial exchange system of the same name, scientist A judges scientist B, who judges C, who judges D, is a more favourable model for organic integration of the scientific world than, for example, a mutual admiration society conducting a restricted exchange of services, or, scarcely better, the exchange of ritual polemics through which colluding adversaries reinforce each other's status. Whereas restricted exchange is compatible with communion in implicit presuppositions, generalized exchange entails a multiplicity and diversity of types of communication and so favours the explication of epistemological assumptions. Moreover, as Michael Polanyi shows, this kind of "continuous network of critics" ensures the compliance of all with the common norms of scientificity by setting up, through the "'transitiveness' of neighbouring appraisals", the control of each over several others (those whom he can and must judge as a specialist) and by several others (those who can and must judge him as specialists) [*Polanyi, text no. 44*]. By continuously confronting each scientist with a critical explication of his own scientific operations and of the presuppositions they imply and so forcing him to make this explication the obligatory accompaniment of his own practice and the communication of his discoveries, this "system of cross-checks" tends to set up and constantly reinforce the capacity for epistemological vigilance in each scientist.[7]

The effects of inter-disciplinary collaboration, which is frequently presented as a scientific panacea, must likewise not be dissociated from the social and intellectual characteristics of the scientific community. Just as contacts between societies with different traditions are one of the occasions when unconscious presuppositions are as it were provoked to make themselves explicit, so discussions between specialists in different disciplines might constitute the best measure of the traditionalism of a scientific body, i.e. of the degree to which it unconsciously excludes from customary discussion the presuppositions which make that discussion possible. Interdisciplinary encounters which, in the case of the social sciences, generally give rise to simple exchanges of "data" or, which amounts to the same thing, of

[7] For an analysis of the function of social control in the "scientific city", see G. Bachelard, *La formation de l'esprit scientifique*, Paris: Vrin, 4th edn., 1965 (1st edn. 1938), Ch. III.

unresolved questions, remind one of the archaic type of transactions in which two groups deposit goods for each other's benefit that they can subsequently collect without having to meet each other.[8]

In short, the scientific community has to provide itself with specific forms of social interchange, and, like Durkheim, one is entitled to see a symptom of its heteronomy in the fact that, in France at least, and even today, it is too often responsive to the non-scientific enticements of intellectual "worldliness": "We believe," wrote Durkheim at the end of The Rules of Sociological Method, "that the time has come for sociology to renounce worldly successes, so to speak, and to take on the character which befits all science. Thus it will gain in dignity and authority what it will perhaps lose in popularity."[9]

[8] To appreciate how much the language in which a group of specialists expresses its problematics owes to the largely unconscious tradition of the discipline, one only has to think of the misunderstandings that arise in dialogue between specialists, even from neighbouring disciplines. The common idea that all the difficulties of inter-disciplinary communication stem from the diversity of languages obscures the fact that speakers enclose themselves in their language because systems of expression are at the same time the schemes of perception and thought which create the objects that are worth talking about.

[9] É. Durkheim, The Rules of Sociological Method, op. cit., p. 163.

Illustrative texts

Remarks on the choice of texts

We have taken the illustration of the principles of sociological science from authors who are radically different in other respects—at the risk of seeming to do violence to the texts by tearing them from their contexts—because we are convinced that it is possible to define the principles of knowledge of the social independently of the theories of the social which separate theoretical schools and traditions. In order to fill what seemed to us to be gaps in the specifically epistemological writing devoted to sociology, we have often drawn on texts originally concerned with the natural sciences. This reflects our intention of applying the classical analyses of the philosophy of science, mutatis mutandis, to the science like others that sociology is or seeks to be. We have included a number of sociological texts from the work of the founders of sociology, in particular the Durkheimian school, because the present-day inattentive recognition of Durkheim's methodology seems to us even more likely to neutralize the epistemological advances that it contains than a deliberate refusal; and, at a deeper level, because the inaugural phase is the most favourable moment for spelling out the principles which make a new type of scientific discourse possible.

Foreword ✓
An epistemology of composition

Bachelard's thinking has to be situated explicitly in relation to the tradition of the philosophy of knowledge and the theory of the sciences, and in particular to the realism of Meyerson and the idealism of Brunschvicg, in order to make clear the synthetic significance of the "philosophy of no", which integrates and moves beyond the acquisitions of previous thinking by constituting epistemology as a reflection on science in progress. By placing himself at the centre of the oscillations, which characterize all scientific thought, between the rectifying power of experimentation and the illusion-breaking and creative power of reason, Bachelard is able to define the philosophy that is actualized in "the incessant polemical action of Reason" as applied rationalism and rational materialism. This epistemology rejects the formalism and fixism of a single, indivisible Reason in favour of a pluralism of rationalisms linked to the scientific domains that they rationalize. Positing as its first axiom the "theoretical primacy of error", it defines the progress of knowledge as an unceasing rectification. It is thus predisposed to provide a language and theoretical assistance to the social sciences, which, in order to constitute their regional rationalism, have to overcome some particularly daunting epistemological obstacles.

1. G. Canguilhem

In *La Dialectique de la durée*, Bachelard declares that he can accept almost everything in Bergsonianism except continuity.[1] This profession of faith seems to us more sincere in what it refuses than in what it retains. Being very resolutely hostile to the idea of continuity, but rather moderately Bergsonian, Bachelard does not accept that perception and science are pragmatic functions in continuity. But it is continuity that he dislikes here even more than pragmatism, for, like Émile Meyerson, neither does he accept that perception and science are speculative functions in continuity linked in their effort to identify the diverse.[2] He is assuredly closer to a position that one might, with some caution, call Cartesian—thinking of the distinction between understanding and imagination—, a position common, in some respects, to Alain and Léon Brunschvicg, according to which science is constituted by a break with perception and as a critique of it. But, though closer to Brunschvicg than Alain, in that, like the former, he feels required to accept and celebrate the subordination of reason to science, the instruction of reason by science,[3] Bachelard nonetheless differs from him in stressing the polemical form, the dialectical manner of the supersession that constitutes knowledge, in which Brunschvicg saw rather the effect of continuous progress, correction no doubt, but which, all in all, only requires the intelligence to be aware of its own standard, a

---

[1] *La dialectique de la durée*, p. 16.
[2] *Le rationalisme appliqué*, pp. 176–177.
[3] *La philosophie du non*, p. 144.

Continuity is not a concrete, complete, concept, at least philosophically

"capacity to transform itself by the very attention it pays to itself".[4] [...]

Situating Bachelard's epistemological position in relation to others must not divert us from the essential point, which is to convey to those who did not experience it a sense of just what an event it was when in 1927 an unusual style appeared in the sphere of French philosophy: not at all worldly, but at once dense, sinewy, and subtle, matured in solitary labour, far from academic modes and models, a rustic philosophical style. Now, the first characteristic of this style is that it states things as they are seen or known, with no effort to seek approval by the use of attenuation and concession, no "as it were's" and "one might even say's" [à la rigueur]. With an "à la rigueur" all rigour is given away, and that is just where Bachelard will not give way. That is why, when he asserts that "science is not a pleonasm for experience",[5] but is constructed against experience, against perception, against all everyday technical activity, Bachelard, who knows that he thereby puts science in a strange situation, is quite unconcerned as to whether the intellectual habits of his contemporaries will enable them to cope with his theses. Science becomes a specifically intellectual operation that has a history but no origins. It is the Genesis of the Real, but its own genesis cannot be told. It can be described as a beginning-anew, but can never be grasped in its infancy. It is not the fructifying of a preknowledge. An archaeology of science is an undertaking that has a meaning, a pre-history of science is an absurdity.

Not in order to simplify this epistemology, but the better to test its coherence, I shall try to extract from it a body of axioms, the duplication of which as a code of intellectual standards reveals to us that their nature is not that of immediately clear self-evidences, but is indeed that of often laboriously gathered and tested instructions. [...]

The first axiom relates to the *Theoretical primacy of error*. "Truth takes on its full meaning only after a polemic. There cannot be a primary truth. There are only primary errors."[6] One notes, in passing, the Pythagorean, Cartesian style of the grammatical form. Primary truth is singular; primary errors, plural. In more lapidary style, the same axiom is stated thus: "A truth against a background of error, such is the form of scientific thought."[7]

The second axiom relates to the *Speculative depreciation of intuition*. "Intuitions are very useful; they serve to be destroyed."[8] This axiom is converted into a standard of confirmation, in accordance with two formulae: "In all circumstances, the *immediate* must give way to the *constructed*."[9] "Every datum must reappear as a result."[10]

[4] *Les âges de l'intelligence*, p. 147.
[5] *Le rationalisme appliqué*, p. 38.
[6] "Idéalisme discursif", in *Recherches philosophiques*, 1934–35, p. 22.
[7] *Le rationalisme appliqué*, p. 48.
[8] *La philosophie du non*, p. 139.
[9] *Ibid.*, p. 144.
[10] *Le matérialisme rationnel*, p. 57.

The third axiom relates to the *Positing of the object as a perspective of ideas*.[11] "We understand the real precisely to the extent that necessity organizes it... . Our thought goes towards the real, it does not start out from it."[12]

It is important to insist on the scope of these three axioms. First of all, it is in a sense a truism to say that science expels error and substitutes itself for ignorance. But equally, philosophers or scientists have too often conceived error as a regrettable accident, a blunder that a little less haste or caution would have spared us, and have regarded ignorance as a corresponding privation of knowledge. Hitherto no one had said with Bachelard's insistent assurance that the mind is initially in itself a pure capacity for error, that error has a positive function in the genesis of knowledge, and that ignorance is not a kind of lacuna or absence but has the structure and vitality of instinct.[13] Similarly, their awareness of the necessarily hypothetico-deductive nature of any science whatsoever had, by the late 19th century, led the philosophers to accept the inadequacy of the notion of intuitive principles, self-evidences, gifts, or graces, sensory or intellectual. But no one had previously devoted as much energy and persistence as Bachelard to asserting that science is constructed against the immediate, against sensations,[14] that "primary self-evidence is not a fundamental truth",[15] that the immediate phenomenon is not the important phenomenon.[16] Critical malevolence is not a painful necessity from which the scientist might wish to be dispensed, for it is not a consequence of science but its essence. The break with the past of concepts, polemics, dialectics: that is all we find after analysis of the means of knowledge. Without exaggeration but not without paradox, Bachelard makes refusal the driving force of knowledge. But, above all, no one had applied more patience, ingenuity, and culture to multiplying the examples given in support of this thesis. The model of this kind of exercise seems to us to lie in the passage in which the example of atomic theory is called upon to show that the benefit of knowledge lies entirely in what the rectification of a concept "cuts out"[17] from an initial intuition or image. "The atom is exactly *the sum of the criticisms* to which its first representation has been subjected."[18] And again: "The diagram of the atom proposed by Bohr a quarter of a century ago has, in this sense, acted as a good image: there is nothing left of it."[19] In an earlier work in which he was much less harsh towards Bohr's schema, Bachelard denounced the "illusory character of

[11] This phrase appears in *Essai sur la connaissance approchée*, p. 246.
[12] *La valeur inductive de la relativité*, pp. 240–241.
[13] *La philosophie du non*, p. 8; *La formation de l'esprit scientifique*, p. 15.
[14] *La formation de l'esprit scientifique*, p. 250.
[15] *La psychanalyse du feu*, p. 9.
[16] *Les intuitions atomistiques*, p. 160.
[17] *La philosophie du non*, p. 139.
[18] *Ibid.*, p. 139.
[19] *Ibid.*, p. 140.

our primary intuitions".[20] For a philosopher who declares that "the real is never what one might think, but what one ought to have thought",[21] the true can only be "the limit of lost illusions".[22]

So it is not surprising that no realism, least of all empirical realism, finds favour as a theory of knowledge in Bachelard's eyes. The real does not exist before or outside science. Science does not detect or capture the real, it indicates the intellectual direction and organization with which "one can be assured that one is approaching the real".[23] Scientific concepts are neither catalogues of sensations nor mental replicas of essences. "Essence is a function of relationship."[24] Having, in his *Essai sur la connaissance approchée*,[25] justified the subordination of the concept to judgement, Bachelard returns to and consolidates this position in his study of relativity physics. The judgement of inherence appears as a particular case of the judgement of relation; the attribute as a function of modes; being, as coincident with relations. "Relationship says everything, proves everything, contains everything."[26] Thought encounters the real on its path towards the true. In the order of judgements of modality, "the assertoric has to be placed far behind the apodictic".[27] This being so, it matters little to Bachelard what label the lovers of academic classifications or the censors of heterodox ideologies seek to fix on what is not his system, but only his line of thought. If he is called an idealist when he approaches science by the royal road of mathematical physics, he answers: *Discursive idealism*—laborious in its dialectics and never triumphant without a reverse. If he is called a materialist when he goes into the chemist's laboratory, he answers: *Rational materialism*—informed, not naïve, active, not docile, a materialism that does not receive its matter but makes its own, which "thinks and works on a world made anew".[28]

For the reality of the world always has to be recreated, being under the responsibility of reason. And reason can never cease to be unreasonable in order to strive to become ever more rational. If reason were merely reasonable, it would one day end up being satisfied with its success, saying yes to its achievements. But the message is always no. How is this perpetually renewed power of negation to be explained? In an admirable formula, Bachelard once said that "we have the power to reawaken the springs".[29] But in the very heart of man there is a spring that never runs dry and so never needs to be reawakened, and it is the very source of that which philosophy has long

[20] *Les intuitions atomistiques*, p. 193.
[21] *La formation de l'esprit scientifique*, p. 13.
[22] "Idéalisme discursif", in *op. cit.*
[23] *La valeur inductive de la relativité*, p. 203.
[24] *Ibid.*, p. 208.
[25] *Essai sur la connaissance approchée*, Ch. II, "La rectification des concepts".
[26] *La valeur inductive de la relativité*, p. 270.
[27] *Ibid.*, p. 245.
[28] *Le matérialisme rationnel*, p. 22.
[29] *Essai sur la connaissance approchée*, p. 290.

attributed to the sleep of the body and the mind, the source of dreams, images, and illusions. It is the permanence of this primal, literally poetic, power that compels reason to strive constantly to deny, criticize, and reduce. The rational dialectic, the essential ingratitude of reason for its repeated successes, therefore merely designates the presence in consciousness of a tireless capacity for diversion of the real, a force that always accompanies scientific thought not as a shadow but as a counterlight [...].

So the mind must be vision in order for reason to be revision, the mind must be poetic in order for reason to be analytic in its technique, and rationalism, psychoanalytical in its intention. Some have been surprised to see a philosophical enterprise that is in such apparent conformity with the constant attitude of rationalism, placed under the sign of psychoanalysis. But this is a quite different undertaking from the optimistic vocation of the Enlightenment or positivism. It is not a question of thinking or calling oneself a rationalist. "Rationalist?" says Bachelard, "That is what I am trying to become."[30] And he explains: "It has been seen as surprising that a rationalist philosopher should devote so much attention to illusions and errors and should constantly need to represent rational values and clear images as rectifications of falsehoods."[31] But, contrary to what was supposed by the rationalists of the 18th and 19th centuries, error is not a weakness but a strength, reverie is not smoke but fire. Like fire, it starts up again incessantly. "We shall devote part of our efforts to showing that reverie endlessly takes up primitive themes, works unceasingly like a primitive mind, in spite of the successes of elaborated thought, even contrary to the lessons of scientific experiments."[32]

It was possible to place hope in the definitive reduction of sense images by the work of insensible reason, so long as it was not suspected to what extent the sensualist imagination can have the deep, renascent vitality of sensuality. [...]

The senses, in all senses of the word, fabulate. One only has to re-read on this subject, and in connection with early research on electricity, the reflections of our philosopher on the sensual character of concrete knowledge[33] and his conclusion concerning the immutability of unconscious values.[34] It is not so easy to be a rationalist as the men of the Enlightenment supposed. Rationalism is a costly philosophy, an unending philosophy, because it is "a philosophy that has had no beginning".[35]

Describing the dialectical subtleties of reason as a riposte to the proliferation of epistemological obstacles, Bachelard has succeeded where so many epistemologists have failed: in understanding anti-science. Émile Meyerson, in

---

[30] *Ibid.*, p. 10.
[31] *Ibid.*, p. 9.
[32] *La psychanalyse du feu*, p. 14.
[33] *Le rationalisme appliqué*, p. 141.
[34] *Ibid.*, note.
[35] *Le rationalisme appliqué*, p. 123.

short, found an easy way out of the difficulties raised for the philosophical intelligence by the resistance that qualified experience, the universe of the living, puts up against the rational effort for the identity of the real. By calling this rebellious core "irrational", Meyerson sought to depreciate it; but in declaring reason justified in "sacrificing" it, he implicitly acknowledged in it some value that he did not hesitate equally to call reality. But two realities are one too many! In fact, Meyerson's epistemology remained based on Manichaeism, having failed to distinguish between the negative and nothing. This is the inevitable fate of any epistemology which imports into philosophy the values exclusively proper to science, and which regards anti-science as disqualified absolutely by and for science. Bachelard, equally though differently attached to science and poetry, reason and imagination, is not in the least Manichaean. He has willingly taken on the role and the risk of a "philosophy of composition" [une philosophie concordataire].[36] When he brings out into the open the latent archetypes of the image-making imagination, fomenting for reason, i.e. against it, the obstacles to science that are the objects of science, the objections to science, he is not playing the Devil's advocate but knows he is the accomplice of the Creator. With Bachelard, once again, after Bergson, continuous creation changes its meaning. It is not only his epistemology that is non-Cartesian,[37] but also, and primarily, his ontology. Continuous creation is not the guarantee of the identity of being or of its habit, but of its naïveté, its renewal. "Instants are distinct because they are fruitful."[38]

Georges Canguilhem
"Sur une épistémologie concordataire"

[36] *L'activité rationaliste de la physique contemporaine*, p. 56.
[37] *Le nouvel esprit scientifique*, p. 135.
[38] *L'intuition de l'instant*, p. 112.

The three degrees of vigilance

First-degree monitoring—waiting for the expected or even alertness to the unexpected—remains a posture of the empiricist mind. Second-degree monitoring presupposes spelling out one's methods and adopting the methodic vigilance that is essential for the methodical application of methods. At this level a mutual monitoring is set up between rationalism and empiricism through the exercise of an applied rationalism which is the precondition for explicit statement of the adequate relationship between theory and experience. Only with third-degree monitoring does distinctively epistemological inquiry appear; and this alone can break free from the "absolute of method"—the system of the "censures of Reason"—and from the false absolutes of the traditional culture which may still be at work in second-degree vigilance. The freedom that this "acute critique" gives, from both traditional culture and the empirical history of the sciences, leads to a "super-naturalizing pragmatism" which seeks the means of moving beyond methods and theories in a re-made history of methods and theories. Thus the sociology of knowledge and culture and, more especially, the sociology of scientific ✶ *education, is an almost indispensable instrument of third-degree monitoring.*

2. G. Bachelard

We can define a particular region of the super-ego which might be called the *intellectual super-ego.* [...]

In the efforts of scientific culture the function of self-monitoring takes composite forms which demonstrate to us the mental action of rationality. By studying it more closely, we shall find a new proof of the specifically second character of rationalism. One is not truly installed in the philosophy of the rational until one understands that one understands and can confidently denounce the errors and semblances of rationalism. In order for self-monitoring to have this confidence, it must in some way itself be monitored. There then come into existence forms of *monitoring of monitoring*, which we shall designate, for the sake of brevity, in exponential form: (monitoring)^2. I shall even indicate the elements of a monitoring of monitoring of monitoring, in other words (monitoring)^3. On this problem of the discipline of the mind, it is even fairly easy to grasp the meaning of an exponential psychology and to appreciate how this psychology can contribute to the ordering of the dynamic elements of experimental and theoretical conviction. The interlinking of psychological facts obeys very diverse causalities depending on their plan of organization. This interlinking cannot be unfolded in the continuous time of life. Setting out such diverse linkages requires hierarchy. This hierarchy cannot dispense with a psychoanalysis of the useless, the inert, the superfluous, and the ineffective. [...]

A physicist monitors his technique at the level of the monitoring of his thoughts. He has constant need for *confidence* in the *normal* operation of his apparatus. Endlessly he renews a certificate of good performance. It is the same for the entirely mental apparatus of correct thought.

But after having suggested the complexity of the problem of monitoring for precise thought, let us now see how to set up the monitoring of monitoring.

Intellectual monitoring, in its simple form, is the expectation of a *definite* fact, the identification of a *clear-cut* event. One does not monitor just anything. Monitoring is directed towards an object which may be more or less well designated but which at least benefits from some type of designation. There is nothing new for a monitoring subject. The phenomenology of pure novelty in the object cannot eliminate the phenomenology of *surprise* in the subject. Monitoring is therefore the consciousness of a subject which has an object—and a consciousness so clear that the subject and its object specify themselves together, coupling more closely as the rationalism of the subject more carefully prepares the technique for monitoring the object that is examined. Consciousness of the expectation of an event must be accompanied by consciousness of mental openness, so that the monitoring of a well-designated event is, in fact, a kind of rhythm analysis of central attention and peripheral attention. However alert and vigilant it may be, simple monitoring is essentially an attitude of the empiricist mind. In this perspective, a fact is a fact, nothing more than a fact. The posture of awareness respects the contingency of facts.

The monitoring-of-monitoring function can really only emerge after a "discourse on method", when practice or thought have found methods and valorized them. Then respect for the method that has been valorized entails attitudes of monitoring which a special monitoring has to maintain. Monitoring thus monitored is then both consciousness of form and consciousness of information. Applied rationalism appears with this "doublet". It is indeed a matter of apprehending *formed facts*, facts which actualize *information principles*.

We can observe, incidentally, at this point, how many documents a teaching of scientific thought provides for an exponential psychology. An education of scientific thought would gain by making explicit this monitoring of monitoring which is the clear awareness of the rigorous application of a method. Here, well-designated method plays the role of a well-psychoanalysed *super-ego* in the sense that mistakes appear in a calm atmosphere; they are not painful, on the contrary they are instructive. One has to have made them in order for the monitoring of monitoring to be alerted and to teach itself. The psychoanalysis of objective knowledge and of rational knowledge works at this level by clarifying the relationship between theory and experiment, form and substance, the rigorous and the approximate, the certain and the probable—all dialectics which require *special censorships* so that one does not pass without precaution from one term to the other. This will very often provide the means of breaking philosophical blockages; so many philosophies presume to impose a super-ego on scientific culture. Some people, claiming allegiance to realism, positivism, or rationalism, dispense with the censorship that should guarantee the limits and the relationship of the rational and the experimental. To draw constant support from a philosophy as from an absolute is to perform a censorship whose justification has not always been examined. The monitoring of monitoring, by working on the two sides of empiricism and rationalism is, in many ways, a mutual psychoanalysis of the two philosophies. The censorships of rationalism and scientific experiment are correlative.

In what circumstances can (monitoring)^3 arise? Quite clearly, when one monitors not only the application of one's method, but the method itself. (Monitoring)^3 will require one to put *method* to the test, require one to risk rational certainties in experiment, or risk a crisis of interpretation of duly observed phenomena. The active super-ego then exercises, one way or another, an acute critique. It calls into question not only the ego of culture, but the antecedent forms of the super-ego of culture. First, of course, the critique bears on the culture imparted by traditional education, then it bears on reasoned culture, on the very history of the rationalization of knowledge. In a more condensed way, we can say that the activity of (monitoring)^3 declares itself absolutely free with respect to all historicity of culture. The history of scientific thought ceases to be a necessary avenue, it is only a beginner's gymnastics which should supply us with examples of intellectual emergences. Even when it seems to follow on from a historical evolution, the monitored culture that we envisage remakes through recurrence a well-ordered history which in no way corresponds to actual history. In this remade history, everything is value. The (super-ego)^3 finds quicker condensations than the examples diluted over historical time. It thinks history, well aware of the weakness of reliving it.

Should it be pointed out that (monitoring)^3 grasps relations between form and end? that it destroys the absolute of method? that it judges method as a stage in the progress of method? At the level of (monitoring)^3, there is no more fragmented pragmatism. Method has to demonstrate a rational goal that has nothing in common with transient utility. Or at least, one has to envisage a super-naturalizing pragmatism, a pragmatism designated as an analogical spiritual exercise, a pragmatism which seeks motives for supersession, transcendence, and which asks if the rules of reason are not themselves censorships to be infringed.

Gaston Bachelard
Le rationalisme appliqué

Introduction
Epistemology and methodology √

Epistemology and reconstructed logic

Sociologists of science observe that scientists' relationship to their practice — at least as scientists reconstruct it when they talk or write about it — is almost always mediated by social representations that are inspired by philosophies often very remote from the reality of the scientific act. In the case of the social sciences, the acts of research are generally reinterpreted in accordance with the canons of methodology, as a reconstructed logic very remote from the "logic-in-use" that is involved in the real process of invention.

Reconstructing the process of research is one of the ways of checking the logical rigour of a piece of research,* but it can have the opposite consequences when it is presented as a reflection of the real process. It then helps to consecrate the dichotomy between the real operations, which are subject to intuition and chance, and the ideal rigour that can more easily be actualized in formal exercises or the replication of surveys.** This being so, a reminder of the difference between the logic-in-use of the real conduct of science and the ideal logic of ex post facto reconstructions should not be taken as an invitation to hyper-empiricism or the adventure of intuitionism, but rather as a call for epistemological vigilance, since it shows that invention can have a logic of its own, different from the logic of demonstration or exposition.

3. A. Kaplan

A reconstructed logic is not meant to be merely a description of what is actually being done by scientists, and for two reasons.

First, because logic is concerned with evaluations, it may be less interested in what is being done than in what is being left undone. But the formation of hypotheses in science and their replacement by more satisfactory ones is, on the whole, a matter of sound operations, and not something illogical or even extralogical. The criticism I am making is that in the "hypothetico-deductive" reconstruction the most important incidents in the drama of science are enacted somewhere behind the scenes. The growth of knowledge is surely basic to the scientific enterprise, even from a logical point of view. The conventional reconstruction presents the denouement, but we remain ignorant of the plot.

Second, a reconstructed logic is not a description but rather an idealization of scientific practice. Not even the greatest of scientists has a cognitive style which is wholly and perfectly logical, and the most brilliant piece of research still betrays its all-too-human divagations. The logic-in-use is embedded in a matrix of an *a*logic-in-use, even an *il*logic-in-use. The reconstruction idealizes the logic of science only in showing us what it *would* be if it were extracted and refined to utmost purity.

(*)See above, section 1.1, p. 14, and see below, J. H. Goldthorpe and D. Lockwood, text no. 6, pp. 100–108.

** See above, section 2.1, p. 35.

This defense is important and, I think, sound—but only up to a point. The idealization may be carried so far that it is useful only for the further development of logic itself, and not for the understanding and evaluation of scientific practice. Reconstructions have been so idealized that, as Max Weber wryly observed, "it is often difficult for the specialized disciplines to recognize themselves with the naked eye".[1] At worst, the logician becomes so absorbed with enhancing the power and beauty of his instrument that he loses sight of the material with which it must work. At best, he commits himself to a questionable Platonism: that the proper way to analyze and understand something is to refer it to its most ideal form, that is, its form abstracted from any concrete embodiment. This is *a* way but it is not the only way; and I am far from convinced that it is always the best way.

The great danger in confusing the logic-in-use with a particular reconstructed logic, and especially a highly idealized one, is that thereby the autonomy of science is subtly subverted. The normative force of the logic has the effect, not necessarily of improving the logic-in-use, but only of bringing it into closer conformity with the imposed reconstruction. It is often said that behavioral science should stop trying to imitate physics. I believe that this recommendation is a mistake: the presumption is certainly in favor of those operations of the understanding which have already shown themselves to be so preeminently successful in the pursuit of truth. What *is* important, I believe, is that behavioral science should stop trying to imitate only what a particular reconstruction claims physics to be.

Abraham Kaplan
The Conduct of Inquiry:
Methodology for Behavioral Science

[1] *The Methodology of the Social Sciences*, Glencoe (Ill.): Free Press, 1949, p. 114.

Part one
The break

1.1 Prenotions and techniques for breaking with them

Prenotions as an epistemological obstacle

Challenging the "truths" of common-sense has become a commonplace of methodological discourse, which is thereby in danger of losing all its critical force. Bachelard and Durkheim show that a point-by-point challenge to the prejudices of common-sense is no substitute for a radical questioning of the principles on which common-sense is based: "Faced with the real, what one thinks one knows clearly obscures what one ought to know. When it presents itself to scientific culture, the mind is never young. It is even very old, as old as its prejudices... . Opinion thinks badly; it does not think: it translates needs into knowledge. In designating objects by their utility, it prevents itself from knowing them... . It would not be sufficient, for example, to rectify it on particular points while maintaining a provisional knowledge as a kind of provisional ethic. The scientific mind forbids us to have an opinion on questions that we do not know, questions that we cannot formulate clearly."* The slowness or the errors of sociological knowledge are not due solely to extrinsic causes, such as the complex and ephemeral nature of the phenomena it deals with, but also to the social functions of the prenotions that stand in the way of sociological science. Spontaneous opinions have such strength not only because they present themslves as an attempt at systematic explanation but also because the functions they fulfil themselves constitute a system.

4. É. Durkheim

At the moment when a new order of phenomena becomes the object of a science they are already represented in the mind, not only through sense perceptions, but also by some kind of crudely formed concepts. Before the first rudiments of physics and chemistry were known, men already possessed notions about physical and chemical phenomena which went beyond pure perception alone. Such, for example, are those to be found intermingled with all religions. This is because reflective thought precedes science, which merely employs it more methodically. Man cannot live among things without forming ideas about them according to which he regulates his behaviour. [...]

These notions or concepts—however they are designated—are of course not legitimate surrogates for things. The products of common experience, their main purpose is to attune our actions to the surrounding world; they are formed by and for experience. Now a representation can effectively perform this function even if it is theoretically false. Several centuries ago Copernicus

* G. Bachelard, *La formation de l'esprit scientifique*, Paris: Vrin, 4th edn. 1965, p. 14.

dispelled the illusions our senses experienced concerning the movements of the heavenly bodies, and yet it is still according to these illusions that we commonly regulate the distribution of our time. For an idea to stimulate the reaction that the nature of a thing demands, it need not faithfully express that nature. It is sufficient for it to make us perceive what is useful or disadvantageous about the thing, and in what ways it can render us service or disservice. But notions formed in this way can only present a roughly appropriate practicality, and then only in the general run of cases. How often are they both dangerous and inadequate! It is therefore not by elaborating upon them, however one treats them, that we will ever succeed in discovering the laws of reality. On the contrary, they are as a veil interposed between the things and ourselves, concealing them from us even more effectively because we believe it to be more transparent. [...]

Indeed the notions just discussed are those *notiones vulgares*, or *praenotions*, which [Bacon] points out as being at the basis of all the sciences, in which they take the place of facts. It is these *idola* which, resembling ghost-like creatures, distort the true appearance of things, but which we nevertheless mistake for the things themselves. It is because this imagined world offers no resistance that the mind, feeling completely unchecked, gives rein to limitless ambitions, believing it possible to construct—or rather reconstruct—the world through its own power and according to its wishes.

If this has been true for the natural sciences, how much more had it to be true for sociology. Men did not wait on the coming of social science to have ideas about law, morality, the family, the state or society itself, for such ideas were indispensable to their lives. It is above all in sociology that these preconceptions, to employ again Bacon's expression, are capable of holding sway over the mind, substituting themselves for things. Indeed, social things are only realised by men: they are the product of human activity. Thus they appear to be nothing save the operationalising of ideas, which may or may not be innate but which we carry within us, and their application to the various circumstances surrounding men's relationships with one another. [...]

The apparent justification for this view derives from the fact that since the details of social life swamp the consciousness from all sides, it has not a sufficiently strong perception of the details to feel the reality behind them. Lacking ties that are firm enough or close enough to us, this all produces the impression upon us that it is clinging to nothing and floating in a vacuum, consisting of matter half unreal and infinitely malleable. This is why so many thinkers have seen in the social organisation mere combinations which are artificial and to some degree arbitrary. But if the details and the special concrete forms elude us, at least we represent to ourselves in a rough, approximate way the most general aspects of collective existence. It is precisely these schematic, summary representations which constitute the prenotions that we employ in our normal way of life. Thus we cannot visualise their existence being called into question, since we see it at the same time as we see our own. Not only are they within us, but since they are the product of repeated experiences, they are invested with a kind of ascendancy and authority, by dint of repetition and the habit which results from it. We feel their resistance when we seek to free ourselves from them, and we cannot fail to regard as real something which pits itself against us. Thus everything conspires to make us see in them the true social reality. [...]

These common notions are not to be encountered only at the basis of the sciences, but are also to be found constantly as the arguments unravel. In our present state of knowledge we do not know exactly what the state is, nor sovereignty, political freedom, democracy, socialism, communism, etc. Thus our method should make us forswear any use of these concepts so long as they have not been scientifically worked out. Yet the words that express them recur continually in the discussions of sociologists. They are commonly used with assurance, as if they corresponded to things well known and well defined, while in fact they evoke in us only confused notions, an amalgam of vague impressions, prejudices and passions. Today we mock at the strange ratiocinations that the doctors of the Middle Ages constructed from their notions of heat and cold, humidity and dryness, etc. Yet we do not perceive that we continue to apply the selfsame method to an order of phenomena which is even less appropriate for it than any other, on account of its extreme complexity.

In the specialised branches of sociology this ideological character is even more marked.

It is particularly so in the case of ethics. [...] Thus all the questions that ethics normally raises relate not to things but to ideas. We must know what constitutes the ideas of law and morality and not what is the nature of morality and law considered in their own right. Moralists have not yet even grasped the simple truth that, just as our representations of things perceived by the senses spring from those things themselves and express them more or less accurately, our representation of morality springs from observing the rules that function before our very eyes and perceives them systematically. Consequently it is these rules and not the cursory view we have of them which constitute the subject matter of science, just as the subject matter of physics consists of actual physical bodies and not the idea that ordinary people have of it. The outcome is that the basis of morality is taken to be what is only its superstructure, namely, the way in which it extends itself to the individual consciousness and makes its impact upon it. [...]

One must systematically discard all preconceptions. Special proof of this rule is unnecessary: it follows from all that we have stated above. Moreover, it is the basis of all scientific method. Descartes' method of doubt is in essence only an application of it. If at the very moment of the foundation of science Descartes prescribed a rule for himself to question all the ideas he had previously accepted, it is because he wished to use only concepts which had been scientifically worked out, that is, constructed according to the method that he devised. All those of another origin had therefore to be rejected, at least for the time being. We have seen that Bacon's theory of the idols has the same significance. The two great doctrines, so often placed in contradiction to each other, agree on this essential point. Thus the sociologist, either when he decides upon the object of his research or in the course of his investigations, must resolutely deny himself the use of those concepts formed outside science and for needs entirely unscientific. He must free himself from those fallacious notions which hold sway over the mind of the ordinary person, shaking off, once and for all, the yoke of those empirical categories that long habit often makes tyrannical. If necessity sometimes forces him to resort to them, let him at least do so in full cognisance of the little value they possess, so as not to assign to them in the investigation a role which they are unfit to play.

Émile Durkheim
The Rules of Sociological Method

Provisional definition as a means of escaping from prenotions

Durkheim's insistence on preliminary definition, so often written off as an obligatory stage in the ritual of didactic exposition, and recently treated to an "operationist" rehabilitation which does it no greater justice, is primarily intended to sweep away prenotions, in other words the pre-constructions of spontaneous sociology, by constructing the system of relations that defines the scientific fact. } FP

5. M. Mauss

It now remains for us to determine the method most appropriate to our subject. Although we think that one should not perpetually stir up questions of methodology, it nonetheless seems useful to explain here the procedures of definition, observation, and analysis that will be applied in the course of this work. It will then be easier to criticize each of our steps and monitor their results.

As soon as prayer, an integral part of ritual, is a social institution, the study has a subject, a thing to which it can and must attend. Whereas, for philosophers and theologians, ritual is a conventional language in which the play of internal images and feelings is imperfectly expressed, for us it becomes the reality itself. For it contains all that is active and living in prayer: it holds in reserve all the meaning that was put into the words, it contains the seed of all that can be deduced from them, even through new syntheses. The social practices and beliefs that are condensed in it are charged with the past and present, and pregnant with the future. So when one studies prayer from this angle, it ceases to be something inexpressible and inaccessible. It becomes a well-defined reality, a concrete datum, something precise, resistant, and fixed, which impresses itself on the observer.

Definition: Though we now know that there is somewhere a system of facts called prayers, we still have only a confused idea of it. We do not know its extent or its exact limits. We shall therefore first of all have to transform this blurred impression into a distinct notion. This is the purpose of definition. There is, of course, no question of defining straightaway the very substance of the facts. Such a definition can only come at the end of the scientific investiga- ← ? tion; the definition we have to make at the outset can only be provisional. It is simply intended to start up the research, to determine the thing to be studied, without prejudicing the results of the study. It is a question of knowing what are the facts that deserve to be called prayers. But this definition, though by whom? provisional, cannot be established too carefully, since it will dominate all the subsequent work. It facilitates the research because it limits the scope of observation. At the same time it gives a methodical character to the verification of hypotheses. It enables us to escape from arbitrariness: we are obliged to } Scope study all the facts of prayer and only those. The critique can then be conducted } ? according to precise rules. To dispute a proposition, one has to show either that the definition was defective and vitiated all the subsequent reasoning; or that a fact that should have entered into the definition has been neglected; or that facts have been taken into account that did not fall under the definition.

By contrast, when the nomenclature has not been established, the author moves imperceptibly from one order of facts to another, or the same order of facts bears different names in the work of different authors. The disadvantages which result from the absence of definition are felt particularly in the science of religions, where there has been so little concern to define. Thus some ethnographers, after telling us that prayer is unknown in a given society, will then quote "religious chants", numerous ritual texts that they have observed there. A preliminary definition will spare us these deplorable inconsistencies and the interminable debates between authors who, on the same subject, are not talking about the same thing.

Because this definition comes at the beginning of research, in other words at a moment when the facts are only known from outside, it can only be made on the basis of external signs. It is solely a matter of delimiting the object of study and consequently marking its outlines. What we need to find are some apparent and sufficiently perceptible characteristics which make it possible to recognize, almost at first sight, everything that is prayer. But on the other hand, these same characteristics must be objective. We must not rely on our impressions, or our prenotions, or those of the milieux we are observing. We shall not say of a religious act that it is a prayer simply because we feel it must be, or because the adepts of a religion give it that name. Just as a physicist defines heat by the expansion of bodies and not by the impression of warmth, so we shall seek in the things themselves the characteristic in terms of which prayer has to be expressed. Defining on the basis of impressions amounts to not defining at all, for nothing is more fluid than an impression; it changes from one individual to another, one people to another; it changes, in a given individual or people, according to their current state of mind. So, when, instead of constituting the scientific notion of prayer—arbitrarily, admittedly, with a concern for logic and a sense of the concrete—, one composes it with the aid of elements as insubstantial as the feelings of individuals, we see it pulled this way and that, to the detriment of the research. The most different things are called prayers, either in the course of the same research, by the same author, or depending on the authors who give the word different meanings, or depending on the civilizations that are studied. In this way, authors are led to set up oppositions between facts that are of the same kind, or to confuse facts that ought to be distinguished. Just as the physicists of the Ancient world gave hot and cold two different natures, so even today an idealist will refuse to admit that there is some kinship between prayer and crude magical incantation. The only way of escaping from distinctions as arbitrary as some confusions is to set aside, once and for all, all these subjective prenotions in order to reach the institution itself. On this condition, the initial definition will in itself be a first gain for research. [...]

When we say "prayer", we do not mean to imply that there exists somewhere a social entity that deserves this name and on which we could immediately speculate. An institution is not an indivisible unit, distinct from the facts that manifest it; it is only their system. Not only does "religion" not exist—there are only particular religions—but each of them is nothing other than a more or less organized set of religious beliefs and practices. Likewise the word "prayer" is only a substantive by which we designate a set of phenomena each of which is individually a prayer. But they all have in common certain specific characteristics which an abstraction can bring out. So we can group them together under a single name which designates all of them and them alone.

But while, in order to constitute this notion, we are in no way bound by everyday ideas, we must not do them unnecessary violence. It is not at all a question of using in an entirely new sense a word that everyone uses, but of substituting a clearer and more distinct conception for the everyday conception, which is a confused one. The physicist did not disfigure the sense of the word "heat" when he defined it by expansion. Similarly, the sociologist will not disfigure the sense of the word "prayer" when he delimits its scope and understanding. His only aim is to replace personal impressions by an objective sign that dissipates ambiguities and confusions and, while avoiding neologisms, prevents play on words.

Marcel Mauss
"La prière"

Logical analysis as an aid to epistemological vigilance

Clarifying one's concepts and formulating one's propositions and hypotheses so as to make them amenable to experimental verification are one of the fundamental conditions for rigour and one of the most effective instruments of epistemological vigilance. In particular, concepts borrowed from ordinary language, such as "conformism" or "embourgeoisement",* have to be examined in order to make their presuppositions explicit, to test their coherence, and to bring out the consequences of the propositions they imply. It would certainly be asking too much of the automatic effects of abstract classification (see above, section 1.6, p. 26–29) to see the formalized diagram put forward by the authors as an all-purpose plan for experimental verification; but at the very least, the logical analysis that can be derived from it brings to light all the ambiguities concealed by the semi-scientific term "embourgeoisement".

6. J. H. Goldthorpe and D. Lockwood

Of late still further economic progress has resulted in a new factor entering into the discussion—that of working class "affluence". And this has led to the claim being made that in yet another way the British class structure is in process of change. It has been argued by a number of writers that the working class, or at least a more prosperous section of it, is losing its identity as a social stratum and is becoming merged into the middle class. In other words, the contention is that today many manual wage-earning workers and their families are becoming socially indistinguishable from the members of other groups —those of blackcoated workers, minor professionals and technicians, for example,—who were previously their social superiors.

This, one should note, is to claim a far more rapid and far-reaching change in class structure than any which could ensue from secular trends in occupational distribution, in the overall distribution of income and wealth or in rates of intergenerational social mobility. It is to claim that, in course of their own lifetimes, large numbers of persons are collectively experiencing not only a marked increase in their standard of living but also a basic change in their way of life and in their status position relative to other groups with whom they are in regular contact. There are implied, thus, as well as economic changes, changes in values, attitudes and aspirations, in behavioural patterns, and in the structure of relationships in associational and community life. [...]

The long-term trends of change which were referred to above have all at some time or another been adduced to help explain shifting patterns of party allegiance; notably, of course, the decline in support for the Labour Party over the past decade or more. But it is in particular the thesis of the *embourgeoisement* of the working class that has been invested with political significance, and especially in relation to the third successive electoral defeat of the Labour Party in 1959. For example, in their study of that election, Butler and Rose have argued that the result and the reports from the constituencies which

---

* Another example of this style of analysis may be found in M. Jahoda, "Conformity and Independence", *Human Relations*, April 1959, pp. 99 ff.

accompanied it, "make it plain that the swing to the Conservatives cannot be dismissed as an ephemeral veering of the electoral breeze. Long term factors were also involved. Traditional working class attitudes had been eroded by the steady growth of prosperity..." In their view, many manual workers are at least "on the threshold of the middle class". The same theme has been taken up by Labour Party "revisionists" such as Crosland. "The swing against Labour" the latter has written "although quantitatively not large, must be taken seriously because it appears to reflect a long-run trend. Moreover, it seems to be causally related to certain underlying social and economic changes... which not merely are irreversible, but are not yet even complete." The forces of change are "gradually breaking down the old barriers between the working and middle classes..." and Labour's support is dwindling because of a crisis in class identity: "People who would be objectively classified as working class in terms of occupation or family background have acquired a middle class income and pattern of consumption, and sometimes a middle class psychology."

It is not our purpose here to consider whether or how far the electoral trend against Labour is in fact related to processes of irreversible change. It is, however, our view that interpretations of Labour's decline of the kind referred to cannot by any means be regarded as conclusive. In the first place, there are various other ways in which Labour's lack of success at the polls might be accounted for without resorting to the thesis of the worker turning middle class. And secondly, there is the elementary point that before this thesis can be usefully introduced as an explanatory factor, it is necessary to have a clear idea of what it is that it states and also, of course, empirical confirmation of its validity. As things stand at present, the requirement of clarity, let alone of proof, has still to be met. [...]

The chief sociological implications of the argument that the more prosperous of the country's manual wage workers are being assimilated into the middle class would appear to be as follows:

(a) That these workers and their families are acquiring a standard of living, in terms of income and material possessions, which puts them on a level with at least the lower strata within the middle class. Here one refers to certain of the specifically economic aspects of class stratification.

(b) That these same workers are also acquiring new social perspectives and new norms of behaviour which are more characteristic of middle class than of working class groups. Here one refers to what may be termed the normative aspect of class.

(c) That being essentially similar to many middle class persons in their economic position and their normative orientation, these manual workers are being accepted by the former on terms of social equality in both formal and informal social interaction. Here one refers to what may be called the relational aspect of class. [...]

For the purposes of this discussion, we shall start by assuming economic parity between groups of working and middle class persons, and thus concentrate on the other two aspects of the problem that we have distinguished; that is, the relational and the normative. These two components of class, as we have treated them, may, it so happens, be directly related to a pair of concepts which by now have wide currency in sociological literature: namely, "membership group" and "reference group". [...]

The case that is relevant to our problem is that in which a person progressively dissociates himself, or is dissociated, from the norms of a membership group, and comes to take as his reference group some other group into which he may or may not be socially accepted. In our view, it is according to this pattern that changes in class structure, in other than a narrow economic sense, must ultimately be understood—as being, that is, a specific form of the general process by which individuals are attached to and detached from social groups. [...]

Interpreted in class terms, [Merton's analysis of the move from membership group to reference group] clearly indicates that the problem of "the worker turning middle class" involves a complex process of *social* change, rather than some straightforward reaction of the individual to altered economic circumstances. It may well be the case that a certain level of affluence is a prerequisite of working class *embourgeoisement*, being the essential means of supporting a middle class style of life and participation in middle class society. But it is an error to take up a naive economic determinism, as some writers appear to have done, and to regard working class prosperity as providing in itself a *sufficient* basis for *embourgeoisement*. This, we would suggest, may be considered as a real possibility only under the following, rather more specific, conditions.

(a)   When working class persons are in some way motivated to reject working class norms and are exposed to, and come to identify with, the norms of middle class groups.

(b)   When they are able, furthermore, to resist the pressure to conformity within their working class membership groups, either by withdrawing from them or as a result of these groups for some reason or other losing their cohesiveness and thus their control over individuals.

(c)   When there are genuine opportunities for them of gaining acceptance into the middle class groups to which they aspire to belong.

Following from this, the actual process of transition could then be seen in terms of a model such as that set out below. This is based on the four different positions which result from a cross-classification of the relational and normative aspects of class.

1963

FIGURE I. "Assimilation through Aspiration"

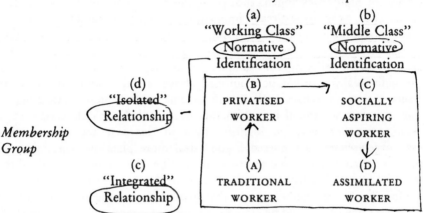

The two sets of alternatives in the worker's class situation are postulated as follows:

(a) that he has a set of norms which are primarily "working class" or
(b) that he has a set of norms which are primarily "middle class" and
(c) that he is socially integrated into a membership group of the class whose norms he shares or
(d) that he is socially isolated from membership groups of the class whose norms he shares.

Understood in terms of this model, then, the process of *embourgeoisement* takes the form of a threefold movement: from (A) to (B), from (B) to (C), and from (C) to (D).

Through using a model of this kind it thus becomes possible to reduce the thesis of *embourgeoisement* to some relatively systematic and unambiguous form, and one in which it could conceivably be tested by empirical research. Moreover, a schematic presentation of this nature has a further merit: that of helping to reveal in the argument various pre-suppositions and assumptions which, on consideration, may be recognised as unwarranted or as unjustifiably crude. Of these, and there are several, probably the most basic is the idea, implicit in all discussion of *embourgeoisement* so far, that this process entails the *assimilation* of working class persons to middle class life-styles and middle class society—which are themselves taken as "given". There are two points, at least, arising in connection with this assumption, which call for comment.

In the first place, one connotation of the thesis of *embourgeoisement*, explicated in this way, is that the "new" working class is moving towards a middle class which is *unchanging* and *homogeneous*. This, however, is an idea which has only to be stated to be seen as untenable. Apart from the major "vertical" distinction between the entrepreneurs and independents on the one hand and the salaried employees on the other, stratification within the middle class is obviously highly developed, though at the same time subtle and far from static. Thus, as we have already implied, it is important that a focus of future research should be on the relationship between the working class and those *specific* middle class groups which appear socially least distant from it. There are reasons for believing, for example, that among lower white-collar workers the individualistic orientation outlined above is today somewhat less pronounced than it was previously or still remains in other middle class groups. If this is in fact so, and if it is with this section of the middle class that the aspiring worker tends to identify, then in this case the occurrence of *embourgeoisement* is rendered a good deal more plausible: certainly more plausible than where *embourgeoisement* must be taken to imply a radical shift in social perspective from the collectivistic to the individualistic pole.

However, once one recognises the possibility that the social outlook of some sections of the middle class may represent a movement away from the "individualism" which has been found characteristic of this class as a whole, then a further and more fundamental issue arises. The idea of *embourgeoisement* as entailing a process of "assimilation through aspiration" to middle class values and norms must now be regarded as but one way of interpreting any ongoing modifications of the class frontier. An alternative hypothesis which suggests itself is that this change may be in the nature of *independent convergence* between the "new" working class and the "new" middle class, rather than the merging of the one into the other.

There are several considerations which would lend support to this point of view. Firstly, as we have already noted, it has not been established that the attitudes and behaviour of the "new" working class are related to aspirations for "middle class" status. Secondly, no convincing case has been put forward to suggest how such aspirations might be generated out of the structure of social relationships in which the workers in question are implicated. Thirdly, there are facts such as the continuing strength of trade union organisation, and the growth especially of white-collar unionism, which cannot easily be accommodated into the conception of *embourgeoisement* as this has been developed so far. If the "convergence" argument is adopted, however, not only does it account for these facts very readily but it is also quite unaffected by the "new" worker's apparent lack of concern with middle class membership. Spelled out in more detail, this argument would claim that convergence in attitudes and behaviour between certain working and middle class groups is the result, primarily, of changes in economic institutions and in the conditions of urban life, which have weakened simultaneously the "collectivism" of the former and the "individualism" of the latter. On the side of the working class, twenty years of near full employment, the gradual erosion of the traditional, work-based community, the progressive bureaucratisation of trade unionism and the institutionalisation of industrial conflict, have all operated in the same direction to reduce the solidary nature of communal attachments and collective action. At the same time, there has been greater scope and encouragement for a more individualistic outlook so far as expenditure, use of leisure time and general levels of aspiration are concerned. Within the white-collar group, on the other hand, a trend in the opposite direction has been going on. Under conditions of rising prices, increasingly large-scale units of bureaucratic administration and reduced chances of upward "career" mobility, lower level white-collar workers, at any rate, have now become manifestly less attached to an unqualified belief in the virtues of "individualism" and more prone to collective, trade union, action of a deliberately apolitical and instrumental type—especially as the nature of many manual workers' philosophy of unionism is steadily coming nearer to that which they themselves find acceptable.

Further clarification of the idea of "convergence" may be obtained if we modify our original individualistic–collectivistic dichotomy in the way shown in Fig. II. Here we incorporate a distinction between the "primacy of means" and the "primacy of aspirations". Means may be primarily collective action or individual effort: aspirations may be primarily orientated to the present and to communal sociability, or to the future position of the nuclear family. The original ideal-type perspectives are now designated as "solidaristic collectivism" and "radical individualism".

Understood in this context, then, solidaristic collectivism implies collectivism (mutual aid) as an end and not just as a means. It is typified by an affective attachment to a local class community as opposed to the utilitarian attachment to a specific economic association which is characteristic of what we have called "instrumental collectivism". In this latter case, the means are still collective action but they are subordinate to the primary goal of the economic and social advancement of the individual nuclear family. The degree to which this family orientation develops, and particularly the degree to which advancement is seen in social rather than in simply economic terms, will of course vary. But in general it may be defined as an orientation to consumption (of goods, time, educational facilities, etc.) which involves the family as an independent unit in decisions about its own future.

Although then it may be suggested that the social perspectives of the "new" working and the "new" middle classes are tending to converge in the way indicated, the proviso must at this point be entered that convergence should not be taken to imply identity. It is reasonable to suppose that instrumental collectivism and family-centredness are present in both strata: but it is also reasonable to expect that the relative emphasis given to the two elements will differ from one stratum to the other. This is because for the "new" working class convergence largely means an adaptation of ends, while for the "new" middle class an adaptation of means. In the former case, convergence implies primarily an attenuation of collectivism of the solidaristic kind, of which an

FIGURE II. "Normative Convergence"

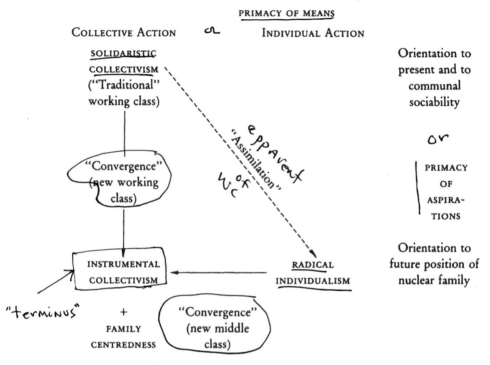

incipient family-centredness is a by-product. In the latter case, the by-product is instrumental collectivism, resulting from an attenuation of radical individualism. Thus, both the new "individualism" of the working class and the new "collectivism" of the middle class, though bringing the two strata into closer approximation, are still likely to remain distinct, in more or less subtle ways, from the attenuated individualism of the middle class and the attenuated collectivism of the working class.

This will perhaps be the more true of the element of individualism; for it would seem most probable that the shift in aspirations among the "new" working class will occur more gradually than the corresponding modification of means among the "new" middle class. We would expect, thus, that the main difference within the area of convergence will be that the new individualism of working class groups will take the form primarily of a desire for the *economic* advancement of the nuclear family, while the attenuated individualism of middle class groups will still be distinguished by a greater sensitivity to status group association and dissociation.

At this point we may return to our earlier distinction between the "privatised" and the "socially aspiring" worker. This, it will be recalled, depends on whether the worker, isolated from his traditional class environment, comes, for whatever reasons, to identify with a middle class status group. In Fig. II both the privatised and the socially aspiring worker belong in the lower left-hand box; in both cases, their social perspectives are seen as converging with those of the "new" middle class. They may, however, be distinguished from each other, we would suggest, by the nature of their individualism. In the case of the privatised worker, whatever individualistic outlook he has developed may be regarded as the result of negative factors (the attenuation of solidaristic collectivism) and as tending thus to centre on economic advancement in terms of commodity consumption. In the case of the socially aspiring worker, on the other hand, there is, in addition, a positive identification with middle class individualism and thus a greater awareness of, and concern with, the consequences of total life-style for status differentiation and status enhancement.

In conclusion, we may attempt to pull together the threads of our argument by using the discussion of this paper as a basis for the following, necessarily tentative, views, concerning the probable effects so far of working class affluence on the British class structure.

(a)   The change which would seem most probable is one which may be best understood as a process of normative convergence between certain sections of the working and middle classes; the focus of the convergence being on what we have termed "instrumental collectivism" and "family centredness". There is as yet, at least, little basis for the more ambitious thesis of *embourgeoisement* in the sense of the large-scale assimilation of manual workers and their families to middle class life-styles and middle class society in general. In particular, there is no firm evidence either that manual workers are consciously aspiring to middle class society, or that this is becoming any more open to them.

(b)   The groups which appear involved in normative convergence cannot be distinguished in terms of economic factors alone. Certainly, on the working class side, affluence is not to be regarded as sufficient in itself to bring about the attenuation of solidaristic collectivism. The process of convergence must rather be seen as closely linked to changes in the structure of social relationships in industrial, community and family life, which are in turn related not only to growing prosperity but also to advances in industrial organisation and technology, to the process of urban development, to demographic trends, and to the evolution of mass communications and "mass culture".

(c)   Even among the "new" working class groups in which instrumental collectivism and family centredness are manifested, status goals seem much less in evidence than economic goals: in other words, the privatised worker would appear far more typical than the socially aspiring worker. The conditions under which status aspirations are generated may be regarded as still more special than those which are conducive to a more individualistic outlook. Thus, we return to the point that normative convergence has to be understood as implying as yet only a rather limited modification of the class frontier.

scope

(d)   Finally, it is consistent with the above views to believe further that the political consequences of working class influence are so far, at least, indeterminate.

The link between "affluence" and "vote" is mediated by the social situation in which the affluent worker finds himself. If this situation is, as we believe, in a great many instances one of "privatisation", and if the prevailing attitudes are those of "instrumental collectivism" and "family centredness", the worker's attachment to the party of his choice is (to follow Duverger) more likely to be "associational" rather than "communal". That is, his instrumental attitude to trade unionism is likely to spill over into politics, and his vote will go to the highest bidder. It is in this section of the working class that Conservative voting, under present circumstances, is likely to be "prosperity voting". But calculative and opportunistic voting of this kind implies a very tenuous political link, and one does not have to conjure up pictures of widespread unemployment to visualise how it might be severed. For once the worker has experienced a rising standard of living, he comes to have certain expectations about the rightfulness of a continuing improvement in the future. Thus, his present political allegiance may readily be switched if his failure to realize these expectations is associated with existing governmental policy. The same logic of "relative deprivation" may also be operative in the case of the socially aspiring worker although the nature of the aspirations here is rather different. But in so far as his aspirations for a rising social status (and not simply a rising standard of living) are not recognised by the status groups to which he orients himself, the radicalisation of his political outlook is one possible consequence of affluence and aspiration which must enter into any estimation of the future alignment of party allegiance.

GOP
+
DJT
iN
2016 ?

John H. Goldthorpe and David Lockwood
"Affluence and the British Class Structure"

1.2   The illusion of transparency and the principle of non-consciousness

Artificialism as the basis of the illusion of reflexiveness

The illusion of transparency stems from the idea that, in order to explain and understand institutions, it is sufficient to understand the intentions of which they are the product. This common-sense idea draws some of its strength from the common attitudes of ethnocentrism or moralism that it supports. The artificialist illusion leads to the illusion of the technocrat who imagines he can create or transform institutions by decree, or the illusion of the evolutionist for whom the past can only provide the example of forms inferior to those of the present. This gives an insight into the essential strength of spontaneous sociology, which derives its psychological coherence from the systematic nature of the illusions it supplies.* Against these illusions, Durkheim points out the complexity of the determinations that a social institution receives from its past and from the system of institutions to which it belongs.

7. É. Durkheim

If one begins by asking what an ideal education must be, abstracted from conditions of time and place, it is to admit implicitly that a system of education has no reality in itself. One does not see in education a collection of practices and institutions that have been organized slowly in the course of time, which are comparable with all the other social institutions and which express them, and which, therefore, can no more be changed at will than the structure of the society itself. But it seems that this would be a pure system of *a priori* concepts; under this heading it appears to be a logical construct. One imagines that men of each age organize it voluntarily to realize a determined end; that, if this organization is not everywhere the same, it is because mistakes have been made concerning either the end that it is to pursue or the means of attaining it. From this point of view, educational systems of the past appear as so many errors, total or partial. No attention need be paid to them, therefore; we do not have to associate ourselves with the faulty observation or logic of our predecessors; but we can and must pose the question without concerning ourselves with solutions that have been given, that is to say, leaving aside everything that has been, we have only to ask ourselves what should be. The lessons of history can, moreover, serve to prevent us from repeating the errors that have been committed.

In fact, however, each society, considered at a given stage of development, has a system of education which exercises an irresistible influence on individuals. It is idle to think that we can rear our children as we wish. There are customs to which we are bound to conform; if we flout them too severely, they take their vengeance on our children. The children, when they are adults,

---

* See above, É. Durkheim, text no. 4, pp. 93–96.

are unable to live with their peers, with whom they are not in accord. Whether they had been raised in accordance with ideas that were either obsolete or premature does not matter; in the one case as in the other, they are not of their time and, therefore, they are outside the conditions of normal life. There is, then, in each period, a prevailing type of education from which we cannot deviate without encountering that lively resistance which restrains the fancies of dissent.

Now, it is not we as individuals who have created the customs and ideas that determine this type. They are the product of a common life, and they express its needs. They are, moreover, in large part the work of preceding generations. The entire human past has contributed to the formation of this totality of maxims that guide education today; our entire history has left its traces in it, and even the history of the peoples who have come before. It is thus that the higher organisms carry in themselves the reflection of the whole biological evolution of which they are the end product. Historical investigation of the formation and development of systems of education reveals that they depend upon religion, political organization, the degree of development of science, the state of industry, etc. If they are considered apart from all these historic causes, they become incomprehensible. Thus, how can the individual pretend to reconstruct, through his own private reflection, what is not a work of individual thought? He is not confronted with a *tabula rasa* on which he can write what he wants, but with existing realities which he cannot create, or destroy, or transform, at will. He can act on them only to the extent that he has learned to understand them, to know their nature and the conditions on which they depend; and he can understand them only if he studies them, only if he starts by observing them, as the physicist observes inanimate matter and the biologist, living bodies.

Émile Durkheim
Education and Sociology

Methodic ignorance

To offer methodical resistance to the illusion of immediate knowledge which is the basis of familiarity with the social world, the sociologist has to posit that the social world is as strange to him as the biological world was to biologists before biology had been constituted. The externality of social phenomena with respect to the individual observer results from the duration and opacity of the past from which they come, and also from the multiplicity of the actors involved in them. The sociologist must therefore posit, as a methodological principle, the alien character of the social universe, which presupposes not only epistemological recognition of the illusory nature of preconceptions, but also the intellectual and ethical conviction that scientific discoveries are neither easy nor intuitively plausible [vraisemblable]. The decision to be ignorant appears as an indispensable methodological precaution in an epistemological situation in which it is so difficult to know that one does not know, and what one does not know.

8. É. Durkheim

We do not say that social facts are material things, but that they are things just as are material things, although in a different way.

What indeed is a thing? The thing stands in opposition to the idea, just as what is known from the outside stands in opposition to what is known from the inside. A thing is any object of knowledge which is not naturally penetrable by the understanding. It is all that which we cannot conceptualise adequately as an idea by the simple process of intellectual analysis. It is all that which the mind cannot understand without going outside itself, proceeding progressively by way of observation and experimentation from those features which are the most external and the most immediately accessible to those which are the least visible and the most profound. To treat facts of a certain order as things is therefore not to place them in this or that category of reality; it is to observe towards them a certain attitude of mind. It is to embark upon the study of them by adopting the principle that one is entirely ignorant of what they are, that their characteristic properties, like the unknown causes upon which they depend, cannot be discovered by even the most careful form of introspection.

The terms being so defined, our proposition, far from being a paradox, might almost pass for a truism if it were not too often still unrecognised in those sciences which deal with man, and above all in sociology. Indeed, in this sense it may be said that any object of knowledge is a thing, except perhaps for mathematical objects. Regarding the latter, since we construct them ourselves, from the most simple to the most complex, it is enough to look within ourselves and to analyse internally the mental process from which they arise, in order to know what they are. But as soon as we consider facts *per se*, when we undertake to make a science of them, they are of necessity unknown for us, *things* of which we are ignorant, for the representations that we have been able to make of them in the course of our lives, since they have been made without method and uncritically, lack any scientific value and must be discarded. The facts of individual psychology themselves are of this nature and must be considered in this light. Indeed, although by definition they are internal to ourselves, the consciousness that we have of them reveals to us neither their inmost character nor their origin. Consciousness allows us to know them well up to a certain point, but only in the same way as our senses make us aware of heat or light, sound or electricity. It gives us muddled impressions of them, fleeting and subjective, but provides no clear, distinct notions or explanatory concepts. This is precisely why during this century an objective psychology has been founded whose fundamental rule is to study mental facts from the outside, namely as things. This should be even more the case for social facts, for consciousness cannot be more capable of knowing them than of knowing its own existence. It will be objected that, since they have been wrought by us, we have only to become conscious of ourselves to know what we have put into them and how we shaped them. Firstly, however, most social institutions have been handed down to us already fashioned by previous generations; we have had no part in their shaping; consequently it is not by searching within ourselves that we can uncover the causes which have given rise to them. Furthermore, even if we have played a part in producing them, we can hardly glimpse, save in the most confused and often even the most imprecise way, the real reasons which have impelled us to act, or the nature of our action. Already, even regarding merely the steps we have taken personally, we know very inaccurately the relatively simple motives that govern us. We believe ourselves disinterested, whereas our actions are egoistic; we think that we are commanded by hatred whereas we are giving way to love, that we are obedient to reason whereas we are the slaves of irrational prejudices, etc. How therefore could we possess the ability to discern more clearly the causes, of a different order of complexity, which inspire the measures taken by the collectivity? For at the very least each individual shares in only an infinitesimally small part of them; we have a host of fellow-fashioners, and what is occurring in their different consciousnesses eludes us.

Thus our rule implies no metaphysical conception, no speculation about the innermost depth of being. What it demands is that the sociologist should assume the state of mind of physicists, chemists and physiologists when they venture into an as yet unexplored area of their scientific field. As the sociologist penetrates into the social world he should be conscious that he is penetrating into the unknown. He must feel himself in the presence of facts governed by laws as unsuspected as those of life before the science of biology was evolved. He must hold himself ready to make discoveries which will surprise and disconcert him. Yet sociology is far from having arrived at this degree of intellectual maturity. While the scientist who studies physical nature feels very keenly the resistances that it proffers, ones which he has great difficulty in overcoming, it really seems as if the sociologist operates among things immediately clear to the mind, so great is the ease with which he seems to resolve the most obscure questions. In the present state of the discipline, we do not really know the nature of the principal social institutions, such as the state or the family, property rights or contract, punishment and responsibility. We are virtually ignorant of the causes upon which they depend, the functions they fulfil, and their laws of evolution. It is as if, on certain points, we are only just beginning to perceive a few glimmers of light. Yet it suffices to glance through works of sociology to see how rare is any awareness of this ignorance and these difficulties. Not only is it deemed mandatory to dogmatise about every kind of problem at once, but it is believed that one is capable, in a few pages or sentences, of penetrating to the inmost essence of the most complex phenomena. This means that such theories express, not the facts, which could not be so swiftly fathomed, but the preconceptions of the author before he began his research.

Émile Durkheim
The Rules of Sociological Method

1895

Levine, Donald
Visions of the sociological tradition
1995

BAM $46
B&N   "   29.56 used

The principle of determinism as the negation of the illusion of transparency

"In order to have a genuine science of social facts, it was necessary to gain the insight that societies contain realities comparable to those which constitute other realms, the insight that societies have a character which we cannot change arbitrarily, and are governed by laws which necessarily derive from this character. In other words, sociology could not emerge until the idea of determinism, which had been securely established in the physical and natural sciences, was finally extended to the social order."* The example of the other sciences was required in order to overcome the tenacious prejudice which accorded a privileged status to the social world. Thus, organicism can be seen as an effort to extend determinism, which was accepted in biology, to the "social realm" in which it was contested and to "fill the gap which had so long been felt to exist between societies and the rest of the universe".** This historical reminder of the difficulty with which the principle of determinism was established in the study of the "social realm" should make it easier to analyse and dispel the subtle forms in which the illusion of transparency still lives on, by showing the true bases of this recurrent illusion, in the coarse and simple form they took in other times.

9. É. Durkheim   1903

Sociology could not appear until men had acquired the sense that societies, like the rest of the world, are subject to laws which of necessity derive from and express their nature. Now this conception was very slow to take form. For centuries, men believed that even minerals were not ruled by definite laws but could take on all possible forms and properties if only a sufficiently powerful will applied itself to them. They believed that certain expressions or certain gestures had the ability to transform an inert mass into a living being, a man into an animal or a plant, and vice versa. This illusion, for which we have a sort of instinctive inclination, naturally persisted much longer in the realm of social phenomena. [...]

It was only at the end of the eighteenth century that people first began to perceive that the social realm, like the other realms of nature, had its own laws. When Montesquieu declared that "The laws are the necessary relationships which derive from the nature of things," he well understood that this excellent definition of natural law applied to social as well as to other phenomena; his book, *The Spirit of Laws*, attempts to show precisely how legal institutions are grounded in man's nature and his milieu. Soon thereafter, Condorcet undertook to reconstruct the order according to which mankind achieved its progress. This was the best way to demonstrate that there was nothing fortuitous or capricious about it but that it depended on determinate causes. At the same time, the economists taught that the phenomena of industrial and commercial life are governed by laws, which they thought they had discovered.

---

* É. Durkheim, "Sociology", trans. J. D. Folmann, in *Émile Durkheim, 1858–1917*, ed. K. H. Wolff, Columbus (Oh.): Ohio State University Press, 1960, p. 376.
** *Ibid*, p. 380.

Although these different thinkers had prepared the way for the conception on which sociology rests, they had as yet only a rather ambiguous and (yet) irresolute notion of what the laws of social life might be. They did not wish to say that social facts link up according to definite and invariable relations which the scholar seeks to observe by procedures analogous to those which are employed in the natural sciences. They simply meant that, given the nature of man, a course was laid out which was the only natural one, the one mankind should follow *if it wished to be in harmony with itself and to fulfil its destiny*; but it was still possible that it had strayed from that path. [...]

It is only at the beginning of the nineteenth century, with Saint-Simon at first, and especially with his disciple, Auguste Comte, that a new conception was definitively brought to light.

Proceeding to the synthetic view of all the constituted sciences of his time in his *Cours de philosophie positive*, Comte stated that they all rested on the axiom that the phenomena with which they dealt are linked according to necessary relationships, that is to say, on the determinist principle. From this fact, he concluded that this principle, which had thus been verified in all the other realms of nature from the realm of mathematics to that of life, must be equally true of the social realm. The resistances which today are opposed to this new extension of the determinist idea must not stop the philosopher. They have arisen with regularity each time that it has been a question of extending to a new realm this fundamental postulate and they always have been overcome. There was a time when people refused to accept that this principle applied even in the world of inanimate objects; it was established there. Next it was denied for living and thinking beings; now it is undisputed there as well.

One can therefore rest assured that these same prejudices which this principle encountered in the attempt to apply it to the social world will last only for a time. Moreover, since Comte postulated as a self-evident truth—a truth which is, moreover, now undisputed—that the individual's mental life is subject to necessary laws, how could the actions and reactions which are exchanged among individual consciousnesses in association not be subjected to the same necessity? *such as?*

Viewed in this way, societies ceased to appear as a sort of indefinitely malleable and plastic matter that men could mould, so to speak, at will; thenceforth, it was necessary to see them as realities whose nature is imposed upon us and which, like all natural things, can only be modified in conformity with the laws which regulate them. Human institutions could be considered no longer as the product of the more or less enlightened will of princes, statesmen, and legislators, but as the necessary result of determinate causes that physically imply them. Given the composition of a nation at a given moment in its history, and the state of its civilization at this same period, a social organization results which is characterized in this or that manner, just as the properties of a physical body result from its molecular constitution. We are thus faced with a stable, immutable order of things, and pure science becomes at once possible and necessary for describing and explaining it, for saying what its characteristics are and on what causes they depend. [...]

Until yesterday we believed that all this was arbitrary and contingent, that legislators or kings could, just like the alchemists of yore, at their pleasure change the aspect of societies, make them change from one type to another. In reality, these supposed miracles were illusory; and how many grave errors have resulted from this yet too widespread illusion! [...]

At the same time that they proclaim the necessity of things, the sciences place in our hand the means to dominate that necessity. Comte even remarks with insistence that of all the natural phenomena, social phenomena are the most malleable, the most accessible to variations and to changes, because they are the most complex. Therefore, sociology in no way imposes upon man a passively conservative attitude; on the contrary, it extends the field of our action by the simple fact that it extends the field of our science. It only turns us away from ill-conceived and sterile enterprises inspired by the belief that we are able to change the social order as we wish, without taking into account customs, traditions, and the mental constitution of man and of societies.

Tarot

how?
in what way?

Émile Durkheim
"Sociology and the Social Sciences"

1960s social unrest

2010s Trump [promise of freedom / tyranny]

[handwritten: 1873-1935]

[handwritten: 1854-1942]

The code and the document

In Simiand's polemic against the positivism of historians such as Seignobos, what is noteworthy is not so much the critiques of a now outmoded factual history, as the principles of a scientific sociology. Refusing to lock sociology in a problematic of subjective intentions which, in defiance of all logic, would make it a science of the accidental, Simiand shows that only the hypothesis of "non-consciousness" makes it possible to proceed to a study of the objective relations among phenomena. By this methodological decision, the sociologist acquires a specific object, the institution, and, at the same time, transforms the questions put to the material, which is no longer treated as a document, i.e. as a subjective testimony as to the intentions of historical actors, but as a set of indices on the basis of which a scientific questioning can constitute objects of specific study, "customs, collective representations, social forms". These are the genuine scientific facts of the sociologist, because they are not consciously, i.e. arbitrarily, recorded by the author of the document.*

[handwritten: MCAE ("the material")?]

10. F. Simiand

The idea that sociology models itself on the other sciences encounters a final objection, stemming from the very conditions of knowledge in the matter that is studied. The *document*, the intermediary between the mind which studies and the fact that is studied, is, as we have seen, very different from a scientific observation. It is made without definite method and for purposes other than the scientific purpose; it therefore is said to have a *subjective* character.

Social science is indeed thereby placed in an inferior position. But it is important to note that here, as in the question of contingency, the objection derives its force from the direction of the historian's mind even more than from the nature of things. If one asks the document, as traditional historians do, for individual events, or even for explanations in terms of motives, actions, individual thoughts, knowledge of which is necessarily obtained only through a mind, then the document is indeed not the stuff of real scientific work. But if research is turned towards the "institution" and not towards the "event", towards the objective relationships among phenomena and not towards the intentions and the ends that are conceived, it is often the case, in reality, that the fact being studied is attained not through a mind, but *directly*. The fact that, in a given language, different words are used to designate the paternal uncle and the maternal uncle is a *direct trace* of a form of family different from our present-day family. A code is not a "document" in the historical sense; it

---

* This definition of the social fact is one of the principles of Durkheim which have most marked his emulators or disciples and which, for most of them, have made possible the most positive scientific gains. Granet, for example, in his work as a sinologist, endeavoured to overcome the distinction between the "authentic" document and the "inauthentic" or reinterpreted document. He was able to escape from this quarrel, which is historically inextricable in the case of the Chinese tradition, by taking as his object (a second-degree, i.e. constructed object) the "schemes" and "stereotypes" according to which the ritual or historical material is shaped in classical Chinese works, and acknowledges his debt for this methodological intention to Durkheim's teaching (M. Granet, *Danses et légendes de la Chine ancienne*, vol. I, Paris: P.U.F., 1959, introduction, pp. 25–37).

is an immediate and direct record of fact, if it is precisely the legal rule that is the object of study. Customs, collective representations, social forms are unconsciously recorded or automatically leave traces in what the historian calls documents. Social phenomena can be grasped in them through a genuine observation, made by the *author of the research*, sometimes an immediate observation, more often a mediated observation (i.e. of the effects or traces of the phenomenon), but not, in any case, through an indirect path, i.e. through the *author of the document*. The critique of knowledge, devised by the methodologists of history and applied by them, as such, to social science, is therefore fully valid only for the object and practice of traditional history. To cover the whole practice of positive social science, and to fix even the best and most fertile part of it, it would have to be done all over again, greatly modified, and considerably expanded.

François Simiand
"Méthode historique et science sociale"

1.3   Nature and culture: substance and system of relations

Nature and history

Marx often showed that one cannot impute the properties or consequences of a social system to "nature" unless one forgets its genesis and its historical functions, i.e. everything that constitutes it as a system of relations. More precisely, he shows that this error of method is so common because of the ideological functions that it fulfils when it succeeds, in imagination at least, in "eliminating history". Thus, by asserting the "natural" character of bourgeois institutions and bourgeois relations of production, the classical economists justified the bourgeois order at the same time as protecting the dominant class against the historical, and therefore transient, character of its domination.

11. *K. Marx*

Economists have a singular method of procedure. There are only two kinds of institutions for them, artificial and natural. The institutions of feudalism are artificial institutions, those of the bourgeoisie are natural institutions. In this they resemble the theologians, who likewise establish two kinds of religion. Every religion which is not theirs is an invention of men, while their own religion is an emanation from God. When they say that present-day relations —the relations of bourgeois production—are natural, the economists imply that these are the relations in which wealth is created and productive forces developed in conformity with the laws of nature. Thus these relations are themselves natural laws independent of the influence of time. They are eternal laws which must always govern society. Thus there has been history, but there is no longer any. There has been history, since there were the institutions of feudalism, and in these institutions of feudalism we find quite different production relations from those of bourgeois society, production relations which the economists try to pass off as natural and as such eternal.

> *Karl Marx*
> The Poverty of Philosophy

The object before us, to begin with, *material production.*

   Individuals producing in society—hence socially determined individual production—is, of course, the point of departure. The individual and isolated hunter and fisherman, with whom Smith and Ricardo begin, belongs among the unimaginative conceits of the eighteenth-century Robinsonades, which in no way express merely a reaction against over-sophistication and a return to a misunderstood natural life, as cultural historians imagine. As little as Rousseau's *contrat social*, which brings naturally independent, autonomous subjects into relation and connection by contract, rests on such naturalism. This is the semblance, the merely aesthetic semblance, of the Robinsonades, great and small. It is, rather, the anticipation of "civil society", in preparation since the sixteenth century and making giant strides towards maturity in the eighteenth. In this society of free competition, the individual appears detached from the natural bonds etc. which in earlier historical periods make him the accessory of a definite and limited human conglomerate. Smith and Ricardo still stand with both feet on the shoulders of the eighteenth-century prophets, in whose imaginations this eighteenth-century individual—the product on one side of the dissolution of the feudal forms of society, on the other side of the new forces of production developed since the sixteenth century—appears as an ideal, whose existence they project into the past. Not as a historic result but as history's point of departure. As the Natural Individual appropriate to their notion of human nature, not arising historically, but posited by nature. This illusion has been common to each new epoch to this day. Steuart avoided this simple-mindedness because as an aristocrat, and in antithesis to the eighteenth century, he had in some respects a more historical footing.

The more deeply we go back into history, the more does the individual, and hence also the producing individual, appear as dependent, as belonging to a greater whole: in a still quite natural way in the family and in the family expanded into the clan [*Stamm*]; then later in the various forms of communal society arising out of the antithesis and fusions of the clans. Only in the eighteenth century, in "civil society", do the various forms of social connectedness confront the individual as a mere means towards his private purposes, as external necessity. But the epoch which produces this standpoint, that of the isolated individual, is also precisely that of the hitherto most developed social (from this standpoint, general) relations. The human being is in the most literal sense a ζῷον πολιτιχόν, not merely a gregarious animal, but an animal which can individuate itself only in the midst of society. Production by an isolated individual outside society—a rare exception which may well occur when a civilized person in whom the social forces are already dynamically present is cast by accident into the wilderness—is as much of an absurdity as is the development of language without individuals living *together* and talking to each other. There is no point in dwelling on this any longer. The point could go entirely unmentioned if this twaddle, which had sense and reason for the eighteenth-century characters, had not been earnestly pulled back into the centre of the most modern economics by Bastiat, Carey, Proudhon etc. Of course it is a convenience for Proudhon et al. to be able to give a historico-philosophic account of the source of an economic relation, of whose historic origins he is ignorant, by inventing the myth that Adam or Prometheus stumbled on the idea ready-made, and then it was adopted, etc. Nothing is more dry and boring than the fantasies of a *locus communis*.

[...]

'social individuals'?

Nature and culture: substance and system of relations. K. Marx   121

Whenever we speak of production, then, what is meant is always production at a definite stage of social development—production by social individuals. It might seem, therefore, that in order to talk about production at all we must either pursue the process of historic development through its different phases, or declare beforehand that we are dealing with a specific historic epoch such as e.g. modern bourgeois production, which is indeed our particular theme. However, all epochs of production have certain common traits, common characteristics. *Production in general* is an abstraction, but a rational abstraction in so far as it really brings out and fixes the common element and thus saves us repetition. Still, this *general* category, this common element sifted out by comparison, is itself segmented many times over and splits into different determinations. Some determinations belong to all epochs, others only to a few. [Some] determinations will be shared by the most modern epoch and the most ancient. No production will be thinkable without them; however, even though the most developed languages have laws and characteristics in common with the least developed, nevertheless, just those things which determine their development, i.e. the elements which are not general and common, must be separated out from the determinations valid for production as such, so that in their unity—which arises already from the identity of the subject, humanity, and of the object, nature—their essential difference is not forgotten. The whole profundity of those modern economists who demonstrate the eternity and harmoniousness of the existing social relations lies in this forgetting. For example. No production possible without an instrument of production, even if this instrument is only the hand. No production without stored-up, past labour, even if it is only the facility gathered together and concentrated in the hand of the savage by repeated practice. Capital is, among other things, also an instrument of production, also objectified, past labour. Therefore capital is a general, eternal relation of nature; that is, if I leave out just the specific quality which alone makes "instrument of production" and "stored-up labour" into capital. The entire history of production relations thus appears to Carey, for example, as a malicious forgery perpetrated by governments.

If there is no production in general, then there is also no general production. Production is always a *particular* branch of production—e.g. agriculture, cattle-raising, manufactures etc.—or it is a *totality*. But political economy is not technology. The relation of the general characteristics of production at a given stage of social development to the particular forms of production to be developed elsewhere (later). Lastly, production also is not only a particular production. Rather, it is always a certain social body, a social subject, which is active in a greater or sparser totality of branches of production. [...]

It is the fashion to preface a work of economics with a general part—and precisely this part figures under the title "production" (see for example J. St. Mill)—treating of the *general preconditions* of all production. This general part consists or is alleged to consist of (1) the conditions without which production is not possible. I.e. in fact, to indicate nothing more than the essential moments of all production. But, as we will see, this reduces itself in fact to a few very simple characteristics, which are hammered out into flat tautologies; (2) the conditions which promote production to a greater or lesser degree, such as e.g. Adam Smith's progressive and stagnant state of society. While this is of value in his work as an insight, to elevate it to scientific significance would require investigations into the periodization of *degrees of productivity* in the development of individual peoples—an investigation which lies outside the proper boundaries of the theme, but, in so far as it does belong there, must be brought in as part of the development of competition, accumulation etc. In the usual formulation, the answer amounts to the general statement that an industrial people reaches the peak of its production at the moment when it arrives at its historical peak generally. In fact. The industrial peak of a people when its main concern is not yet gain, but rather to gain. Thus the Yankees over the English. Or, also, that e.g. certain races, locations, climates, natural conditions such as harbours, soil fertility etc. are more advantageous to production than others. This too amounts to the tautology that wealth is more easily created where its elements are subjectively and objectively present to a greater degree.

But none of all this is the economists' real concern in this general part. The aim is, rather, to present production—see e.g. Mill—as distinct from distribution etc., as encased in eternal natural laws independent of history, at which opportunity *bourgeois* relations are then quietly smuggled in as the inviolable natural laws on which society in the abstract is founded. This is the more or less conscious purpose of the whole proceeding.

Karl Marx
Grundrisse: Foundations of
the Critique of Political Economy

Nature as a psychological invariant and the fallacy of inverting cause and effect

Recourse to psychological explanations stops analysis in its tracks, because it provides too easily the sense of immediate self-evidence. By invoking "simple natures" such as the "propensities", "instincts", or "tendencies" of a human nature, one is liable to offer as an explanation precisely what needs to be explained and, in particular, to locate the principles of institutions such as the family in the magic of the sentiments aroused by those very institutions. "So one should not, as Mr. Spencer does, present social life as the simple resultant of individual natures, since, on the contrary, it is rather the latter which come from the former. Social facts are not the simple development of individual natures, but the second are in large part only the prolongation of the first within consciousnesses.... . The contrary point of view exposes the sociologist, at every moment, to mistaking the cause for the effect, and conversely. For example, if, as often happens, we see in the organization of the family the logically necessary expression of human sentiments inherent in every consciousness, we are reversing the true order of facts. On the contrary, it is the social organization of the relations of kinship which has determined the respective sentiments of parents and children. They would have been completely different if the social structure had been different, and the proof of this is that paternal love is unknown in a great many societies." Durkheim shows that in order to grasp the specificity of the* natura naturans *invoked by prescientific discourse, one has to treat it as* natura naturata, *a cultivated nature.*

12. É. Durkheim

A purely psychological explanation of social facts cannot therefore fail to miss completely all that is specific, i.e. social, about them.

What has blinkered the vision of many sociologists to the insufficiency of this method is the fact that, taking the effect for the cause, they have very often highlighted as causal conditions for social phenomena certain psychical states, relatively well defined and specific, but which in reality are the consequence of the phenomena. Thus it has been held that a certain religiosity is innate in man, as is a certain minimum of sexual jealousy, filial piety or fatherly affection, – Murdoch etc., and it is in these that explanations have been sought for religion, marriage and the family. But history shows that these inclinations, far from being inherent in human nature, are either completely absent under certain social conditions or vary so much from one society to another that the residue left after eliminating all these differences, and which alone can be considered of psychological origin, is reduced to something vague and schematic, infinitely removed from the facts which have to be explained. Thus these sentiments result from the collective organisation and are far from being at the basis of it. It has not even been proved at all that the tendency to sociability was originally a congenital instinct of the human race. It is much more natural to see in it a product of social life which has slowly become organised in us, because it is an observable fact that animals are sociable or otherwise, depending on whether

---

* É. Durkheim, *On the Division of Labor in Society*, trans. G. Simpson, New York: Macmillan, 1933, pp. 349–350.

their environmental conditions force them to live in common or cause them to shun such a life. And even then we must add that a considerable gap remains between these well determined tendencies and social reality.

Furthermore, there is a means of isolating almost entirely the psychological factor, so as to be able to measure precisely the scope of its influence: this is by seeking to determine how race affects social evolution. Ethnic characteristics are of an organic and psychical order. Social life must therefore vary as they vary, if psychological phenomena have on society the causal effectiveness attributed to them. Now we know of no social phenomenon which is unquestionably dependent on race, although we certainly cannot ascribe to this proposition the value of a law. But we can at least assert that it is a constant fact in our practical experience. Yet the most diverse forms of organisation are to be found in societies of the same race, while striking similarities are to be observed among societies of different races. The city state existed among the Phoenicians, as it did among the Romans and the Greeks; we also find it emerging among the Kabyles. The patriarchal family was almost as strongly developed among the Jews as among the Hindus, but it is not to be found among the Slavs, who are nevertheless of Aryan race. By contrast, the family type to be found among the Slavs exists also among the Arabs. The maternal family and the clan are observed everywhere. The precise nature of judicial proofs and nuptial ceremonies is no different among peoples most unlike from the ethnic viewpoint. If this is so, it is because the psychical element is too general to predetermine the course of social phenomena. Since it does not imply one social form rather than another, it cannot explain any such forms. It is true that there are a certain number of facts which it is customary to ascribe to the influence of race. Thus this, in particular, is how we explain why the development of literature and the arts was so rapid and intense in Athens, so slow and mediocre in Rome. But this interpretation of the facts, despite being the classic one, has never been systematically demonstrated. It seems to draw almost all its authority from tradition alone. We have not even reflected upon whether a sociological explanation of the same phenomena was not possible, yet we are convinced that this might be successfully attempted. In short, when we hastily attribute to aesthetic and inherited faculties the artistic nature of Athenian civilisation, we are almost proceeding as did men in the Middle Ages, when fire was explained by phlogiston and the effects of opium by its soporific powers.

Finally, if social evolution really had its origin in the psychological make-up of man, one fails to see how this could have come about. For then we would have to admit that its driving force is some internal motivation within human nature. But what might such a motivation be? Would it be that kind of instinct of which Comte speaks, which impels man to realise increasingly his own nature? But this is to reply to one question by another, explaining progress by an innate tendency to progress, a truly metaphysical entity whose existence, moreover, has in no way been demonstrated. For the animal species, even those of the highest order, are not moved in any way by a need to progress, and even among human societies there are many which are content to remain stationary indefinitely. Might it be, as Spencer seems to believe, that there is a need for greater happiness, which forms of civilisation of ever increasing complexity might be destined to realise more and more completely? It would then be necessary to establish that happiness grows with civilisation, and we have explained elsewhere all the difficulties to which such a hypothesis gives rise. Moreover, there is something else: even if one or other of these postulates were conceded, historical development would not thereby become more intelligible; for the explanation which might emerge from it would be purely teleological. We have shown earlier that social facts, like all natural phenomena, are not explained when we have demonstrated that they serve a purpose. After proving conclusively that a succession of social organisations in history which have become increasingly more knowledgeable have resulted in the greater satisfaction of one or other of our fundamental desires, we would not thereby have made the source of these organisations more comprehensible. The fact that they were useful does not reveal to us what brought them into existence. We might even explain how we came to conceive them, by drawing up a blueprint of them beforehand, so as to envisage the services we might expect them to render—and this is already a difficult problem. But our aspirations, which would thereby become the purpose of such organisations, would have no power to conjure them up out of nothing. In short, if we admit that they are the necessary means to attain the object we have in mind, the question remains in its entirety: How, that is to say, from what, and in what manner, have these means been constituted?

Hence we arrive at the following rule: *The determining cause of a social fact must be sought among antecedent social facts and not among the states of the individual consciousness.* Moreover, we can easily conceive that all that has been stated above applies to the determination of the function as well as the cause of a social fact. Its function can only be social, which means that it consists in the production of socially useful effects. Undoubtedly it can and indeed does happen that it has repercussions which also serve the individual. But this happy result is not the immediate rationale for its existence. Thus we can complement the preceding proposition by stating: *The function of a social fact must always be sought in the relationship that it bears to some social end.*

Émile Durkheim
The Rules of Sociological Method

The sterility of explaining historical specificities by universal tendencies

Through his practice of historical analysis and his constant recourse to the comparative method, Max Weber was particularly aware of the tautological verbalism of psychological explanations in terms of the tendencies of human nature. Explanation of capitalist conduct by reference to an auri sacra fames, *supposed to have reached its apogee in the modern period, combines two types of historical reduction in a contradictory way: the splintering of real totalities into a dust of facts isolated from their context and intended to illustrate a trans-historical explanation; and evolutionist reduction of a specific system of behaviours to an original institution relative to which it introduces no essential novelty.*

One might contrast this text, in which Weber systematically constructs the specific features of modern capitalism, with Sombart's argument in The Quintessence of Capitalism. *Having acknowledged that "there can be infinite variation in the spirit of economic life, in other words, that the soul qualities required for the performance of economic acts can vary from case to case, as will the general ideas and principles which govern economic activity as a whole", Sombart nonetheless then yields to the temptation to explain a singular historical formation in terms of a "generality" attractive to common-sense. For Sombart, it is "the greed of gold and the love for money" that constitutes the common origin of the historically very diverse forms developed by the Germanic, Slav, and Celtic peoples. "Everything points to an early appearance of a desire for gold and its possession among the European peoples in their prime, certainly at least among the upper classes."* Thus a whole part of his method consists in searching, through anecdotal memories illustrating the penchant for accumulation, or moral protests against the "mammonization of all areas of life", for traces of this love of gold and money, which, in various forms, is seen as a constant factor of economic life.*

13. *M. Weber*

The impulse to acquisition, pursuit of gain, of money, of the greatest possible amount of money, has in itself nothing to do with capitalism. This impulse exists and has existed among waiters, physicians, coachmen, artists, prostitutes, dishonest officials, soldiers, nobles, crusaders, gamblers, and beggars. One may say that it has been common to all sorts and conditions of men at all times and in all countries of the earth, wherever the objective possibility of it is or has been given. It should be taught in the kindergarten of cultural history that this naïve idea of capitalism must be given up once and for all. Unlimited greed for gain is not in the least identical with capitalism, and is still less its spirit. Capitalism *may* even be identical with the restraint, or at least a rational tempering, of this irrational impulse. But capitalism is identical with the pursuit of profit, and forever *renewed* profit, by means of continuous, rational, capitalistic enterprise. For it must be so: in a wholly capitalistic order of society, an individual capitalistic enterprise which did not take advantage of its opportunities for profit-making would be doomed to extinction. [...]

A state of mind such as that expressed in the passages we have quoted from Franklin, and which called forth the applause of a whole people, would both

---

* W. Sombart, *The Quintessence of Capitalism: A Study of the History and Psychology of the Modern Business Man*, trans. M. Epstein, London: Fisher Unwin, 1915, pp. 25–26.

in ancient times and in the Middle Ages* have been proscribed as the lowest sort of avarice and as an attitude entirely lacking in self-respect. It is, in fact, still regularly thus looked upon by all those social groups which are least involved in or adapted to modern capitalistic conditions. This is not wholly because the instinct of acquisition was in those times unknown or undeveloped, as has often been said. Nor because the *auri sacra fames*, the greed for gold, was then, or now, less powerful outside of bourgeois capitalism than within its peculiar sphere, as the illusions of modern romanticists are wont to believe. The difference between the capitalistic and pre-capitalistic spirits is not to be found at this point. The greed of the Chinese Mandarin, the old Roman aristocrat, or the modern peasant, can stand up to any comparison. And the *auri sacra fames* of a Neapolitan cab-driver or *barcaiuolo*, and certainly of Asiatic representatives of similar trades, as well as of the craftsmen of southern European or Asiatic countries, is, as anyone can find out for himself, very much more intense, and especially more unscrupulous than that of, say, an Englishman in similar circumstances.

The universal reign of absolute unscrupulousness in the pursuit of selfish interests by the making of money has been a specific characteristic of precisely those countries whose bourgeois-capitalistic development, measured according to Occidental standards, has remained backward. As every employer knows, the lack of *coscienziosità* of the labourers of such countries, for instance Italy as compared with Germany, has been, and to a certain extent still is, one of the principal obstacles to their capitalistic development. Capitalism cannot make use of the labour of those who practise the doctrine of undisciplined *liberum arbitrium*, any more than it can make use of the business man who seems absolutely unscrupulous in his dealings with others, as we can learn from Franklin. Hence the difference does not lie in the degree of development of any impulse to make money. The *auri sacra fames* is as old as the history of man. But we shall see that those who submitted to it without reserve as an uncontrolled impulse, such as the Dutch sea-captain who "would go through hell for gain, even though he scorched his sails", were by no means the representatives of that attitude of mind from which the specifically modern capitalistic spirit as a mass phenomenon is derived, and that is what matters. At all periods of history, wherever it was possible, there has been ruthless acquisition, bound to no ethical norms whatever. [...]

Now, however, the Occident has developed capitalism both to a quantitative extent, and (carrying this quantitative development) in types, forms, and directions which have never existed elsewhere. All over the world there have been merchants, wholesale and retail, local and engaged in foreign trade.

* Weber has just quoted some texts that he regards as expressing the "spirit of capitalism": in them, Franklin preaches an ascetic morality whose supreme goal is to produce ever more money, at the cost of a life dominated by calculation and the concern to secure a return on money, which is "generous and prolific by nature".

Loans of all kinds have been made, and there have been banks with the most various functions, at least comparable to ours of, say, the sixteenth century. Sea loans, *commenda*, and transactions and associations similar to the *Kommanditgesellschaft*, have all been widespread, even as continuous businesses. Whenever money finances of public bodies have existed, money-lenders have appeared, as in Babylon, Hellas, India, China, Rome. They have financed wars and piracy, contracts and building operations of all sorts. In overseas policy they have functioned as colonial entrepreneurs, as planters with slaves, or directly or indirectly forced labour, and have farmed domains, offices, and, above all, taxes. They have financed party leaders in elections and *condottieri* in civil wars. And, finally, they have been speculators in chances for pecuniary gain of all kinds. This kind of entrepreneur, the capitalistic adventurer, has existed everywhere. With the exception of trade and credit and banking transactions, their activities were predominantly of an irrational and speculative character, or directed to acquisition by force, above all the acquisition of booty, whether directly in war or in the form of continuous fiscal booty by exploitation of subjects.

The capitalism of promoters, large-scale speculators, concession hunters, and much modern financial capitalism even in peace time, but, above all, the capitalism especially concerned with exploiting wars, bears this stamp even in modern Western countries, and some, but only some, parts of large-scale international trade are closely related to it, to-day as always.

But in modern times the Occident has developed, in addition to this, a very different form of capitalism which has appeared nowhere else: the rational capitalistic organization of (formally) free labour. Only suggestions of it are found elsewhere. Even the organization of unfree labour reached a considerable degree of rationality only on plantations and to a very limited extent in the *Ergasteria* of antiquity. In the manors, manorial workshops, and domestic industries on estates with serf labour it was probably somewhat less developed. Even real domestic industries with free labour have definitely been proved to have existed in only a few isolated cases outside the Occident. The frequent use of day labourers led in a very few cases—especially State monopolies, which are, however, very different from modern industrial organization—to manufacturing organizations, but never to a rational organization of apprenticeship in the handicrafts like that of our Middle Ages.

Rational industrial organization, attuned to a regular market, and neither to political nor irrationally speculative opportunities for profit, is not, however, the only peculiarity of Western capitalism. The modern rational organization of the capitalistic enterprise would not have been possible without two other important factors in its development: the separation of business from the household, which completely dominates modern economic life, and closely connected with it, rational book-keeping. A spatial separation of places of work from those of residence exists elsewhere, as in the Oriental bazaar and in the *ergasteria* of other cultures. The development of capitalistic associations with their own accounts is also found in the Far East, the Near East, and in antiquity. But compared to the modern independence of business enterprises, those are only small beginnings. The reason for this was particularly that the indispensable requisites for this independence, our rational business book-keeping and our legal separation of corporate from personal property, were entirely lacking, or had only begun to develop. The tendency everywhere else was for acquisitive enterprises to arise as parts of a royal or manorial *household* (of the *oikos*), which is, as Rodbertus has perceived, with all its superficial similarity, a fundamentally different, even opposite, development.

However, all these peculiarities of Western capitalism have derived their significance in the last analysis only from their association with the capitalistic organization of labour. Even what is generally called commercialization, the development of negotiable securities and the rationalization of speculation, the exchanges, etc., is connected with it. For without the rational capitalistic organization of labour, all this, so far as it was possible at all, would have nothing like the same significance, above all for the social structure and all the specific problems of the modern Occident connected with it. Exact calcula-tion—the basis of everything else—is only possible on a basis of free labour.

Max Weber
The Protestant Ethic and the Spirit
of Capitalism

1.4   Spontaneous sociology and the powers of language

The nosography of language

We think, said Bacon, that we govern our words, yet it is they that govern us unawares and entangle us in the deceptions of their false appearances. But—contrary to the rationalist tradition of the Lingua universalis *or the* Characteristica generalis—*it is not sufficient to substitute the perfect logic of a constructed language for the uncertainties of that* idolum fori, *ordinary language. One also has to analyse the logic of ordinary language, which, just because it is so ordinary, passes unnoticed. Only such a critique can bring to light the false problematics and fallacious categories which are purveyed by everyday language and which always threaten to sneak back in the erudite guise of the most formalized language.*

14. *M. Chastaing* (φ)

Wittgenstein treats philosophers like people suffering from an illness and invents a *new method* [II, 26]* that will cure them. How? By *calming* them. How will it dispel their anxiety? By resolving their problems? No: by dissolving them [48, 51, 91, 155].

What are they suffering from? From mistaken ways of talking [47]. They use the same words as us—"knowledge", "being", "I", "object", and so on [48]—but they do not use them either as we do or as they themselves *humbly* use words like "table", "kitchen", or "tennis" [44]. When they ask "Does a colonel think?", are they asking the same question that we unfortunately sometimes ask [126]? When they confess: "I cannot know your feelings", shall we say: "Try!"? Either they interpret our ordinary expressions *oddly* [19], or their oddness is expressed in extraordinary turns of phrase [47]. Either, in their disorder, they no longer understand either our everyday language or their own,[1] or they invent a language as incomprehensible as that of a madman who orders "Milk me sugar" [138]. Their problems stem from their linguistic disorders [51]. To be precise: from their disobeying the rules of *language games*.[2]

Now, "the meaning of a word or a set of words is determined by the system

---

* The numbers in square brackets refer to *Philosophical Investigations*, Oxford: Blackwell, 1953. The numbers preceded by I and II refer to pages in G. E. Moore, "Wittgenstein's Lectures", *Mind*, 1954 and 1955.

[1] "When we do philosophy, we are like savages, primitive people, who hear the expressions of civilized men, put a false interpretation on them, and then draw the queerest conclusions from them" [79]. M. Macdonald translates: philosophers "use ordinary words while depriving them of their ordinary function" ("The Philosopher's Use of Analogy", *Logic and Language*, I, p. 82, 1955).

[2] Wittgenstein uses the expression *Sprachspiel* (language game) sometimes to designate the *system* [I, 6] of a language, sometimes the use of this language, i.e. speech, and sometimes speech and the acts with which it is intertwined [5]. He illustrates the expression, like Saussure, by comparing language to a game of chess.

of rules which fixes its use"[3] [I, 298]. Philosophical statements therefore have no meaning[4] [48]. And every philosopher, lost in the fog [222] of his absurdities, merely repeats "I don't know my way about".[5]

The main symptoms of his disorientation:

1. Being "out of play": Sufferers remove words from the texts in which we use them, extract sentences from their usual contexts, and so produce "unusual" utterances which they endow with an absolute meaning, whereas our utterances only have meaning in relation to the conditions—verbal or otherwise—in which we have learned to play with them. For example, they ask, outside of all the *games* in which words have roles and therefore outside of all language,[6] questions like "Is this simple or complex?" "Is this a mental state?" [21, 61].

Some diagnostic signs:

a) *Contradictions* [50]: A man who asks "Can one play chess without the queen?" "Can I feel your tooth-ache?" "Is a tiger without stripes a tiger?"[7] is a philosopher. If he has learned to say "tiger" to name a carnivore with stripes, surely he contradicts himself in talking about a tiger without stripes?

b) *Hidden essences* [43]: The philosopher who seeks teeth in a hen's beak finds invisible teeth there; he is looking for the meaning of the words "being" and "object", but he has deprived them of any visible meaning by abstracting them from the *circumstances* from which they sprang and of which they are manifestly signs,[8] so he has to imagine that the looked-for meaning is *hidden* in ideas or spiritual *essences* which the words signify[9] (as a scratch on a stone signifies buried treasure), then invent an *intuition* [84] which enables him to grasp "in a flash" [80] the hidden essence of beings and objects [48].

c) *Definitions* [73]: When a seeker after hidden essences asks you "What is a game?", isn't he hoping that you will provide a *definitive answer* [43]? When philosophers ask questions, they are looking for definitions. But how can we explain to them where games end and where they begin [33–36]?[10] Haven't we

---

[3] M. Schlick attributes this formulation to Wittgenstein ("Meaning and Verification", *Philosophical Review*, p. 341, 1936).

[4] See B. Farrell, "An Appraisal of Therapeutic Positivism", *Mind*, 1946.

[5] "*Ein philosophisches Problem hat die Form: 'Ich kenne mich nicht aus'*" [49].

[6] "It is only in a language that I can mean something by something" [18]. A very "Saussurian" formula.

[7] Wittgenstein's examples (J. Wisdom, "Other Minds", *Mind*, p. 370, 1940).

[8] The meaning of a word is therefore "mediated" by the circumstances in which it is used. P. F. Strawson sees "hostility to the doctrine of non-mediation" as one of the constant features of the *Philosophical Investigations* (*Mind*, pp. 92, 98, 1951).

[9] Cf. "Where our language suggests a body and there is none: there, we should like to say, is a spirit." [18].

[10] Linguists talk exactly like Wittgenstein: "Where, for example, does the genus *pot* begin and end, or the genus *marmite*?" (A. Dauzat, *La géographie linguistique*, Paris, 1922, p. 123).

learned to talk of children's games, the Olympic Games, mathematical games, playing on words, etc.? And therefore learned to extend the field of games endlessly? Our *concept* "game" seems *open-ended* [31–33].[11]

Remedy: bring words and sentences back *home* to the situations in which they are used [48, 155]. In the event of philosophical crisis, take the offending words and ask: "In what circumstances do we say them?" [48, 61, 188; II, 19].

2. The common denominator: Sufferers fight back: they want to define *what is common*, in all circumstances, to every game; they wish to contemplate the essence of Art in which all arts commune. And they attack: in order for us to apply a common name, like "game" or "art", to different activities, these activities *must* have a common denominator.

Does this mean that, in order to talk about *vol*, the *vol* of an aviator has to have *something in common* with the *vol* of a robber?[12] Our hunting ancestors moved from one *vol* to another through "birds of prey" and poaching. We move *gradually* from one use of the word *bureau* to another, without thinking of an Idea of Bureau to which a table cloth, a desk, an office, a company, and a government agency would all have to belong.[13] The semantics of gradual transitions dispels the mystery of too general ideas [II, 17].

The remedy, therefore: Don't say "There *must* be something common" to all the substances, qualities, or actions designated by the same word, but *look* and *see* whether there is anything common to all. [31] Look at the way the word "occupation" *functions* and see whether "a worker's occupation" has anything in common with "occupation of premises"; whether wit is "dry" like land and land "dry" like some champagne;[14] whether the life of the verb "take" is as simple as that of a specialist verb like *écobuer*.

Learn to understand, through *examples, how words work* [31–32, 51, 109]. Take a few doses of examples, as required, from treatises of semantics.

3. One-sided diet [155]: To be sure, some philosophers avoid feeding their speculations on examples; but others "nourish their thinking with only one kind of example". They end up forgetting that other kinds exist. This leads them to universalize particular ways of speaking: they turn "some" into "all", a part into the whole [3, 13, 18, 37, 110, 155]. Watch them at work: metaphysicians who *substitute* "identical" for "the same", although the two are only sometimes synonymous [91]; psychologists who assume that *a* motive is *the*

---

[11] See M. Chastaing, "Jouer n'est pas jouer", *Journal de psychologie normale et pathologique*, no. 3, pp. 303–326, 1959.

[12] The verb *voler* (steal) is said to derive from its homograph meaning "fly", though this etymology is disputed [translator's note].

[13] *Bureau* — from *bure*, rough cloth — can mean all these things in French [translator].

[14] See R. Wells, "Meaning and Use", *Word*, p. 24, August 1951. In this issue of *Word*, Wittgenstein's philosophy converges with structural linguistics (see S. Ullmann, "The Concept of Meaning in Linguistics", *Archivum Ling.*, pp. 18–29, 1956). But convergence is not influence. Was Wittgenstein influenced by linguists? Has he influenced linguistics?

motive. Often philosophers of language, they are in the habit of treating all words as names and all names as proper names [18–20; I, 9].

Remedy: explicit specification. Formulate the special conditions in which words X have meaning Y, expressly restricting this meaning with sample conditions: "In *this* case...", "In *these* cases...". Sometimes it will be sufficient to say: "In a large number of cases...".

To prepare this remedy, supplement the formula already prescribed—"In what circumstances do we say that...?"—with the question: "Aren't there circumstances in which we speak differently?" If, for example, you are tempted to define games as competitions, ask not only "Which games?" but also: "Are there games without competitors? And which ones?". Through your questions you will learn to *compare* the different uses of the word "game" [3, 20, 30, 32, 50].

4. The "category error":[15] Because philosophers do not practise comparing the semantic domains of their words, they make the mistake of confusing these domains [24, 13]. Their language then resembles tennis with goals, or a ring in which boxers of different categories fight [231]. Could they be imitating the humorists for whom the "category error" is a law? No. They are not offering their *grammatical jokes* as jokes [47]. They are quite serious when they treat psychology as analogous to physics [151] or "thinking" as parallel to "talking" [217], when they say that Miss N. has a "self" in the same way that she has blonde hair,[16] or that the mind has opinions in the same sense that Mr. N. has opinions [151], when they confuse the *reasons* for dreaming with the *causes* of the dream [II, 20–21], our actual language with a logical language [46], or the meaning of a word with the word itself [49]. They are quite serious when they take "illustrated turns of speech" for empirical propositions, and *metaphors*, in which words move from their semantic field to an alien field [I, 5, 292], for ordinary expressions.

Remedy: a few "commutation" exercises.[17] Practice asking: "In the circumstances in which I say A, can I commute A and say B? And can I therefore say either A *or* B, or A *and* B?" Ask, for example; "Can I say 'Am I suffering?' as I say 'Am I in love?'; or say 'For a second I felt deep grief' as I say 'For a second I felt violent pain'?"—and you will no longer succumb to the temptation to put love and grief in the category of *sensations* where you place pain and even suffering [61, 154, 174]. Ask: "Can I say that I speak with words *and*

[15] See G. Ryle, *The Concept of Mind*, Cambridge, 1951, pp. 16–18.
[16] J. E. Thomson, "The Argument from Analogy and our Knowledge of Other Minds", *Mind*, p. 343, 1951.
[17] A word much favoured by "glossematicians". Justified by the 20th remark, in which, like them, Wittgenstein makes the word the smallest "commutation unit" which can have the value of a sentence [8, 9], and by remark 558 in which he uses the famous "substitution test" to identify the meaning of a word [149] (see L. Hjelmslev, *Prolegomena to a Theory of Language*, Baltimore, Indiana: Waverley Press, 1953, p. 66).

sentences?[18] That a chess-player plays with pieces *and* gambits?" And you will no longer be tempted to set words at the same level as statements.

In this way, through questions in which you use one sentence in contrast with others, one word in opposition to others [9, 90], learn to recognize both the semantic differences that everyday language systematically establishes and the errors of philosophers who violate the "system of differences" (Saussure) of their language.

This remedy, like the previous ones, thus proceeds from a psychoanalysis, the rule of which is as follows: in order to be cured, philosophers have to be made conscious of their verbal eccentricities;[19] to become conscious of these eccentricities, they have to recover awareness of ordinary language which, because it is ordinary, passes unnoticed [43–49]. They have to be *recalled* [50] to linguistic order, through a *clear* exposition of our ways of talking [6, 51, 133, 167]. The therapist who, like Descartes, loves order and clarity,[20] teaches nothing, like Socrates: opening up ordinary language, he never offers anything but *banalities* [42, 47, 50; II, 27].[21]

Maxime Chastaing
"Wittgenstein et le problème de la connaissance d'autrui"

---

[18] See G. Ryle, "Ordinary Language", *Philosophical Review*, 1953.
[19] "Philosophical problems arise when language *goes on holiday*" [19].
[20] Malebranche was already applying Wittgenstein's method (*Recherche de la vérité*, VI, 2, 7).
[21] "Philosophy only states what everyone admits" [156].

Metaphorical schemes in biology

Because they offer an immediate, overall understanding, common schemes — images or analogies — have the power to block the development of scientific knowledge of phenomena. To release the heuristic value of notions such as "cell" or "tissue", biological thought had to succeed in neutralizing the emotional or social connotations that these words derived from their common usage. Most often, like Harvey, who had to repress the image of "irrigation" in order to be able to formulate the hypothesis of the circulation of the blood, one has to be able to break irrevocably with a system of images that prevents the formulation of a coherent theory. More generally, use of an analogy, even if it is not absolutely adequate, may make it possible to see the ambiguities of a less adequate analogy, if it is itself controlled by a theoretical intention. The metaphor of the organism as a society enabled biology to break with the technological representation of the body; but this analogy was in turn rectified by the development of biological theory.

15. G. Canguilhem

With the cell, we are in the presence of a biological object whose affective overdetermination is indisputable and considerable. The psychoanalysis of knowledge now boasts enough successes to be able to claim the dignity of a genre to which one may make a few contributions, even without a systematic intention. Everyone will find in his memories of natural history lessons the image of the cellular structure of living beings. This image has an almost canonical constancy. The schematic representation of an epithelium is the image of a honeycomb. "Cell" is a word that does not make us think of a monk or a prisoner, but of bees. Haeckel pointed out that wax cells filled with honey are the complete counterpart of vegetable cells filled with cell sap. However, the hold that the idea of the cell exerts over people's minds does not seem to us to be due to this completeness of correspondence. But might it not rather be that in consciously borrowing the term "cell", to designate the element of the living organism, from the beehive, the human mind was also, almost unconsciously, borrowing the idea of the co-operative labour of which the honey is the product? As the alveolus is the element of an edifice, so the bees are, in Maeterlinck's phrase, individuals entirely absorbed by the republic. In fact, the cell is a notion that is both anatomical and functional, the notion of an elementary material and an individual labour that is partial and subordinate. What is certain is that, at a greater or lesser distance, the affective and social values of co-operation and association overhang the development of cell theory. [...]

The term "tissue" deserves some attention. The French word *tissu* comes, as we know, from *tistre*, an archaic form of the verb *tisser*, to weave.* If the word "cell" struck us as charged with implicit affective and social implications, the word "tissue" seems to us no less fraught with extra-theoretical implications. "Cell" makes us think of bees and not man; *tissu* makes us think of man and

* The primary meaning of French *tissu* is therefore "cloth, fabric" (translator).

not the spider. "Tissue" is par excellence the work of man. The cell, with its canonical hexagonal form, is the image of a self-enclosed whole. But "tissue" is the image of a continuity in which any interruption is arbitrary, in which the product proceeds from an activity that is always open to continuation. One cuts, here or there, according to one's needs. Moreover, a cell is a fragile thing, made to be admired, looked at but not touched lest it be destroyed. By contrast, tissue is there to be touched, felt, squeezed, in order to appreciate its texture, suppleness, and softness. It is folded and unfurled, unrolled in superimposed waves on the merchant's counter. [...]

Blood and sap flow like water. Channelled water irrigates the soil; blood and sap must irrigate, too. It was Aristotle who assimilated the distribution of the blood from the heart to the irrigation of a garden through channels. And Galen thought in just the same way. But irrigating the soil means in the end being lost in the soil. And that is exactly the obstacle to the understanding of circulation. Harvey is celebrated for the experiment in which he applied a ligature to the veins of the arm, the swelling of which below the point of constriction is one of the experimental proofs of circulation. Now, this experiment had already been done in 1603 by Fabricio d'Aquapendente—and it is quite possible that it was done earlier—who concluded from it the regulatory function of the valves of the veins, but thought their role was to prevent the blood from accumulating in the limbs and lower body. What Harvey added to the sum of observations made before him is this, which is both simple and capital: in an hour, the left ventricle sends into the body, through the aorta, a weight of blood three times greater than the weight of the body. Where does so much blood come from and where does it go? Furthermore, if an artery is opened, the organism is bled white. This led to the idea of a possible closed circuit. "I asked myself," says Harvey, "if everything would not be explained by circular movement of the blood." It was then that, by repeating the experiment of ligature, Harvey was able to give a coherent meaning to all the observations and experiments. It can be seen how the discovery of the circulation of the blood was first, and perhaps essentially, the substitution of a concept designed to "cohere" precise obervations made on the organism at different points and at different times, for another concept, that of irrigation, directly imported into biology from the domain of human technology. The reality of the biological concept presupposes abandoning the convenience of the agricultural concept of irrigation.

Georges Canguilhem
La connaissance de la vie

It is physiology that gives the key to organic totalization, a key which anatomy had not been able to supply. The organs, the systems of a highly differentiated organism, do not exist for themselves, they exist for the cells, for the innumerable anatomical radicals, creating for them the internal environment, kept in constant composition through the compensation of deviations that is necessary for them. The result is that their association, i.e. their social type of relationship, provides the elements with the collective means of living a separate life. "If one could produce at every moment an environment identical to that which the action of the neighbouring parts creates continuously for a given elementary organism, the latter *would live in freedom exactly as in society.*" The part depends on a whole which is only constituted for its maintenance. By bringing down the study of all functions to the level of the cell, general physiology accounts for the fact that the structure of the total organism is subordinated to the functions of the part. The organism, made up of cells, is made for the cells, for parts which are themselves wholes of lesser complexity.

The use of an economic and political model gave the 19th-century biologists the means of understanding that which the use of a technological model had not previously allowed. The relation of the parts to the whole is a relation of *integration*—and this latter concept has made its fortune in nerve physiology—of which the end is the part, since the part is no longer a piece or an instrument, but an individual. In the period during which what was to become very positively the cell theory depended as much on philosophical speculation as on microscopic exploration, the term *monad* was often used to designate the anatomical element, before the term *cell* came to be generally and definitively preferred. In particular, it is under the name *monad* that Auguste Comte refuses the cell theory. The indirect but real influence of Leibnizian philosophy on the first philosophers and biologists who imagined the cell theory entitles us to say of the cell what Leibniz says of the monad, that it is *pars totalis*. It is not an instrument, a tool, it is an individual, a subject of functions. Claude Bernard often uses the term *harmony* to give an idea of what he means by organic totality. It is not difficult to recognize here too a weakened echo of Leibniz's language. Thus, with the recognition of the cellular form as the morphological element of any organized body, the concept of organization changes its meaning. The whole is no longer the result of an assemblage of organs, it is a totalization of individuals. In the 19th century, in a parallel and simultaneous way, the term *part* loses its traditional arithmetical sense, because of the constitution of set theory, and its traditional anatomical sense, because of the constitution of cell theory.

About thirty years after the death of Claude Bernard, did the technique of *in vitro* culture of explanted cells (developed by Carrel in 1910 but invented by Jolly in 1903) provide experimental proof that the organism is constructed as a liberal-type society—for it is the society of his time that Claude Bernard takes as a model—in which the conditions of individual life are respected and could be prolonged outside the association, subject to the artificial provision of an appropriate environment? In fact, in order for the element in the free state, i.e.

freed from the inhibitions and stimulations that it undergoes as a result of its integration in the whole, to be able to live in the free state as in society, the environment that is provided has to age at the same rate as itself, which amounts to making elementary life lateral with respect to the whole of which the artificial environment constitutes the equivalent—lateral and not independent. Moreover, life in the free state forbids a return to the state of society, which is a proof that the freed part has irreversibly lost its character as a part. As Etienne Wolff observes: "The association of cells previously dissociated has never resulted in the reconstitution of the structural unity. Synthesis has never followed analysis. By an illogical use of language, we often give the name *tissue cultures* to anarchic cell proliferations which respect neither the structure nor the cohesion of the tissue from which they are derived." In short, an organic element can only be called an element in the non-separated state. In this sense one must recall Hegel's formula, that it is the whole that realizes the relationship of the parts among themselves, so that outside of the whole there are no parts.

On this point, therefore, experimental embryology and cytology have rectified the concept of organic structure that Claude Bernard too closely associated with a social model which was perhaps, all in all, no more than a metaphor. Reacting against the use of mechanical models in physiology, Bernard once wrote: "The larynx is a larynx and the lens of the eye the lens of the eye, which means to say that their mechanical or physical conditions are not realized anywhere other than in the living organism." The same is true of social models in biology as of mechanical models. Although the concept of a totality regulating organic development and functioning has remained an at least formally invariant concept of biological thought since the time when Bernard was one of the first to verify its experimental efficacy, it nonetheless has to be recognized that its fate has ceased to be linked to that of the social model which initially underpinned it. The organism is not a society, even when like a society it presents a structure of organization. Organization, in the most general sense, is the solution of a problem concerning the conversion of competition into compatibility. An organism and a society each organize themselves in their own ways. Just as Bernard said "The larynx is a larynx", so we may say that the model of the organism is the organism itself.

Georges Canguilhem
"Le tout et la partie dans la pensée biologique"

1.5 The temptation to prophesy

The prophéticism of the professor and the intellectual

The situation of the professor, facing an audience of adolescents more eager for "personal touches" than attentive to the austere rules of scientific work, clearly creates a particular temptation to practise one type of prophesy. But Weber's analysis also makes it possible to understand, mutatis mutandis, *how the sociologist is tempted to betray the demands of research whenever he consciously or unconsciously indulges the expectations of an intellectual audience which looks to sociology for total answers to human problems that rightly belong to everyone, and especially intellectuals.*

Weber's analysis should be borne in mind when reading the text by Bennett M. Berger. The disillusionment aroused in intellectuals by sociologists who confine themselves to their specialism and refuse to be intellectuals illustrates a contrario *the invitation to prophéticism implied in the expectations of the intellectual mass audience, eager for "thought-provoking" overviews, pronouncements on ultimate values, reflections on the "great issues" of the day, or unjustified and portentously dramatic systematizations designed to inspire an existential frisson.*

16. *M. Weber*

The examination of one's conscience would perhaps show that the fulfillment of our postulate is especially difficult, just because we reluctantly refuse to enter the very alluring area of values without a titillating "personal touch". Every teacher has observed that the faces of his students light up and they become more attentive when he begins to set forth his personal evaluations, and that the attendance at his lectures is greatly increased by the expectation that he will do so. Everyone knows furthermore that in the competition for students, universities in making recommendations for advancement, will often give a prophet, however minor, who can fill the lecture halls, the upper hand over a much superior scholar who does not present his own preferences. Of course, it is understood in those cases that the prophecy should leave sufficiently untouched the political or conventional preferences which are generally accepted at the time. [...]

An unprecedented situation exists when a large number of officially accredited prophets do not do their preaching on the streets, or in churches or other public places or in sectarian conventicles, but rather feel themselves competent to enunciate their evaluations on ultimate questions "in the name of science" in governmentally privileged lecture halls in which they are neither controlled, checked by discussion, nor subject to contradiction. It is an axiom of long standing, which Schmoller on one occasion vigorously espoused that what took place in the lecture hall should be held separate from the arena of public discussion. Although it is possible to contend that even scientifically this may have its disadvantages, I take the view that a "lecture" should be different from a "speech". The calm rigor, matter-of-factness and sobriety of the lecture declines with definite pedagogical losses, when the substance and manner of public discussion are introduced, in the style of the press. This privilege of freedom from outside control seems in any case to be appropriate only to the sphere of the specialized qualifications of the professor. There is, however, no specialized qualification for personal prophecy, and for this reason it is not entitled to that privilege of freedom from external control. Furthermore, there should be no exploitation of the fact that the student, in order to make his way, must attend certain educational institutions and take courses with certain teachers, with the result that in addition to what is required, i.e., the stimulation and cultivation of his capacity for observation and reasoning, and a certain body of factual information, the teacher slips in his own uncontradictable evaluations, which though sometimes of considerable interest, are often quite trivial.

Like everyone else, the professor has other facilities for the diffusion of his ideals. When these facilities are lacking, he can easily create them in an appropriate form, as experience has shown in the case of every honest attempt. But the professor should not demand the right as a professor to carry the marshal's baton of the statesman or reformer in his knapsack. This is just what he does when he uses the unassailability of the academic chair for the expression of political (or cultural-political) evaluations. In the press, in public meetings, in associations, in essays, in every avenue which is open to every other citizen, he can and should do what his God or dæmon demands.

Max Weber
The Methodology of the Social Sciences

Δ=65

17. B. M. Berger (1957) vs (2022)

[Most of the criticism of sociologists is inspired by the idea that "the most basic function of intellectuals in the Western tradition" is "to comment on and interpret the meaning of contemporary experience".]

It would be a mistake to assume that, because the intellectual is conceived in the image of the literary man, his essential property is that he is an artist or a student of literature. His identification as an intellectual rests not on the aesthetic value of his novels, plays, poems, essays, or literary criticism, but on his assumption, through them, of the role of *commentator on contemporary culture and interpreter of contemporary experience*. [...]

In our time literary men have pre-empted the intellectual's role because of (A) their maximal freedom from the parochial demands of technical specialization (B) their freedom (within their status as literary men) to make large and uncompromising judgments about values, and (C) their maximal freedom from institutional restraints.

A. *Specialization.* Intellectuals, I have said, are commentators on contemporary culture and interpreters of contemporary experience; they are critics, liberal or conservative, radical or reactionary, of contemporary life. The range of their competence is not circumscribed; it includes nothing less than the entire cultural life of a people. If they are academic men, they may be specialists in various subjects; but their professional specialties do not generally interfere with their being intellectuals. In the humanities, and particularly in literature, a specialty usually consists of *expertise* regarding a given historical period and the figures important to one's discipline who are associated with it: Dr. Johnson and the English literature of the eighteenth century; the significance of Gide in the French literature of the twentieth century; Prince Metternich and the history of Europe after 1815; Kant, Hegel, and German Idealism 1750–1820. Specialties like these do not militate against one's assuming the role of the intellectual, because the traditions of humanistic study encourage the apprehension of cultural wholes; they encourage commentary and interpretation regarding the "backgrounds"—social, cultural, intellectual, spiritual—of the subject matter one is expert about. The humanities—and particularly literature—offer to intellectuals a professional status which impedes little if at all the fulfillment of their function as intellectuals. [...]

it's 1957

B. *Values.* In commenting on contemporary culture and in interpreting contemporary experience, intellectuals are under no seriously sanctioned injunction to be "detached" or "objective". Unlike the sociologist, who functions under the rule of strict separation between facts and values, the intellectual is expected to judge and evaluate, to praise and blame, to win adherents to his point of view and to defend his position against his intellectual enemies. In the context of free debate among intellectuals, the exercise of this function takes the form of polemics; in an academic context, it develops into the phenomenon of "schools of thought". The point is that, whereas in sociology the existence of schools of thought is an embarrassment to everyone (since it is a constant reminder that not enough is *known*—in science, opinion is tolerated only where facts are not available), in the humanities the existence of schools of thought is accepted as normal and proper, because the humanities actively encourage evaluation, the development of point of view, and heterogeneity of interpretation.

1957

C. *Freedom from Institutional Restraints.* Literary men have been able, more than members of other intellectual professions, to resist the tendencies toward the bureaucratization of intellectual life. This has been possible because of the large market for fiction in the United States, and because of the opportunities of selling critical and interpretive articles to the high- and middle-brow magazines, which, in spite of repeated protestations to the contrary, continue to flourish in this country. The ability of free lance writers to support them-

1.1.

1.11.

selves without depending upon a salary from a university or other large organization maximizes their freedom to be critics of contemporary life. Such opportunities are not typically available to sociologists. In addition, major sociological research is increasingly "team" research, while literary and humanistic research in universities is still largely a matter of individual scholarship. Obviously, collective responsibility for a work restrains the commentaries and interpretations of its authors; the individual humanistic scholar, usually responsible only to himself, is free from the restraints imposed by the conditions of collective research.

The purpose of this discussion of the intellectuals has been to highlight the fact that although sociology has arrogated to itself the right to *expertise* regarding society and culture, its commitment to the traditions of science (narrow specialization, objectivity, and team research) militates against sociologists assuming the role of the intellectual. [...] When the sociologist arrogates *expertise* regarding the affairs of contemporary men, he is perceived as saying, in effect, that he *knows* more about the affairs of contemporary men than the intellectual does; and once this implication is received into the community of intellectuals, the issue is joined. The fact of this implication becomes one more fact of contemporary experience to which the intellectuals can devote their critical faculties—and with considerable relish, because the implication seems to threaten the basis of their right to the position which, as intellectuals, they hold.

Even those intellectuals with sympathies for the goals of sociology often exhibit a fundamental underestimation of the consequences of its commitment to science. The characteristic plea of these people is an exhortation to "grapple with the *big* problems". Although this advice is without doubt well intentioned, it characteristically underestimates the degree to which the mores of science and the responsibility of foundations and university research institutes can command the type of work sociologists do. I mean by this simply that the sociologist is responsible to the community of social scientists for the *scientific* value of his work, and that university research institutes are sensitive to charges of financing "biased" or "controversial" research (a possibility that is maximized when one deals with the "big problems"). And when the "big problems" *are* grappled with, for example, in books like *The American Soldier* and *The Authoritarian Personality*, or in other types of work like *The Lonely Crowd*, *White Collar*, and *The Power Elite*, controversy and polemic follow. For the sympathetic intellectual's exhortation to the sociologist to "grapple with the big problems" says, in effect, "don't be a scientist, be a humanist; be an intellectual." This implication is supported by the respectful (if not totally favorable) reception given by intellectuals to the works of Riesman and Mills (least encumbered with the trappings of science), and their utter hostility to

sociologist vs intellectual
author?

works like _The American Soldier_, which fairly bristles with the method of science.*

There is one more source of the intellectual's hostility to sociology that I would like to examine, a source that was anticipated by Weber in his lecture on science as a vocation. For if it is true that intellectualization and rationalization, to which science commits itself and of which it is a part, means "that principally there are no mysterious incalculable forces that come into play, but rather that one can, in principle, master all things by calculation," then it is not only true, as Weber said, that "the world is disenchanted," but also true that the social scientist is perceived as challenging that tradition of humanism and art which has subsisted on the view that the world _is_ enchanted, and that man is the mystery of mysteries. [...]

Intellectuals in this tradition seem to believe that the fulfillment of the goals of social science necessarily means that the creative powers of man will be "explained away", that his freedom will be denied, his "naturalness" mechanized, and his "miraculousness" made formula; that Cummings' "feelingly illimitable individual"[1] will be shown up as a quite limited and determined "social product", whose every mystery and transcendence can be formulated, if not on a pin, then within the framework of some sociological theory. It is no wonder, then, that a vision as fearsome as this can provoke the simultaneous convictions that a science of society is both impossible and evil.

Bennett M. Berger
"Sociology and the Intellectuals: An Analysis of a Stereotype"

---

* The author notes elsewhere that "with the publication and reception of _The Lonely Crowd_, David Riesman emancipated himself, in the eyes of the community of intellectuals, from bearing the burden of identification as a 'sociologist'; that is to say, he became an intellectual."

[1] E. E. Cummings, _six nonlectures_, Cambridge: Harvard University Press, 1955, pp. 110–111.

1.6   Theory and the theoretical tradition

Architectonic reason and polemical reason

Scientific theory progresses through rectifications, that is, by integrating the critiques that tend to destroy the imagery of the earliest stages. Coherent knowledge is the product of polemical reason, not architectonic reason; one cannot neglect the labour of criticism and dialectical synthesis without condemning oneself to the spurious reconciliations of traditional syntheses.   dialectal vs traditional synthesis

18. G. Bachelard

Let us try, however, to grasp some of the principles of coherence in the activity of the philosophy of no. [...]

Nobody understood the value of the successive rectifications of the various atomic plans better than Eddington. After having recalled the diagram proposed by Bohr which likened the atomic system to a miniature planetary system, Eddington warns that one must not take this system too literally.[1] "The orbits can scarcely refer to an actual motion in space, for it is generally admitted that the ordinary conception of space breaks down in the interior of an atom; nor is there any desire nowadays to stress the suddenness or discontinuity conveyed by the word 'jump'. It is found also that the electron cannot be localized in the way implied by the picture. In short, the physicist draws up an elaborate plan of the atom and then proceeds critically to erase each detail in turn. What is left is the atom of modern physics!" We would express the same thoughts differently. It does indeed seem to us quite impossible to understand the atom of modern physics without calling forth the history of its imagery, taking up once again the realist forms and the rationalist forms, and making explicit the epistemological profile. The history of the various plans becomes, at this point, an absolutely unavoidable pedagogical scheme. Anyway we look at it, what has been cut out of the image must be included in the rectified concept. We would almost be inclined to say, then, that the atom is exactly *the sum of the criticisms* to which its first representation has been subjected. Coherent knowledge is a product, not of architectonic reasoning, but of polemical reasoning. By means of dialectics and criticisms, surrationalism somehow determines a *super-object*. This super-object is the result of a critical objectification, of an objectivity which only retains that part of the object which it has criticized. As it appears in contemporary microphysics the atom is the absolute type of the super-object. In its relationships with images, the super-object is essentially the non-image. Intuitions are very useful: they serve to be destroyed. By destroying its original images, scientific thought discovers its organic laws. The noumenon is revealed by dialectizing one by one all the

[1] T. Eddington, *New Pathways in Science*, Cambridge: Cambridge University Press, 1935, p. 259.

principles of the phenomenon. The diagram of the atom proposed by Bohr a quarter of a century ago has, in this sense, acted as a good image: there is nothing left of it. But it has suggested "no" often enough so that it keeps its indispensable role as initiatory pedagogy. These "no's" are happily coordinated; they are the real constituents of contemporary microphysics.

Gaston Bachelard
The Philosophy of No

= the group — The leader as nucleus?
                              (empty?)

Part Two
Constructing the object

Handwritten margin notes: Physical | Mental; verbal subject; concrete in the mind; Research; Could st population be otherwise composed? (races, IV)

The method of political economy

Marx outlines the principles of his research method in the Introduction to the Grundrisse of 1857. He rejects both Hegel's "illusion of conceiving the real as the product of thought concentrating itself", and the naïveté of the empiricists who seek to take as their scientific object the "real" object in its concrete totality, for example the population of a real society, without seeing that this means being forced to accept the abstractions of common-sense by refusing the work of scientific abstraction which always brings into play a historically and socially constituted problematic. The "concrete in the mind" that research eventually reconstructs remains distinct from the "real subject [which] retains its autonomous existence outside the head just as before".

19. K. Marx *(Need to read more)*

When we consider a given country politico-economically, we begin with its population, its distribution among classes, town, country, the coast, the different branches of production, export and import, annual production and consumption, commodity prices etc.

It seems to be correct to begin with the real and the concrete, with the real precondition, thus to begin, in economics, with e.g. the population, which is the foundation and the subject of the entire social act of production. However, on closer examination this proves false. The population is an abstraction if I leave out, for example, the classes of which it is composed. These classes in turn are an empty phrase if I am not familiar with the elements on which they rest. E.g. wage labour, capital, etc. These latter in turn presuppose exchange, division of labour, prices, etc. For example, capital is nothing without wage labour, without value, money, price etc. Thus, if I were to begin with the population, this would be a chaotic conception [*Vorstellung*] of the whole, and I would then, by means of further determination, move analytically towards ever more simple concepts [*Begriff*], from the imagined concrete towards ever thinner abstractions until I had arrived at the simplest determinations. From there the journey would have to be retraced until I had finally arrived at the population again, but this time not as the chaotic conception of a whole, but as a rich totality of many determinations and relations. The former is the path historically followed by economics at the time of its origins. The economists of the seventeenth century, e.g., always begin with the living whole, with population, nation, state, several states, etc.; but they always conclude by discovering through analysis a small number of determinant, abstract, general — *Models ?* relations such as division of labour, money, value, etc. As soon as these individual moments had been more or less firmly established and abstracted, there began the economic systems, which ascended from the simple relations, such as labour, division of labour, need, exchange value, to the level of the state, exchange between nations and the world market. The latter is obviously the scientifically correct method. The concrete is concrete because it is the concentration of many determinations, hence unity of the diverse. It appears in the process of thinking, therefore, as a process of concentration, as a result, not as a point of departure, even though it is the point of departure in reality and hence also the point of departure for observation [*Anschauung*] and conception. Along the first path the full conception was evaporated to yield an abstract determination; along the second, the abstract determinations lead towards a reproduction of the concrete by way of thought. In this way Hegel fell into the illusion of conceiving the real as the product of thought concentrating itself, probing its own depths, and unfolding itself out of itself, by itself, whereas the method of rising from the abstract to the concrete is only the way in which thought appropriates the concrete, reproduces it as the concrete in the mind. But this is by no means the process by which the concrete itself comes into being. For example, the simplest economic category, say e.g. exchange value, presupposes population, moreover a population producing in specific relations; as well as a certain kind of family, or commune, or state, etc. It can never exist other than as an abstract, one-sided relation within an already given, concrete, living whole. As a category, by contrast, exchange value leads an antediluvian existence. Therefore, to the kind of consciousness —and this is characteristic of the philosophical consciousness—for which conceptual thinking is the real human being, and for which the conceptual world as such is thus the only reality, the movement of the categories appears as the real act of production—which only, unfortunately, receives a jolt from the outside—whose product is the world; and—but this is again a tautology —this is correct in so far as the concrete totality is a totality of thoughts, concrete in thought, in fact a product of thinking and comprehending; but not in any way a product of the concept which thinks and generates itself outside or above observation and conception; a product, rather, of the working-up of observation and conception into concepts. The totality as it appears in the head, as a totality of thoughts, is a product of a thinking head, which appropriates the world in the only way it can, a way different from the artistic, religious, practical and mental appropriation of this world. The real subject retains its autonomous existence outside the head just as before; namely as long as the head's conduct is merely speculative, merely theoretical. Hence, in the theoretical method, too, the subject, society, must always be kept in mind as the presupposition.

Karl Marx
Grundrisse: Foundations of
the Critique of Political Economy

The positivist illusion of presuppositionless science

Max Weber's particular conception of how to construct the object of research makes reference to a representation of the epistemological role of values which gives a specific character and specific premises to his theory of knowledge of the social. However, his critique of the illusion that, without any theoretical presupposition, the scholar is able to determine what is "essential" and what is "accidental" in a phenomenon vigorously exposes the methodological contradictions of the positivist image of the scientific object. Not only is knowledge of regularities—albeit an irreplaceable instrument—not in itself capable of explaining singular historical configurations considered in their specificity, but regularities are identified on the basis of a problematic that determines the "accidental" and the "essential" in relation to the problems posed, without it ever being possible to give a realist definition of these two terms.

20. M. Weber

The justification of the *one-sided* analysis of cultural reality from specific "points of view"—in our case with respect to its economic conditioning—emerges purely as a technical expedient from the fact that training in the observation of the effects of qualitatively similar categories of causes and the repeated utilization of the same scheme of concepts and hypotheses (*begrifflich-methodischen Apparates*) offers all the advantages of the division of labor. It is free from the charge of arbitrariness to the extent that it is successful in producing insights into interconnections which have been shown to be valuable for the casual explanation of concrete historical events. However—the "*one-sidedness*" and the unreality of the purely economic interpretation of history is in general only a special case of a principle which is generally valid for the scientific knowledge of cultural reality. [...]

There is no absolutely "objective" scientific analysis of culture—or put perhaps more narrowly but certainly not essentially differently for our purposes—of "social phenomena" independent of special and "one-sided" viewpoints according to which—expressly or tacitly, consciously or unconsciously—they are selected, analyzed and organized for expository purposes. The reasons for this lie in the character of the cognitive goal of all research in social science which seeks to transcend the purely *formal* treatment of the legal or conventional norms regulating social life.

The type of social science in which we are interested is an *empirical science* of concrete *reality* (*Wirklichkeitswissenschaft*). Our aim is the understanding of the characteristic uniqueness of the reality in which we move. We wish to understand on the one hand the relationships and the cultural significance of individual events in their contemporary manifestations and on the other the causes of their being historically *so* and not *otherwise*. Now, as soon as we attempt to reflect about the way in which life confronts us in immediate concrete situations, it presents an infinite multiplicity of successively and coexistently emerging and disappearing events, both "within" and "outside" ourselves. The absolute infinitude of this multiplicity is seen to remain undiminished even when our attention is focused on a single "object," for instance, a concrete act of exchange, as soon as we seriously attempt an exhaustive description of *all* the individual components of this "individual phenomena", to say nothing of explaining it casually. All the analysis of infinite reality which the finite human mind can conduct rests on the tacit assumption that only a finite portion of this reality constitutes the object of scientific investigation, and that only it is "important" in the sense of being "worthy of being known". But what are the criteria by which this segment is selected? It has often been thought that the decisive criterion in the cultural sciences, too, was in the last analysis, the "regular" recurrence of certain casual relationships. The "laws" which we are able to perceive in the infinitely manifold stream of events must — according to this conception — contain the scientifically "essential" aspect of reality. As soon as we have shown some causal relationship to be a "law", i.e., if we have shown it to be universally valid by means of comprehensive historical induction or have made it immediately and tangibly plausible according to our subjective experience, a great number of similar cases order themselves under the formula thus attained. Those elements in each individual event which are left unaccounted for by the selection of their elements subsumable under the "law" are considered as scientifically unintegrated residues which will be taken care of in the further perfection of the system of "laws". Alternatively they will be viewed as "accidental" and therefore scientifically unimportant *because* they do not fit into the structure of the "law"; in other words, they are not typical of the event and hence can only be the objects of "idle curiosity". Accordingly, even among the followers of the Historical School we continually find the attitude which declares that the ideal which all the sciences, including the cultural sciences, serve and towards which they should strive even in the remote future is a system of propositions from which reality can be "deduced". As is well known, a leading natural scientist believed that he could designate the (factually unattainable) ideal goal of such a treatment of cultural reality as a sort of "*astronomical*" knowledge.

Let us not, for our part, spare ourselves the trouble of examining these matters more closely — however often they have already been discussed. The first thing that impresses one is that the "astronomical" knowledge which was referred to is not a system of laws at all. On the contrary, the laws which it presupposes have been taken from other disciplines like mechanics. But it too concerns itself with the question of the *individual* consequence which the working of these laws in an unique *configuration* produces, since it is these individual configurations which are *significant* for us. Every individual constellation which it "explains" or predicts is causally explicable only as the consequence of another equally individual constellation which has preceded it. As far back as we may go into the grey mist of the far-off past, the reality to which the laws apply always remains equally *individual*, equally *undeducible*

The Big "Cultural" Bang?

from laws. A cosmic "primeval state" which had no individual character or less individual character than the cosmic reality of the present would naturally be a meaningless notion. But is there not some trace of similar ideas in our field in those propositions sometimes derived from natural law and sometimes verified by the observation of "primitives", concerning an economic-social "primeval state" free from historical "accidents", and characterized by phenomena such as "primitive agrarian communism", sexual "promiscuity", etc., from which individual historical development emerges by a sort of fall from grace into concreteness?

[...] Let us assume that we have succeeded by means of psychology or otherwise in analyzing all the observed and imaginable relationships of social phenomena into some ultimate elementary "factors", that we have made an exhaustive analysis and classification of them and then formulated rigorously exact laws covering their behavior.—What would be the significance of these results for our knowledge of the *historically* given culture or any individual phase thereof, such as capitalism, in its development and cultural significance? As an analytical tool, it would be as useful as a textbook of organic chemical combinations would be for our knowledge of the biogenetic aspect of the animal and plant world. In each case, certainly an important and useful preliminary step would have been taken. In neither case can concrete reality be deduced from "laws" and "factors". This is not because some higher mysterious powers reside in living phenomena (such as "dominants", "entelechies", or whatever they might be called). This, however, a problem in its own right. The real reason is that the analysis of reality is concerned with the *configuration* into which those (hypothetical!) "factors" are arranged to form a cultural phenomenon which is historically significant to us. Furthermore, if we wish to "explain" this individual configuration "causally" we must invoke other equally individual configurations on the basis of which we will explain it with the aid of those (hypothetical!) "laws".

The determination of those (hypothetical) "laws" and "factors" would in any case only be the first of the many operations which would lead us to the desired type of knowledge. The analysis of the historically given individual configuration of those "factors" and their *significant* concrete interaction, conditioned by their historical context and especially the *rendering intelligible* of the basis and type of this significance would be the next task to be achieved. This task must be achieved, it is true, by the utilization of the preliminary analysis but it is nonetheless an entirely new and *distinct* task. The tracing as far into the past as possible of the individual features of these historically evolved configurations which are *contemporaneously* significant, and their historical explanation by antecedent and equally individual configurations would be the third task. Finally the prediction of possible future constellations would be a conceivable fourth task.

For all these purposes, clear concepts and the knowledge of those (hypothetical) "laws" are obviously of great value as heuristic means—but only as such. Indeed they are quite indispensable for this purpose. But even in this function their limitations become evident at a decisive point. In stating this, we arrive at the decisive feature of the method of the cultural sciences. We have designated as "cultural sciences" those disciplines which analyze the phenomena of life in terms of their cultural significance. The *significance* of a configuration of cultural phenomena and the basis of this significance cannot however be derived and rendered intelligible by a system of analytical laws (*Gesetzesbegriffen*), however perfect it may be, since the significance of cultural events presupposes a *value-orientation* towards these events. The concept of culture is a *value-concept*. Empirical reality becomes "culture" to us because and insofar as we relate it to value ideas. It includes those segments and only those segments of reality which have become significant to us because of this value-relevance. Only a small portion of existing concrete reality is colored by our value-conditioned interest and it alone is significant to us. It is significant because it reveals relationships which are important to us due to their connection with our values. Only because and to the extent that this is the case is it worthwhile for us to know it in its individual features. We cannot discover, however, what is meaningful to us by means of a "presupposition-less" investigation of empirical data. Rather perception of its meaningfulness to us is the presupposition of its becoming an *object* of investigation. Meaningfulness naturally does not coincide with laws as such, and the more general the law the less the coincidence. For the specific meaning which a phenomenon has for us is naturally *not* to be found in those relationships which it shares with many other phenomena.

The focus of attention on reality under the guidance of values which lend it significance and the selection and ordering of the phenomena which are thus affected in the light of their cultural significance is entirely different from the analysis of reality in terms of laws and general concepts. Neither of these two types of the analysis of reality has any necessary logical relationship with the other. They can coincide in individual instances but it would be most dis-astrous if their occasional coincidence caused us to think that they were not distinct *in principle*. The *cultural significance* of a phenomenon, e.g., the significance of exchange in a money economy, can be the fact that it exists on a mass scale as a fundamental component of modern culture. But the historical fact that it plays this role must be causally explained in order to render its cultural significance understandable. The analysis of the *general* aspects of exchange and the technique of the market is a—highly important and indispen-sable—*preliminary task*. For not only does this type of analysis leave unanswered the question as to how exchange historically acquired its fundamental significance in the modern world; but above all else, the fact with which we are primarily concerned, namely, the *cultural significance* of the money-economy, for the sake of which we are interested in the description of exchange technique and for the sake of which alone a science exists which deals with that technique—is not derivable from any "law". The *generic features* of exchange, purchase, etc., interest the jurist—but we are concerned with the analysis of *the cultural significance* of the concrete *historical* fact that today exchange exists on a mass scale. When we require an explanation, when we wish to understand what distinguishes the social-economic aspects of our culture for instance from that of antiquity in which exchange showed precisely the same generic traits as it does today and when we raise the question as to where the significance of "money economy" lies, logical principles of quite heterogeneous derivation enter into the investigation. We will apply those concepts with which we are provided by the investigation of the general features of economic mass phenomena—indeed, insofar as they are relevant to the meaningful aspects of our culture, we shall use them as *means* of exposition. The *goal* of our investigation is not reached through the exposition of those laws and concepts, precise as it may be. The question as to what should be the object of universal conceptualization cannot be decided "presuppositionlessly" but only with reference to the *significance* which certain segments of that infinite multiplicity which we call "commerce" have for culture. We seek knowledge of an historical phenomenon, meaning by historical: significant in its individuality (*Eigenart*). And the decisive element in this is that only through the presupposition that a finite part alone of the infinite variety of phenomena is significant, does the knowledge of an individual phenomenon become logically meaningful. Even with the widest imaginable knowledge of "laws", we are helpless in the face of the question: how is the *causal explanation* of an *individual* fact possible—since a *description* of even the smallest slice of reality can never be exhaustive? The number and type of causes which have influenced any given event are always infinite and there is nothing in the things themselves to set some of them apart as alone meriting attention. A chaos of "existential judgments" about countless individual events would be the only result of a serious attempt to analyze reality "without presuppositions". And even this result is only seemingly possible, since every single perception discloses on closer examination an infinite number of constituent perceptions which can never be exhaustively expressed in a judgement. Order is brought into this chaos only on the condition that in every case only a *part* of concrete reality is interesting and *significant* to us, because only it is related to the *cultural values* with which we approach reality. Only certain sides of the infinitely complex concrete phenomenon, namely those to which we attribute a general *cultural significance*—are therefore worthwhile knowing. They alone are objects of causal explanation.

Max Weber
The Methodology of the Social Sciences

"Treat social facts as things"

In protesting against misreadings of this precept, Durkheim indicates that he meant it to be not the first principle of a social philosophy but the methodological rule which is the sine qua non for construction of the sociological object. This is indeed the meaning of the arguments through which he seeks to forearm sociological analysis against the temptations of spontaneous sociology by inviting the researcher to give priority to morphological or institutional aspects, i.e. the most objective forms of social life. This text deserves attention because, from the very beginning, it gave rise to readings which, though contradictory, were equally unfaithful and, having become classic, it remains liable to be glanced at without being read.

21. É. Durkheim

The first and most basic rule is *to consider social facts as things.* [...]

Social phenomena are things and should be treated as such. To demonstrate this proposition one does not need to philosophise about their nature or to discuss the analogies they present with phenomena of a lower order of existence. Suffice to say that they are the sole *datum* afforded the sociologist. A thing is in effect all that is given, all that is offered, or rather forces itself upon our observation. To treat phenomena as things is to treat them as *data*, and this constitutes the starting point for science. Social phenomena unquestionably display this characteristic. What is given is not the idea that men conceive of value, because that is unattainable; rather is it the values actually exchanged in economic transactions. It is also not some conception or other of the moral ideal; it is the sum total of rules that in effect determine behaviour. It is not the idea of utility or wealth; it is all the details of economic organisation. Social life may possibly be merely the development of certain notions, but even if this is assumed to be the case, these notions are not revealed to us immediately. They cannot therefore be attained directly, but only through the real phenomena that express them. We do not know *a priori* what ideas give rise to the various currents into which social life divides, nor whether they exist. It is only after we have traced the currents back to their source that we will know from where they spring.

Social phenomena must therefore be considered in themselves, detached from the conscious beings who form their own mental representations of them. They must be studied from the outside, as external things, because it is in this guise that they present themselves to us. If this quality of externality proves to be only apparent, the illusion will be dissipated as the science progresses and we will see, so to speak, the external merge with the internal. But the outcome cannot be anticipated, and even if in the end social phenomena may not have all the features intrinsic to things, they must at first be dealt with as if they had. This rule is therefore applicable to the whole of social reality and there is no reason for any exceptions to be made. Even those phenomena which give the greatest appearance of being artificial in their arrangement should be considered from this viewpoint. *The conventional character of a practice or an institution should never be assumed in advance.* If, moreover, we are allowed to invoke personal experience, we believe we can state with confidence that by following this procedure one will often have the satisfaction of seeing the apparently most arbitrary facts, after more attentive observation, display features of constancy and regularity symptomatic of their objectivity. [...]

[The transition from the "ideological method" to the objective method has to be made in sociology as it has already been made in psychology. So long as it knows how to use them, sociology has specific means for achieving the break with reflexive analysis, for] social facts display much more naturally and immediately all the characteristics of a thing. Law is enshrined in legal codes, the events of daily life are registered in statistical figures and historical monuments, fashions are preserved in dress, taste in works of art. By their very nature social facts tend to form outside the consciousness of individuals, since they dominate them. To perceive them in their capacity as things it is therefore not necessary to engage in an ingenious distortion.

i.e. suicide as an individual act/choice vs a social phenomenon [handwritten annotation]

                                                              Emile Durkheim
                                                  The Rules of Sociological Method

[margin handwritten notes: "thus a kind of objectivity", "← ?", "E-state structuralism"]

The proposition which states that social facts must be treated as things—the proposition which is at the very basis of our method—is among those which have stirred up the most opposition. It was deemed paradoxical and scandalous for us to assimilate to the realities of the external world those of the social world. This was singularly to misunderstand the meaning and effect of this assimilation, the object of which was not to reduce the higher forms of being to the level of lower ones but, on the contrary, to claim for the former a degree of reality at least equal to that which everyone accords to the latter. Indeed, we do not say that social facts are material things, but that they are things just as are material things, although in a different way.

What indeed is a thing? The thing stands in opposition to the idea, just as what is known from the outside stands in opposition to what is known from the inside. A thing is any object of knowledge which is not normally penetrable by the understanding. It is all that which we cannot conceptualize as an idea by the simple process of intellectual analysis. It is all that which the mind cannot understand without going outside itself, proceeding progressively by way of observation and experimentation from those features which are the most external and readily accessible to those which are the least visible and the most profound. To treat facts of a certain order as things is therefore not to place them in that or that category of reality; it is to observe towards them a certain attitude of mind. It is to embark upon the study of them by adopting the principle that one is entirely ignorant of what they are, that their characteristic properties, like the unknown causes on which they depend, cannot be discovered by even the most careful form of introspection.

Émile Durkheim
The Rules of Sociological Method, *Preface to the Second Edition*

Cartesian

2.1 "The abdications of empiricism"

The epistemological vector

The classical philosophy of science sought to force the scientist's work into a set of pre-formed alternatives; reversing this project, Bachelard insists that the philosopher must "change [his] language... to reflect the subtlety of contemporary thought". Thus, instead of seeing the "tranquil eclecticism" of scientists as an index of the philosophical unconsciousness of science, Bachelard takes as his object the "metaphysical impurity" of scientific procedure and is led to challenge the pretension of "intuitive systems of metaphysics" to give an account of scientific rationalism. The "rectified rationalism" of science shows that a rationalism that has corrected a priori assumptions (with, for example, "the weakening of Euclid's postulates in non-Euclidean geometry") can no longer be a closed system.

22. G. Bachelard

Since William James it has often been repeated that every cultivated man necessarily subscribes to some system of metaphysics. To my mind it is more accurate to say that every man who attempts to learn science makes use not of one but of two metaphysical systems. Both are natural and cogent, implicit rather than explicit, and tenacious in their persistence. And one contradicts the other. For convenience let us attach provisional names to the two fundamental philosophical attitudes that coexist so peacefully in the modern scientific mind: rationalism and realism, to use the classical terminology. Is proof required that such tranquil eclecticism does indeed exist? Consider, then, the following proposition: "Science is a product of the human mind, a product that conforms to both the laws of thought and the outside world. Hence it has two aspects, one subjective, the other objective; and both are equally necess-ary, for it is as impossible to alter the laws of the mind as it is to change the laws of the Universe."[1] This rather odd metaphysical assertion can be pursued in two possible directions: the first leading to a rationalism at one remove, according to which the laws of the universe would merely reflect the laws of the mind; the second leading to a universal realism, one of whose principles would be that the laws of the mind, being instances of universal laws, must be absolutely invariable.

The philosophy of science has done nothing to purify itself since Bouty enunciated the above proposition. It would not be difficult to show that, in forming scientific judgments, the most determined rationalist daily submits to the instruction of a reality whose ultimate structure eludes him, while the most uncompromising realist does not hesitate to make simplifying assumptions just as if he believed in the principles on which the rationalist position is based. One may as well admit that, as far as the philosophy of science is concerned,

[1] Edmond Bouty, *La vérité scientifique* (1908), p. 7.

there is no such thing as absolute realism or absolute rationalism, and that judgments of scientific thought should not be couched in terms of general philosophical attitudes. Sooner or later scientific thought will become the central subject of philosophical controversy; science will show philosophers how to replace intuitive, immediate systems of metaphysics with systems whose principles are debatable and subject to experimental validation. What does it mean to say that science can "rectify" metaphysics? As an example of what I have in mind, consider how "realism" changes, losing its naive immediacy, in its encounter with scientific skepticism. Similarly, "rationalism" need not be a closed system; *a priori* assumptions are subject to change (witness the weakening of Euclid's postulates in non-Euclidean geometry, for example). It should therefore be of some interest to take a fresh approach to the philosophy of science, to examine the subject without preconceptions and free of the straitjacket imposed by the traditional vocabulary of philosophy. Science in effect creates philosophy. Philosophy must therefore modify its language if it is to reflect the subtlety and movement of contemporary thought. It must also respect the oddly ambiguous requirement that all scientific ideas be interpreted in both realistic and rationalistic terms. For that reason perhaps we ought to take as our first object of contemplation, our first fact needing explanation, the metaphysical impurity entailed by the double meaning of the phrase *scientific proof*, which can refer either to confirmation by experiment or to demonstration by logic, to palpable reality or to the mind that reasons.

It is fairly easy, moreover, to explain why any scientific philosophy must have such a dualistic base: The very fact that the philosophy of science is a philosophy that *applies* to another discipline means that it cannot preserve the unity and purity of speculative philosophy. Any work of science, no matter what its point of departure, cannot become fully convincing until it crosses the boundary between the theoretical and the experimental: *Experimentation must give way to argument, and argument must have recourse to experimentation.* Every application is a form of transcendence. I intend to show that this duality exists in even the simplest scientific investigations, that is, that the phenomenology of science divides, according to one set of epistemological polarities, into two realms, that of the picturesque and that of the comprehensible (which is just another way of saying that science may be viewed in either realistic or rationalistic terms). If we could somehow place ourselves at the frontiers of scientific knowledge and there observe the psychology of the scientific mind, we would find that it has been a concern of contemporary science to overcome the contradictions of metaphysics. Yet the orientation of the epistemological "vector" seems clear. It surely points from the rational to the real and not, as all philosophers from Aristotle to Bacon professed, from the real to the general. To put it another way, the application of scientific thought seems to me to tend essentially toward reality (*nous paraît essentielle-*

ment réalisante). Accordingly, the purpose of this book will be to demonstrate what might be called the realization of the rational or, more generally, the realization of mathematics.

Gaston Bachelard
The New Scientific Spirit

read?

2.2 Hypotheses or presuppositions

The instrument is a theory in action

Taken literally, the comparison of techniques with tools could lead to a purely technical critique of techniques. Elihu Katz's analysis of the progressive development of the hypothesis that the transmission of the information diffused by the modern media takes place in two stages shows, however, that the limitations of techniques constitute hidden incitements to orient research in a particular direction and that omissions are at the same time indications. Thus, because the random sample and the opinion poll focus on subjects detached from the network of relationships in which they act and communicate, these techniques lead one to hypostatize an artefact obtained by abstraction. Working on individuals who are in a sense "desocialized", one can only explain the authority of opinion leaders by psychological qualities. To dispel the surreptitious indications suggested by the presuppositions of a technique, something more than technological refinement is required: studies which seek to reconstitute the complete network of communication on the basis of the relationships which link subjects two by two remain trapped by their initial abstraction. Only a break with methodological automatisms can lead one to study the whole set of social relations in a complete community, from which the networks of influences can then be deduced so that there is no further need to ask the respondents to bring them out in place of the sociologist.

23. E. Katz (1957)

Analysis of the process of decision-making during the course of an election campaign led the authors of *The People's Choice* to suggest that the flow of mass communications may be less direct than was commonly supposed. It may be, they proposed, that influences stemming from the mass media first reach "opinion leaders" who, in turn, pass on what they read and hear to those of their every-day associates for whom they are influential. This hypothesis was called "the two-step flow of communication"[1]

The hypothesis aroused considerable interest. The authors themselves were intrigued by its implications for democratic society. It was a healthy sign, they felt, that people were still most successfully persuaded by give-and-take with other people and that the influence of the mass media was less automatic and less potent than had been assumed. For social theory, and for the design of communications research, the hypothesis suggested that the image of modern urban society needed revision. The image of the audience as a mass of disconnected individuals hooked up to the media but not to each other could not be reconciled with the idea of a two-step flow of communication implying, as it did, networks of interconnected individuals through which mass communications are channeled.

Of all the ideas in *The People's Choice*, however, the two-step flow hypo-

[1] P. F. Lazarsfeld, B. Berelson, and H. Gaudet, *The People's Choice*, New York: Columbia University Press, 1948 (2nd edition), p. 151.

thesis is probably the one that was least well documented by empirical data. And the reason for this is clear: the design of the study did not anticipate the importance which interpersonal relations would assume in the analysis of the data. Given the image of the atomized audience which characterized so much of mass media research, the surprising thing is that interpersonal influence attracted the attention of the researchers at all. [...]

Essentially, three distinct sets of findings seem to have been involved:
a) *the impact of personal influence* [... which] appears to have been both more frequent and more effective than the mass media in influencing voting deci-sions; [...]

b) *the flow of personal influence*: opinion leaders are to be found on every level of society and presumably, therefore, are very much like the people whom they influence; [...]

c) *the opinion leaders and the mass media*: compared with the rest of the population, opinion leaders were found to be considerably more exposed to the radio, to the newspapers and to magazines, that is, to the formal media of communication.

  Now the argument is clear: If word-of-mouth is so important, and if word-of-mouth specialists are widely dispersed, and if these specialists are more exposed to the media than the people whom they influence, then perhaps "ideas often flow from radio and print to opinion leaders and from these to the less active sections of the population". [...]

  For studying the flow of influence as it impinges on the making of decisions, the study design of *The People's Choice* had several advantages. Most import-ant was the panel method which made it possible to locate changes almost as soon as they occurred and then to correlate change with the influences reaching the decision-maker. Secondly, the unit of effect, the decision, was a tangible indicator of change which could readily be recorded. But for studying that part of the flow of influence which had to do with contacts among people, the study design fell short, since it called for a random sample of individuals abstracted from their social environments. It is this traditional element in the design of survey research which explains the leap that had to be made from the available data to the hypothesis of the two-step flow of communication.

  Because every man in a random sample can speak only for himself, opinion leaders in the 1940 voting study had to be located by self-designation, that is, on the basis of their own answers to the two advice-giving questions cited above. In effect, respondents were simply asked to report whether or not they were opinion leaders. Much more important than the obvious problem of validity posed by this technique is the fact that it does not permit a comparison of leaders with their respective followers, but only of leaders and non-leaders in general. The data, in other words, consist only of two statistical groupings:

people who said they were advice-givers and those who did not. Therefore, the fact that leaders were more interested in the election than non-leaders cannot be taken to mean that influence flows from more interested persons to less interested ones. To state the problem drastically, it may even be that the leaders influence only each other, while the uninterested non-leaders stand outside the influence market altogether. Nevertheless, the temptation to assume that the non-leaders are the followers of the leaders is very great, and while *The People's Choice* is quite careful about this, it cannot help but succumb. [...]

The authors themselves point out that a far better method would have been based on "asking people to whom they turn for advice on the issue at hand and then investigating the interaction between advisers and advisees. But that procedure would be extremely difficult, if not impossible, since few of the related 'leaders' and 'followers' would happen to be included in the sample." As will be shown immediately, this is perhaps the most important problem which succeeding studies have attempted to solve.

[Katz then considers two subsequent studies which have approached the problems that The People's Choice *had raised. The first one (Rovere), conducted in a small town, identified as opinion leaders those who were mentioned several times in the respondents' answers to the question "Who influences you?", and so "proceeded from the persons influenced to those who are designated as influential". Thus, "whereas the voting study regards any advice-giver as an opinion leader if he influences even one other person", the leaders singled out by this study "were almost certainly wielders of wider influence".*

The second study (Decatur) tried to go further by focussing on the "advisor-advisee dyad", which the previous study had not considered because the initial sample of respondents was only used to identify leaders.]

Just as the dyad could be constructed by proceeding from an advisee to his adviser, it was also possible to begin the other way around by talking first to a person who claimed to have acted as an adviser, and then locating the person he said he had influenced. The Decatur study tried this too. Using the same kind of self-designating questions employed in the voting study, persons who designated themselves as influential were asked to indicate the names of those whom they had influenced. By "snowballing" to the people thus designated, there arose the opportunity not only to study the interaction between adviser and advisee but also to explore the extent to which people who designated themselves as influential were confirmed in their self-evaluations by those whom they allegedly had influenced. Proceeding in this way, the researchers hoped to be able to say something about the validity of the self-designating technique.

The authors of *The People's Choice* had said that "asking people to whom they turn and then investigating the interaction between advisers and advisees... would be extremely difficult if not impossible." And, in fact, it proved to be extremely difficult. Many problems were encountered in the field

The People's Choice

work, the result of which was that not all the "snowball" interviews could be completed. In many parts of the analysis of the data, therefore, it was necessary to revert to comparisons of leaders and non-leaders, imputing greater influence to groups with higher concentrations of self-designated leadership. Yet, in principle it was demonstrated that a study design taking account of interpersonal relations was both possible and profitable to execute.

But about the time it became evident that this goal was within reach, the goal itself began to change. It began to seem desirable to take account of chains of influence longer than those involved in the dyad; and hence to view the adviser-advisee dyad as one component of a more elaborately structured social group.

These changes came about gradually and for a variety of reasons. First of all, findings from the Decatur study and from the later Elmira study revealed that the opinion leaders themselves often reported that their own decisions were influenced by still other people. It began to seem desirable, therefore, to think in terms of the opinion leaders of opinion leaders. Secondly, it became clear that opinion leadership could not be viewed as a "trait" which some people possess and others do not, although the voting study sometimes implied this view. Instead, it seemed quite apparent that the opinion leader is influential at certain times and with respect to certain substantive areas by virtue of the fact that he is "empowered" to be so by other members of his group. Why certain people are chosen must be accounted for not only in demographic terms (social status, sex, age, etc.) but also in terms of the structure and values of the groups of which both adviser and advisee are members. Thus, the unexpected rise of young men to opinion leadership in traditional groups, when these groups faced the new situations of urbanization and industrialization, can be understood only against the background of old and new patterns of social relations within the group and of old and new patterns of orientation to the world outside the group. [...]

One other factor shaped the direction of the new program as well. Reflecting upon the Decatur study, it became clear that while one could talk about the role of various influences in the making of fashion *decisions by individuals*, the study design was not adequate for the study of fashion in the aggregate —*fashion as a process of diffusion*—as long as it did not take account of either the content of the decision or the time factor involved. The decisions of the "fashion changers" studied in Decatur might have cancelled each other out: while Mrs. X reported a change from Fashion A to Fashion B, Mrs. Y might have been reporting a change from B to A. What is true for fashion is true for any other diffusion phenomenon: to study it, one must trace the flow of some specific item over time. Combining this interest in diffusion with that of studying the role of more elaborate social networks of communication gave birth to a new study which focused on (1) a specific item, (2) diffusion over time, (3) through the social structure of an entire community.

See

[This third study was conducted to determine the way in which doctors make decisions to adopt new drugs. It made use of objective indices (an audit of prescriptions on file in the local pharmacies of the cities studied), and it precisely located the interviewees within their networks of relationships.]

Altogether, compared with the earlier studies, the drug study imposes a more objective framework—both psychological and sociological—on the decision. First of all, the decision-maker himself is not the only source of information concerning his decision. Objective data from the prescription record are used as well. Secondly, the role of different influences is assessed not only on the basis of the decision-maker's own reconstruction of the event, but also on the basis of objective correlations from which inferences concerning the flow of influence can be drawn. For example, doctors who adopted the new drug early were more likely to be participants in out-of-town medical specialty meetings than those who adopted it later.

Similarly, it is possible to infer the role of social relations in doctor's decision-making not only from the doctor's own testimony concerning the role of social influences but also from the doctor's "location" in the interpersonal networks mapped by the sociometric questions. Thus, on the basis of sociometric data, it is possible to classify doctors according to their integration into the medical community, or the degree of their influence, as measured by *the number of times* they are named by their colleagues as friends, discussion-partners, and consultants. They can also be classified according to their membership in one or another network or clique, as indicated by *who* names them. Using the first measure makes it possible to investigate whether or not the more influential doctors adopt a drug earlier than those who are less influential. From the second kind of analysis one can learn, for example, whether or not those doctors who belong to the same sub-groups have similar drug-use patterns. In this way, it becomes possible to weave back and forth between the doctor's own testimony about his decisions and the influences involved, on the one hand, and the more objective record of his decisions and of the influences to which he has been exposed, on the other hand.

Note that the networks of social relations in this study are mapped "prior" to the introduction of the new drug being studied, in the sense that friendship, consultation, and so on, are recorded independently of any particular decision the doctor has made. The study is concerned with the potential relevance of various parts of these sociometric structures to the transmission of influence. For example, it is possible to point to the parts of the structure which are "activated" upon the introduction of a new drug, and to describe the sequence of diffusion of the drug as it gains acceptance by individuals and groups in the community. While the Decatur study could hope to examine only the particular face-to-face relationship which had been influential in a given decision, the drug study can locate this relationship against the background of the entire web of *potentially* relevant relationships within which the doctor is embedded.

[These successive changes in research method have made it possible to obtain results which clarify and fill out the initial hypothesis, in particular by establishing:
—that personal influence has more impact than the direct influence of the mass media;
—that primary groups have a high degree of homogeneity in opinions;
—that the role of the mass media is not simple but ranges from "informing" to the "legitimating" of opinions;
—that opinion leaders do not have an overall authority, valid for all spheres, but that their authority is limited to particular spheres;
—that they therefore do not have substantial characteristics separating them from those they influence, but are distinguished by the qualities ascribed to them (competence, etc.) and by their social position;
—that opinion leaders are both more exposed to the media and more affected by them in their decisions.]

The central methodological problem in each of the studies reviewed has been how to take account of interpersonal relations and still preserve the economy and representativeness which the random, cross-sectional sample affords. Answers to this problem range from asking individuals in the sample to describe the others with whom they interacted (Elmira), to conducting "snowball" interviews with influential–influencee dyads (Decatur), to interviewing an entire community (drug study). Future studies will probably find themselves somewhere in between. For most studies, however, the guiding principle would seem to be to build larger or smaller social molecules around each individual atom in the sample.

Elihu Katz
"The Two-Step Flow of Communication:
An Up-To-Date Report on an Hypothesis"

Print

The statistician needs to know what he is doing

Simiand, seeing the statistical method as a form of the experimental method, tries to identify the specificity of the epistemology of sociology, not in a jealous reaffirmation of the originality of sociological methods but in a methodical comparison of the methods of the natural sciences and the methods of sociology.* The facts that the sociologist manipulates are in a sense doubly abstract, firstly as statistical facts, abstracted from empirical reality (like the facts on which the physicist works) and secondly as sociological facts abstracted from individual manifestations. Being collective in nature, social facts are not fully realized in any individual phenomenon, so that "non-correspondence with some objective reality... does not stare one in the face". Reflection on statistical technique and on the elaboration it performs on the facts must therefore be carried out anew for every piece of research.

24. F. Simiand

Let us transpose into the statistical domain the conditions for correct abstraction taught by the methodology of the positive sciences. We shall then see that the first precaution to be taken in order not to deceive others, and ourselves, with our statistical abstractions is to take care that our expressions of complex facts, our averages, indices, and coefficients are not the result of perfunctory arithmetic, arbitrary combinations of figures with figures, but that they too are modelled on the concrete complexity, respect the articulations of the real, and express something that is both distinct and true in relation to the multiplicity of individual cases to which they correspond. Let us observe, on the other hand, that what can mislead us, and does in fact often mislead us in the use of statistical abstractions, *is not that they are abstractions, but that they are bad abstractions.*

We never see a physicist determining the density of a cluster of miscellaneous objects; for, manifestly, since this cluster has no physical identity, the datum would have no scientific interest. We never see a botanist grouping his observations on plants five months by five months, ten months by ten months, because manifestly vegetation grows according to the cycle of the year or twelve months. Still closer to us, and already in the statistical domain, we never see a biologist determining and studying an average of the sizes of the various animals in a zoo.

And yet we find examples, even in work of some repute, of price indexes indiscriminately based on prices of all categories—raw materials with finished products, goods with services, wages, and rents—although the movements of these various groups of prices are often so different either in meaning, or rate, as to make a common expression, which blurs everything, necessarily meaningless or misleading if attention is not paid to these differences.

Even more often we see statistical data grouped and studied by five-year or ten-year averages, for elements whose characteristic variations appear in cycles

* See above, Introduction, pp. 2–3, and below, E. Wind, text no. 37, pp. 214–217.

either longer or shorter than such periods, and often irregular. The picture that such tables give us will therefore mask the essential feature of the element that is being studied, instead of bringing it to light, and it can only mislead us.

Many more examples might be given, but these will suffice to show first, where we should see the real difference, from this point of view, between the ordinary experiment of the positive sciences and the statistical experiment, and then where we can seek a remedy for the inferiority of the latter from this same point of view.

The difference between the two kinds of research is not that one operates on realities and the other on abstractions, but that, in the material experimentation of the positive sciences, bad abstraction, without sufficient correspondence with reality, with no objective basis, often immediately stands out as such with a physical, material self-evidence. In statistical research, on the other hand, figures as such never refuse to be combined with other figures; the correspondence or non-correspondence with some objective reality is not here, in general, a fact that "stares one in the face".

In material experiments, in the midst of the complexity presented by nature, the scientist carefully isolates certain elements which have a recognized or suspected relationship with certain others; but, if he is mistaken as to the relationship, if he forgets some essential element, he is obliged to notice it, because, materially, the expected phenomenon does not occur. The statistician, too, carefully isolates certain elements within the complex "given" from others that he suspects are related to them. But this is an operation of the mind: there is hardly ever any factitious experience available; the statistician does not materially remove or introduce any factor. And consequently, the reality or non-reality of the perceived relationship cannot manifest itself to him in a material way.

Indeed, it is clear that there is a potential risk of a vicious circle. Often statistical expression is necessary to bring out and, one might even say, to constitute the statistical fact, and yet we need to know in advance what this statistical fact is, and how it behaves, in order to choose the appropriate basis and nature of statistical expression.

But it can be seen, at the same time, how statistical research can move closer to the conditions through which physical experimentation distinguishes good abstraction from bad abstraction. [...]

In order to have some correspondence with a reality, the first condition is that our statistical expressions should be established on a basis presenting a certain homogeneity, or on a basis having an appropriate, opportune extension.

It is doubtless also clear that the individual cases covered by a statistical datum always present some degree of more or less complex homogeneity (otherwise there would be no need for statistical expression to represent them together) and that the homogeneity can therefore only be relative; that the appropriate extension will also vary, not only according to the data, but according to the problems, and again can only be relative. But the example of experimentation in the positive sciences shows us that the choice of the statistical abstractions to be adopted will not on that account be arbitrary, if it aims to be well founded.

We cannot count here on material self-evidence; we must therefore try to protect ourselves through intellectual precautions. Let us proceed carefully, with attempts, tests, counter-tests, and comparisons.

Precisely because there are good and bad averages, averages that have meaning and others that have none, we must *mistrust averages*, monitor and compare the indications of averages of one type with those of another, other indices, and complementary data. We should retain only those which, after being tested, appear to us to have genuine substance and to correspond to some collective reality.

The same is true of the other modes of statistical expression. Nowadays, for example, because of the considerable movement of prices and their consequences, everyone readily talks, thinks, and argues in terms of "index numbers". They are used as proof and argument for the most diverse and sometimes the most opposing theses. But before making such use of them, how many people take the time and trouble to learn how these index numbers are established, on what bases, by what methods, what they mean and do not mean? Irving Fisher has pointed out that to represent a set of prices and quantities, one can establish an unlimited number of index number formulae, which are far from having the same meaning or the same uses. For the purpose of his study, he limits himself to drawing up only *forty-four* of these possible formulae, indicating the characteristics of each with respect to this or that condition. Stanley Jevons used a geometric mean for particular response and for a particular problem. Wesley C. Mitchell, for other reasons and with equal success for the problem he was studying, used a median, accompanied by quartiles and deciles. The various index numbers most often cited and invoked at present are often established in rather different conditions and on rather different bases. Is all that unimportant? Or should it not be considered, depending on the questions studied and even depending on the conclusions one seeks to draw? Or—precisely because of these differences—should they not be used as reciprocal complements or as useful comparisons, for particular questions, and in order to demonstrate the limits of their value and their legitimate use?

François Simiand
Statistique et expérience: Remarques de méthode

2.3 The spurious neutrality of techniques: constructed object or artefact

The interview and the forms of organization of experience

David Riesman has shown some of the biases that can affect interviews, inasmuch as this technique presupposes—but generally has no means of monitoring—the interviewee's capacity to respond to the "interpersonal conventions of the interview". As a particular case of social exchange, it does not escape the "conventions governing what one should say or withhold", "which vary with social class, region and ethnic group".* As a social interaction, the interview situation tends to be interpreted by analogy with other relationships (confidences, recrimination, friendly discussion, etc.), the models of which may differ from one group to another. Finally, the relationship with a sociologist is no more than a particular case of the relationship with strangers, who as a matter of honour must not be allowed to see one's most private feelings or opinions: the interview situation may thus call into play a group's whole ethic. "We may understand why working-class people often seem not very 'oncoming' to social workers, seem evasive and prepared to give answers designed to put off rather than to clarify. At the back of the announcement that 'Ah keep meself to meself' there can be a hurt pride. It is difficult to believe that a visitor from another class would ever realise imaginatively all the ins-and-outs of one's difficulties—there is an anxiety not to 'show y'self up', to defend oneself against patronage."**

Because little thought is generally given to the differential effect of survey techniques depending on the respondents' social position, it seemed useful to reproduce here a study in the sociology of communication which aims to examine something that is normally treated as an instrument of study, and sometimes even as a means of absolute measurement of certain "aptitudes" (cf. Lerner's use of the respondents' ability to master the interview situation as an index of their capacity for innovation).*** Leonard Schatzman and Anselm Strauss show that the interview involves techniques of communication and forms of organization of experience in which the middle and lower classes differ systematically. To draw out all the implications of their argument would require one to renounce the illusion of the neutrality of techniques and, in this case, to find the means of monitoring and making allowance for the effects of the interview situation.

25. L. Schatzman and A. Strauss

Common assumptions suggest that there may be important differences in the thought and communication of social classes. Men live in an environment which is mediated through symbols. By naming, identifying, and classifying, the world's objects and events are perceived and handled. Order is imposed through conceptual organization, and this organization embodies not just anybody's rules but the grammatical, logical, and communicative canons of groups. Communication proceeds in terms of social requirements for comprehension, and so does "inner conversation" or thought. Both reasoning and

---

* D. Riesman, "The Sociology of the Interview", in *Abundance for What?*, New York: Doubleday, 1964, pp. 492–513.

** R. Hoggart, *The Uses of Literacy*, London: Chatto & Windus, 1957, p. 68.

*** See above, section 2.3, p. 41–43.

speech meet requirements of criticism, judgment, appreciation, and control. Communication across group boundaries runs the danger—aside from sheer language difficulties—of being blocked by differential rules for the ordering of speech and thought.[1]

If these assumptions are correct, it follows that there should be observable differences in communication according to social class and that these differences should not be merely matters of degree of preciseness, elaboration, vocabulary, and literary style. It follows also that the modes of thought should be revealed by modes of speaking.

Our data are the interview protocols gathered from participants in a disaster. [...] Approximately 340 interviews were available, representing random sampling of several communities ravaged by a tornado. Cases were selected by extreme position on educational and income continuums. Interviewees were designated as "lower" if education did not go beyond grammar school and if the annual family income was less than two thousand dollars. The "upper" group consisted of persons with one or more years of college education and annual incomes in excess of four thousand dollars. [...]

Differences between the lower and upper groups were striking; and, once the nature of the difference was grasped, it was astonishing how quickly a characteristic organization of communication could be detected and described from a reading of even a few paragraphs of an interview. The difference is not simply the failure or success—of lower and upper groups, respectively—in communicating clearly and in sufficient detail for the interviewer's purposes. Nor does the difference merely involve correctness or elaborateness of grammar or use of a more precise or colourful vocabulary. The difference is a considerable disparity in (*a*) the number and kinds of perspectives utilized in communication; (*b*) the ability to take the listener's role; (*c*) the handling of classifications; and (*d*) the frameworks and stylistic devices which order and implement the communication.

PERSPECTIVE OR CENTERING

By perspective or centering is meant the standpoint from which a description is made. Perspectives may vary in number and scope. The flexibility with which one shifts from perspective to perspective during communication may vary also.

Lower class.—Almost without exception any description offered by a lower-class respondent is a description as seen through his *own eyes*; he offers his own perceptions and images directly to the listener. His best performance is a straight, direct narrative of events as he saw and experienced them. He

[1] Cf. E. Cassirer, *An Essay on Man*, New Haven, 1944; S. Langer, *Philosophy in a New Key*, New York, 1948; A. R. Lindesmith and A. L. Strauss, *Social Psychology*, New York, 1949, pp. 237–252; G. Mead, *Mind, Self, and Society*, Chicago, 1934; C. W. Mills, "Language, Logic, and Culture", *American Sociological Review*, IV (1939), pp. 670–680.

often locates himself clearly in time and place and indicates by various connective devices a rough progression of events in relation to his activities. But the developmental progression is only in relation to himself. Other persons and their acts come into his narrative more or less as he encountered them. [...] The speaker's images vary considerably in clarity but are always his own. Although he may occasionally repeat the stories of other persons, he does not tell the story as though he were the other person reconstructing events and feelings. He may describe another person's act and the motive for it, with regard to himself, but this is the extent of his role-taking—he does not assume the role of another toward still others, except occasionally in an implicit fashion: "Some people was helping other people who was hurt." This limitation is especially pronounced when the behavior of more than two or three persons is being described and related. Here the description becomes confused: At best the speaker reports some reactions, but no clear picture of interaction emerges. The interaction either is not noticed or is implicitly present in the communication ("We run over there to see about them, and they was alright"). Even with careful probing the situation is not clarified much further. The most unintelligible speakers thoroughly confound the interviewer who tries to follow images, acts, persons, and events which seem to come out of nowhere and disappear without warning.

Middle class.—The middle class can equal the best performance of the lower class in communicating and elaborating a direct description. However, description is not confined to so narrow a perspective. It may be given from any of several standpoints: for instance, another person, a class of persons, an organization, an organizational role, even the whole town. The middle-class speaker may describe the behavior of others, including classes of others, from their standpoints rather than from his, and he may include sequences of acts as others saw them. Even descriptions of the speaker's own behavior often are portrayed from other points of view.

CORRESPONDENCE OF IMAGERY BETWEEN SPEAKER AND LISTENER

Individuals vary in their ability to see the necessity for mediating linguistically between their own imagery and that of their listeners. [...] When the context of the item under discussion is in physical view of both, or is shared because of similarity of past experience, or is implicitly present by virtue of a history of former interaction, the problem of context is largely solved. But when the context is neither so provided nor offered by the speaker, the listener is confronted with knotty problems of interpretation. In the accounts of the most unintelligible respondents we found dream-like sets of images with few connective, qualifying, explanatory, or other context-providing devices. Thus, the interviewer was hard pressed to make sense of the account and was forced to probe at every turn lest the speaker figuratively run away with the situation. The respondents were willing and often eager to tell their stories, but intention to communicate does not always bring about clear communication. The latter involves, among other requirements, an ability to hear one's words as others hear them.

Lower class.—Lower-class persons displayed a relative insensitivity to disparities in perspective. At best, the respondent corrected himself on the exact time at which he performed an act or became aware that his listener was not present at the scene and so located objects and events for him. On occasion he reached a state of other-consciousness: "You can't imagine if you wasn't there what it was like." However, his assumption of a correspondence in imagery is notable. There is much surnaming of persons without genuine identification, and often terms like "we" and "they" are used without clear referents. The speaker seldom anticipates responses to his communication and seems to feel little need to explain particular features of his account. He seldom qualifies an utterance, presumably because he takes for granted that his perceptions represent reality and are shared by all who were present. Since he is apt to take so much for granted, his narrative lacks depth and richness and contains almost no qualifications and few genuine illustrations. The hearer very often is confronted with a descriptive fragment that supposedly represents a more complete story. The speaker may then add phrases like "and stuff like that" or "and everything". Such phrasing is not genuine summation but a substitute for detail and abstraction. Summary statements are virtually absent, since they signify that speakers are sensitive to the needs of listeners. Certain phrases that appear to be summaries—such as "That's all I know" and "That's the way it was"—merely indicate that the speaker's knowledge is exhausted. Other summary-like phraseologies, like "It was pitiful", appear to be asides, reflective of self-feeling or emotion rather than résumés of preceding detail.

Middle class.—The middle-class respondent also makes certain assumptions about the correspondence of the other's images with his own. Nevertheless, in contrast with the lower group, he recognizes much more fully that imagery may be diverse and that context must be provided. Hence he uses many devices to supply context and to clarify meaning. He qualifies, summarizes, and sets the stage with rich introductory material, expands themes, frequently illustrates, anticipates disbelief, meticulously locates and identifies places and persons—all with great complexity of detail. He depends less on saying "You know"; he insists upon explaining if he realizes that a point lacks plausibility or force. Hence he rarely fails to locate an image, or series of images, in time or place. Frequent use of qualification is especially noteworthy. This indicates not only multiple centering but a very great sensitivity to listeners, actual and potential—including the speaker himself.

In short, the middle-class respondent has what might be called "communication control", at least in such a semiformal situation as the interview. Figuratively, he stands between his own images and the hearer and says, "Let me introduce you to what I saw and know." It is as though he were directing a movie, having at his command several cameras focused at different perspectives, shooting and carefully controlling the effect. By contrast, the lower-class respondent seems himself more like a single camera which unreels the scene to the audience. [...] The middle-class person—by virtue, we would presume, of his greater sensitivity to his listener—stands more outside his experience. He does not so much tell you what he saw as fashion a story about what he saw. The story may be accurate in varying degrees, although, in so far as it is an organized account, it has both the virtues and the defects of organization. The comparative accuracies of middle- and lower-class accounts are not relevant here; the greater objectivity of the former merely reflects greater distance between narrator and event.

In organizing his account, the middle-class respondent displays parallel consciousness of the other and himself. He can stop midstream, take another direction, and, in general, exert great control over the course of his communication. The lower-class respondent seems to have much less foresight, appearing to control only how much he will say to the interviewer, or whether he will say it at all, although presumably he must have some stylistic controls not readily observable by a middle-class reader.

CLASSIFICATIONS AND CLASSIFICATORY RELATIONS
Lower class.—Respondents make reference mainly to the acts and persons of particular people, often designating them by proper or family names. This makes for fairly clear denotation and description, but only as long as the account is confined to the experiences of specific individuals. There comes a point when the interviewer wishes to obtain information about classes of persons and entire organizations as well as how they impinged upon the respondent, and here the lower-class respondent becomes relatively or even wholly inarticulate. At worst he cannot talk about categories of people or acts because, apparently, he does not think readily in terms of classes. Questions about organizations, such as the Red Cross, are converted into concrete terms, and he talks about the Red Cross "helping people" and "people helping other people" with no more than the crudest awareness of how organizational activities interlock. At most the respondent categorizes only in a rudimentary fashion: "Some people were running; other people were looking in the houses." The interviewer receives a sketchy and impressionistic picture. Some idea is conveyed of the confusion that followed upon the tornado, but the organizing of description is very poor. The respondent may mention classes in contrasting juxtaposition (rich and poor, hurt and not-hurt), or list groups of easily perceived, contrasting actions, but he does not otherwise spell out relations between these classes. Neither does he describe a scene systematically in terms of classes that are explicitly or clearly related, a performance which would involve a shifting of viewpoint.

It is apparent that the speakers think mainly in particularistic or concrete terms. Certainly classificatory thought must exist among many or all the respondents; but, in communicating to the interviewer, class terms are rudimentary or absent and class relations implicit: relationships are not spelled out or are left vague. Genuine illustrations are almost totally lacking, either because these require classifications or because we—as middle-class observers—do not recognize that certain details are meant to imply classes.

Middle class.—Middle-class speech is richly interlarded with classificatory terms, especially when the narrator is talking about what he saw rather than about himself. Typically, when he describes what other persons are doing, he classifies actions and persons and more often than not explicitly relates class to class. Often his descriptions are artistically organized around what various categories of persons were doing or experiencing. When an illustration is offered, it is clear that the speaker means it to stand for a general category. Relief and other civic organizations are conceived as sets or classes of co-ordinated roles and actions; some persons couch their whole account of the disaster events in organizational terms, hardly deigning to give proper names or personal accounts. In short, concrete imagery in middle-class communication is dwarfed or overshadowed by the prevalence and richness of conceptual terminology. Organization of speech around classifications comes readily, and undoubtedly the speaker is barely conscious of it. It is part and parcel of his formal and informal education. This is not to claim that middle-class persons always think with and use classificatory terms, for doubtless this is not true. Indeed, it may be that the interview exacts from them highly conceptualized descriptions. Nonetheless, we conclude that, in general, the thought and speech of middle-class persons is less concrete than that of the lower group.

ORGANIZING FRAMEWORKS AND STYLISTIC DEVICES

One of the requirements of communication is that utterances be organized. The principle of organization need not be stated explicitly by the speaker or recognized by the listener. Organizing frames can be of various sorts. Thus an ordering of the respondents' description is often set by the interviewer's question, or the speaker may set his own framework ("There is one thing you should know about this"). The frame can be established jointly by both interviewer and respondent, as when the former asks an open-ended question within whose very broad limits the respondent orders his description in ways that strike him as appropriate or interesting. The respondent, indeed, may organize his account much as though he were telling a special kind of story or drama, using the interviewer's questions as hardly more than general cues to what is required. The great number of events, incidents and images which must be conveyed to the listener may be handled haphazardly, neatly, dramatically, or sequentially; but, if they are to be communicated at all, they must be ordered somehow. Stylistic devices accompany and implement these organizing frames, and the lower and upper groups use them in somewhat different ways.

Lower class. — The interviewer's opening question, "Tell me your story of the tornado", invites the respondent to play an active role in organizing his account; and this he sometimes does. However, with the exception of one person who gave a headlong personal narrative, the respondents did not give long, well-organized, or tightly knit pictures of what happened to them during and after the tornado. This kind of general depiction either did not occur to them or did not strike them as appropriate.

The frames utilized are more segmental or limited in scope than those used by the middle class. They appear to be of several kinds and their centering is personal. One is the personal narrative, with events, acts, images, persons, and places receiving sequential ordering. Stylistic devices further this kind of organization: for instance, crude temporal connectives like "then", "and", and "so" and the reporting of images or events as they are recollected or as they appear in the narrative progression. Asides may specify relationships of kinship or the individuals' location in space. But, unless the line of narrative is compelling to the speaker, he is likely to wander off into detail about a particular incident, where the incident in turn then provides a framework for mentioning further events. Likewise, when a question from the interviewer breaks into the narrative, it may set the stage for an answer composed of a number of images or an incident. Often one incident becomes the trigger for another, and, although some logical or temporal connection between them may exist for the speaker, this can scarcely be perceived by the interviewer. Hence the respondent is likely to move out of frames quickly. The great danger of probes and requests for elaboration is that the speaker will get far away from the life-line of his narrative — and frequently far away from the interviewer's question. As recompense the interviewer may garner useful and unexpectedly rich information from the digressions, although often he needs to probe this material further to bring it into context. General questions are especially likely to divert the speaker, since they suggest only loose frames. [...] If a question is asked that concerns abstract classes or is "above" the respondent — a query, say, about relief organizations — then very general answers or concrete listing of images or triggering of images are especially noticeable. When the interviewer probes in an effort to get some elaboration of an occurrence or an expansion of idea, he commonly meets with little more than repetition or with a kind of "buckshot" listing of images or incidents which is supposed to fill out the desired picture. The lack of much genuine elaboration is probably related to the inability to report from multiple perspectives. [...]

With the lower-class respondent the interviewer, as a rule, must work very hard at building a comprehensive frame directly into the interview. This he does by forcing many subframes upon the respondent. He asks many questions about exact time sequence, placement and identification of persons, expansion of detail, and the like. [...]

The devices used to implement communication are rather difficult to isolate, perhaps because we are middle class ourselves. Among the devices most readily observable are the use of crude chronological notations (e.g., "then, ... and then"), the juxtaposing or direct contrasting of classes (e.g., rich and poor), and the serial locating of events. But the elaborate devices that characterize middle-class interviews are strikingly absent.

Middle class.—Without exception middle-class respondents imposed over-all frames of their own upon the entire interview. Although very sensitive generally to the needs of the interviewer, they made the account their own. This is evidenced sometimes from the very outset; many respondents give a lengthy picture in answer to the interviewer's invitation, "Tell me your story." The organizing frame may yield a fluid narrative that engulfs self and others in dense detail; it may give a relatively static but rich picture of a community in distress; or, by dramatic and stage-setting devices, it may show a complicated web of relationships in dramatic motion. The entire town may be taken as the frame of reference and its story portrayed in time and space.

Besides the master-frame, the middle-class respondent utilizes many subsidiary frames. Like the lower-class person, he may take off from a question. But, in doing so—especially where the question gives latitude by its generality or abstractness—he is likely to give an answer organized around a sub-frame which orders his selection and arrangement of items. He may even shift from one image to another, but rarely are these left unrelated to the question which initially provoked them. He is much more likely also to elaborate than to repeat or merely to give a scattered series of percepts. [...]

Because he incorporates multiple perspectives, the respondent can add long asides, discuss the parallel acts of other persons in relation to himself, make varied comparisons for the enrichment of detail and comprehension—and then can return to the original point and proceed from there. Often he does this after first preparing his listener for the departure and concludes the circuit with a summary statement or a transitional phrase like "well—anyhow" that marks the end of the digression. [...]

Only if the situation in which the respondent spoke is carefully taken into account will we be on safe ground in interpreting class differences. Consider, first, the probable meaning of the interview for the middle-class respondents. Although the interviewer is a stranger, an outsider, he is a well-spoken, educated person. He is seeking information on behalf of some organization, hence his questioning not only has sanction but sets the stage for both a certain freedom of speech and an obligation to give fairly full information. The respondent may never before have been interviewed by a research organization, but he has often talked lengthily, fairly freely, and responsibly to organizational representatives. At the very least he has had some experience in talking to educated strangers. We may also suppose that the middle-class style of living often compels him to be very careful not to be misunderstood. So he becomes relatively sensitive to communication *per se* and to communication with others who may not exactly share his viewpoints or frames of reference.

Communication with such an audience requires alertness, no less to the meanings of one's own speech than to the possible intent of the other's. Role-taking may be inaccurate, (often) but it is markedly active. Assessing and anticipating reactions to what he has said or is about to say, the individual develops flexible and ingenious ways of correcting, qualifying, making more plausible, explaining, rephrasing—in short, he assumes multiple perspectives and communicates in terms of them. A variety of perspectives implies a variety of ways of ordering or framing detail. Moreover, he is able to classify and to relate classes explicitly, which is but another way of saying that he is educated to assume multiple perspectives of rather wide scope.

It would certainly be too much to claim that middle-class persons always react so sensitively. Communication is often routinized, and much of it transpires between and among those who know each other so well or share so much in common that they need not be subtle. Nor is sensitive role-taking called forth in so-called "expressive behavior", as when hurling invective or yelling during a ball game. With the proviso that much middle-class speech is uttered under such conditions, it seems safe enough to say that people of this stratum can, if required, handle the more complex and consciously organized discourse. In addition to skill and perspicacity, this kind of discourse requires a person who can subtly keep a listener at a distance while yet keeping him in some degree informed.

Consider now, even at risk of overstating the case, how the interview appears to the lower group. The interviewer is of higher social class than the respondent, so that the interview is a "conversation between the classes". It is entirely probable that more effort and ability are demanded by cross-class conversation of this sort than between middle-class respondent and middle-class interviewer. It is not surprising that the interviewer is often baffled and that the respondent frequently misinterprets what is wanted. [...] The lower-lcass person in these Arkansas towns infrequently meets a middle-class person in a situation anything like the interview. Here he must talk at great length to a stranger about personal experiences, as well as recall for his listener a tremendous number of details. Presumably he is accustomed to talking about such matters and in such detail only to listeners with whom he shares a great deal of experience and symbolism, so that he need not be very self-conscious about communicative technique. He can, as a rule, safely assume that words, phrases, and gestures are assigned approximately similar meanings by his listeners. But this is not so in the interview or, indeed, in any situation where class converses with class in nontraditional modes.

There still remains the question of whether the descriptions of perceptions and experiences given by the lower-class respondent are merely inadequate or whether this is the way he truly saw and experienced. Does his speech accurately reflect customary "concrete" modes of thought and perception, or is it that he perceives in abstract and classificatory terms, and from multiple perspectives, but is unable to convey his perceptions? [...]

In any situation calling for a description of human activities it is necessary to utilize motivational terminology, either explicitly or implicitly, in the very namings of acts. In the speech of those who recognize few disparities of imagery between themselves and their listeners, explicit motivational terms are sparse. The frequent use among the lower class of the expression "of course" followed by something like "They went up to see about their folks" implies that it is almost needless to say what "they" did, much less to give the reason for the act. The motive ("to see about") is implicit and terminal, requiring neither elaboration nor explanation. Where motives are éxplicit ("They was needin' help, so we went on up there"), they are often gratuitous and could just as well have been omitted. [...] To the speaker it was quite clear why people did what they did. There was no need to question or to elaborate on the grounds for acts. Under probing the respondent did very little better: he used motivational terms but within a quite narrow range. The terms he used ordinarily reflected kinship obligations, concern for property, humanitarian ("help") sentiments, and action from motives of curiosity ("We went down to see"). [...]   A reasons → same act

Middle-class persons exhibit familiarity with a host of distinct "reasons" for performing particular acts. Their richness in thinking allows activities to be defined and described in a great variety of ways. Here, indeed, is an instrument for breaking down diffuse images ("They was runnin' all over") into classes of acts and events. The middle-class person is able to do this, for one thing, because he possesses an abstract motivational terminology. Then, too, the fine and subtle distinctions for rationalizing behavior require devices for insuring that they will be grasped by the hearer. In a real sense the need to explain behavior can be linked with the need to communicate well—to give a rational account as well as to be objective. Hence, there is a constant flow of qualifying and generalizing terms linked with motivational phraseology ("I don't kow why, but it could be he felt there was no alternative...").

It is not surprising to find the middle class as familiar with elements of social structure as with individual behavior. Assuredly, this familiarity rests not only upon contact with institutions but upon the capacity to perceive and talk about abstract classes of acts. The lower-class person, on other hand, appears to have only rudimentary notions of organizational structure—at least of relief and emergency agencies. Extended contact with representatives of them, no doubt, would familiarize him not only with organizations but with thinking in organizational, or abstract, terms. The propensity of the lower class to state concretely the activities of relief organizations corroborates the observation of Warner that the lowest strata have little knowledge or "feel" for the social structures of their communities. It also suggests the difficulty of conveying to them relatively abstract information through formal media of communication.

Leonard Schatzman and Anselm Strauss
"Social Class and Modes of Communication"

Too bad they didn't employ a
WC interviewer | or try to

Subjective images and objective frame of reference

J. H. Goldthorpe and D. Lockwood do not simply criticize the procedure, which has long been contested, of trying to study the distance between the classes by asking individuals to situate themselves in the social structure. They also show that every technique has to be questioned, both as regards its adequacy to the problem posed (knowledge of the subjects' opinions is no substitute for an objective grasp of relations between groups) and as regards the type of abstraction, which may be good or bad, that it performs. To ask subjects to define the position they assign to themselves in the social structure without seeking to know that social structure and, in particular, the representation that the subjects form of it, is to treat a "Gestalt" as a "series of separate and unrelated responses".*

26. *J. H. Goldthorpe and D. Lockwood*

The evidence of opinion and attitude surveys that have been taken as relevant to the thesis of *embourgeoisement* can be briefly summarised as follows. In a number of studies carried out in recent years, and covering relatively large numbers of manual workers, some sizeable proportion of the latter—ranging from 10 to over 40 per cent—have in each instance claimed to belong to the middle class. In some of the studies, though by no means in all, it has then also been shown how this claim in some degree correlates with other expressions of "middle classness"—for example, voting Conservative. On this basis the argument has been advanced that working class consciousness is weakening and that many manual workers are now no longer willing to identify themselves with others in basically the same objective class position, but see themselves, rather, as forming part of a higher social stratum along with white-collar workers, independents and so on.

Our criticism of this argument is directed primarily at the method of investigation that is chiefly involved, that is, the attempt to ascertain individuals' perception of their position in the class structure and their class identification by means of a poll-type interview. [...]

In the first place, it is known that responses to such a question as "To which social class would you say you belonged" may vary significantly depending on whether the respondent is given a pre-determined choice of class categories or whether categorisation is left "open". Secondly, it is also known that where pre-determined categories are used (which is usually the case), wide variations can again be produced in the pattern of response according to the particular class designations which are offered—for example, according to whether "lower class" is used instead of, or in addition to, "working class" or not at all. Thirdly, and perhaps most importantly, it has become evident that responses to questions on class identification which are nominally similar, and which will thus be grouped together by the investigator, may in fact have very different meanings for the various persons making them. This is because such

---

* To replace this critique of the techniques commonly used in social stratification surveys in the general discussion in which it occurs, see above, text no. 6.

responses will be influenced not only by the form of question that is put, which can for any given sample be held constant, but *also* by respondents' own images of their society and of its class structure, which, it is known, tend to be highly variable. Thus, the same question will be answered in terms of many different, and perhaps widely different, frames of reference. For instance, in the case of a manual worker claiming to be "middle class", it is possible that this statement might mean, among other things, any of the following:

(a) that the respondent does not identify with, and wishes to distinguish himself from, those he sees as forming the lowest strata in society; such as, for example, casual labourers or those on the verge of poverty;

(b) that he sees his position as being in the middle of a broadly defined working class (from an objective point of view) which largely constitutes his own social world; that is to say, he regards himself, for example as being superior to less skilled or less well paid workers but as below such persons as foremen, policemen, garage superintendents and so on;

(c) that he feels he is at least the equal of many white-collar workers, small businessmen, etc. in *economic* terms—that is, in terms of income and material possessions;

(d) that he has aspirations towards a *style of life* which he realises is at least different from what would usually be thought of as working class; or finally

(e) that he has a *family background* which he regards as middle class.

With these considerations in mind, then, it can only be concluded that the findings of class identification studies conducted via poll-type questioning are of very little sociological value. It would seem virtually impossible to interpret such data in any way that would provide reliable indications of respondents' class awareness or class consciousness; the scope for arbitrary variation and ambiguity is far too great. And certainly, we would claim, there can be no valid basis here for the argument that significant numbers of manual workers are now seeking to present themselves as members of "authentic" middle class groups, or that they are even aspiring to such membership.

John H. Goldthorpe and David Lockwood
"Affluence and the British Class Structure"

Categories of native language and construction of scientific facts

Claude Lévi-Strauss suggests that if Mauss needs to resort to a native category, hau, in order to explain the mechanism of gift and counter-gift, this is because, misled by the categories of his language, he has distinguished three operations and therefore three different obligations, "giving, receiving, returning", where there is only an act of exchange which analysis cannot break. Mauss would not have had to look for a force capable of explaining the return gift if, instead of uncritically accepting a theory which is only the conscious statement of "unconscious necessity whose explanation lies elsewhere", he had relied on the native language, which, as he himself observes, has "only one word to designate buying and selling, lending and borrowing", operations that the suggestions of his own language lead him to regard as antithetical.

27. C. Lévi-Strauss

Are we not dealing with a mystification, an effect quite often produced in the minds of ethnographers by indigenous people? Not, of course, by "indigenous people" in general, since no such beings exist, but by a given indigenous group, about whom specialists have already pondered problems, asked questions and attempted answers. In the case in point, instead of applying his principles consistently from start to finish, Mauss discards them in favour of a New Zealand theory—one which is immensely valuable as an ethnological document; yet it is nothing other than a theory. The fact that Maori sages were the first people to pose certain problems and to resolve them in an infinitely interesting but strikingly unsatisfactory manner does not oblige us to bow to their interpretation. *Hau* is not the ultimate explanation for exchange; it is the conscious form whereby men of a given society, in which the problem had particular importance, apprehended an unconscious necessity whose explanation lies elsewhere.

We may infer that Mauss is seized by hesitation and scruples at the most crucial moment. He is no longer quite sure whether he must draw a picture of indigenous theory, or construct a theory of indigenous reality. He is very largely right to be unsure, for indigenous theory is much more directly related to indigenous reality than a theory developed from our own categories or problems would be. So it was a very great progress, at the time when Mauss was writing, to approach an ethnographic problem from the starting-point of his New Zealand or Melanesian theory, rather than to call upon Western notions such as animism, myth or participation. But indigenous or Western, theory is only ever a theory. At best, it offers us a path of access; for, whether they be Fuegians or Australian Aboriginals, the interested parties' beliefs are always far removed from what they actually think or do. Once the indigenous conception has been isolated, it must be reduced by an objective critique so as to reach the underlying reality. We have very little chance of finding that reality in conscious formulations; a better chance, in unconscious mental structures to which institutions give us access, but a better chance yet, in language. *Hau* is a product of indigenous reflection; but reality is more conspicuous in certain linguistic features which Mauss does not fail to note, although he does not make as much of them as he should. "Papuan and Melanesian," he notes, "have only one word to designate buying and selling, lending and borrowing. Antithetical operations are expressed by the same word." That is ample proof that the operations in question are far from "antithetical"; that they are just two modes of a selfsame reality. We do not need *hau* to make the synthesis, because the antithesis does not exist. The antithesis is a subjective illusion of ethnographers, and sometimes also of indigenous people who, when reasoning about themselves—as they quite often do—behave like ethnographers, or more precisely, like sociologists; that is, as colleagues with whom one may freely confer.

Claude Lévi-Strauss
Introduction to the Work of Marcel Mauss

But the methodological principles implied by this critique are not sufficient to define how the ethnologist must construct his objects. It is not enough to be on guard against the native theory and to resort to the language as the privileged site of unconscious structures. Mauss pointed out elsewhere that the divisions performed by any given language have no privilege vis-à-vis the constructs of the sociologist, who should not necessarily submit to the categories of the native language.

28. M. Mauss

It is not indispensable for a social phenomenon to attain verbal expression in order for it to exist. What one language says in one word, others say in several words. It is not even necessary at all that they should express it: the notion of cause is not explicit in the transitive verb, but it is nonetheless there.

*   In order for the existence of a particular principle of mental operations to be sure, it is necessary and sufficient that these operations should only be explicable through it. No one has questioned the universality of the notion of the sacred, and yet it would be difficult indeed to cite a particular word in Sanskrit or Greek corresponding to the Latin *sacer*. One would say, in the one case, pure (*medhya*), sacrificial (*yajniya*), divine (*devya*), terrible (*ghora*); in the other, holy (ιερός) or (ἅγιος), venerable (σεμνός), just (θέσμος), respectable (αἰδέσιμος). And yet the Greeks and the Hindus clearly had a very exact and very strong awareness of the sacred.

Marcel Mauss
"*Introduction à l'analyse de quelques phénomènes religieux*"

refer to Skuovetz observations

Simulation?

Spurious neutrality of techniques: construct or artefact. B. Malinowski   183

The most complete statement of the rules for constructing the scientific object is given by Malinowski, when he considers how to classify the various types of gifts, payments, and commercial transactions that he observed among the Trobrianders. One must avoid the form of ethnocentrism that consists in introducing "artificial categories", dictated by our —Sim? *own terminology and our own criteria, into the description, and the native terminology is one means of achieving this; but "it must also be remembered that this is not a miraculous short cut", since, at the level of institutions and behaviours, there are unconscious "principles of arrangement" that the ethnologist has to extract in order to check the classification spontaneously offered by the native language. Thus, contrary to a popular image of ethnological method, characterized by fidelity to the concrete detail, Malinowski's argument shows that the concern for concrete description of behaviour is precisely aimed at enabling the ethnologist to avoid being the victim of the spontaneous categories of language, whether his own or that of the subjects he studies.**

29. B. Malinowski (1922)

I have on purpose spoken of forms of exchange, of gifts and counter-gifts, rather than of barter or trade, because, although there exist forms of barter pure and simple, there are so many transitions and gradations between that and simple gift, that it is impossible to draw any fixed line between trade on the one hand, and exchange of gifts on the other. Indeed, the drawing of any lines to suit our own terminology and our own distinctions is contrary to sound method. In order to deal with these facts correctly it is necessary to give a complete survey of all forms of payment or present. In this survey there will be at one end the extreme case of pure gift, that is an offering for which nothing is given in return. Then, through many customary forms of gift or payment, partially or conditionally returned, which shade into each other, there come forms of exchange, where more or less strict equivalence is observed, arriving finally at real barter. In the following survey I shall roughly classify each transaction according to the principle of its equivalence.

Such tabularised accounts cannot give the same clear vision of facts as a concrete description might do, and they even produce the impression of artificiality, but, and this must be emphatically stated, I shall not introduce here artificial categories, foreign to the native mind. Nothing is so misleading in ethnographic accounts as the description of facts of native civilisations in terms of our own. This, however, shall not be done here. The principles of arrangement, although quite beyond the comprehension of the natives, are nevertheless contained in their social organisation, customs, and even in their linguistic terminology. This latter always affords the simplest and surest means of approach towards the understanding of native distinctions and classifications. But it also must be remembered that, though important as a clue to native ideas, the knowledge of terminology is not a miraculous short-cut into the native's mind. As a matter of fact, there exist many salient and extremely important features of Trobriand sociology and social psychology, which are

My FP?

* See above, section 1.4.

not covered by any term, whereas their language distinguishes sub-divisions
and subtleties which are quite irrelevant with regard to actual conditions.
Thus, a survey of terminology must always be supplemented by a direct
analysis of ethnographic fact and inquiry into the native's ideas, that is, by
collecting a body of opinions, typical expressions, and customary phrases by
direct cross-questioning. The most conclusive and deepest insight, however,
must always be obtained by a study of behaviour, by analysis of ethnographic
custom and concrete cases of traditional rules.

Bronislaw Malinowski
Argonauts of the Western Pacific

2.4   Analogy and construction of hypotheses

The use of ideal types in sociology

Contrary to what is gratuitously assumed by those who complain of his "constructivism", Weber's methodology of the ideal type does not put forward an instrument of proof intended to take the place of the search for empirical regularities or the historical work of causal explanation. When it is a question of explaining "singular historical constellations" (social formations, cultural configurations, events), the ideal-typical constructions of the sociologist can "make a contribution" by leading to the formulation of hypotheses and suggesting questions to be put to reality; in themselves, they provide no knowledge of reality. Nor does the "complete adequacy on the level of meaning" that the ideal type has to achieve in order to fulfil its role of revealing hidden relations justify the frequent use of "interpretive sociology" as a basis for a social psychology that would aim to construct its objects by reference to "motivations" and the subjective meaning of actions. It can be seen here that "possible meaning" has nothing in common with the "subjective meaning" of lived experience; Weber explicitly presents the hypothesis of the non-conscious nature of the cultural meaning of actions as the principle of interpretive sociology.

30. M. Weber

We have taken for granted that sociology seeks to formulate type concepts and generalized uniformities of empirical process. This distinguishes it from history, which is oriented to the causal analysis and explanation of individual actions, structures, and personalities possessing cultural significance. The empirical material which underlies the concepts of sociology consists to a very large extent, though by no means exclusively, of the same concrete processes of action which are dealt with by historians. An important consideration in the formulation of sociological concepts and generalizations is the contribution that sociology can make toward the causal explanation of some historically and culturally important phenomenon. As in the case of every generalizing science the abstract character of the concepts of sociology is responsible for the fact that, compared with actual historical reality, they are relatively lacking in fullness of concrete content. To compensate for this disadvantage, sociological analysis can offer a greater precision of concepts. This precision is obtained by striving for the highest possible degree of adequacy on the level of meaning. It has already been repeatedly stressed that this aim can be realized in a particularly high degree in the case of concepts and generalizations which formulate rational processes. But sociological investigation attempts to include in its scope various irrational phenomena, such as prophetic, mystic, and affectual modes of action, formulated in terms of theoretical concepts which are adequate on the level of meaning. In *all* cases, rational or irrational, sociological analysis both abstracts from reality and at the same time helps us to understand it, in that it shows with what degree of approximation a concrete historical phenomenon can be subsumed under one or more of these concepts. For example, the same historical phenomenon may be in one aspect feudal, in another patrimonial, in another bureaucratic, and in still another charismatic. In order to give a precise meaning to these terms, it is necessary for the sociologist to formulate pure ideal types of the corresponding forms of action which in each case involve the highest possible degree of logical integration by virtue of their complete adequacy on the level of meaning. But precisely because this is true, it is probably seldom if ever that a real phenomenon can be found which corresponds exactly to one of these ideally constructed pure types. The case is similar to a physical reaction which has been calculated on the assumption of an absolute vacuum. Theoretical differentiation (*Kasuistik*) is possible in sociology only in terms of ideal or pure types. It goes without saying that in addition it is convenient for the sociologist from time to time to employ average types of an empirical statistical character, concepts which do not require methodological discussion. But when reference is made to "typical" cases, the term should always be understood, unless otherwise stated, as meaning *ideal* types, which may in turn be rational or irrational as the case may be (thus in economic theory they are always rational), but in any case are always constructed with a view to adequacy on the level of meaning.

It is important to realize that in the sociological field as elsewhere, averages, and hence average types, can be formulated with a relative degree of precision only where they are concerned with differences of degree in respect to action which remains qualitatively the same. Such cases do occur, but in the majority of cases of action important to history or sociology the motives which determine it are qualitatively heterogeneous. Then it is quite impossible to speak of an "average" in the true sense. The ideal types of social action which for instance are used in economic theory are thus unrealistic or abstract in that they always ask what course of action would take place if it were purely rational and oriented to economic ends alone. This construction can be used to aid in the understanding of action not purely economically determined but which involves deviations arising from traditional restraints, affects, errors, and the intrusion of other than economic purposes or considerations. [...] The procedure would be very similar in employing an ideal type of mystical orientation, with its appropriate attitude of indifference to worldly things, as a tool for analysing its consequences for the actor's relation to ordinary life—for instance, to political or economic affairs. The more sharply and precisely the ideal type has been constructed, thus the more abstract and unrealistic in this sense it is, the better it is able to perform its functions in formulating terminology, classifications, and hypotheses. In working out a concrete causal explanation of individual events, the procedure of the historian is essentially the same. Thus in attempting to explain the campaign of 1866, it is indispensable both in the case of Moltke and of Benedek to attempt to construct imaginatively how each, given fully adequate knowledge both of his own situation and of that of his opponent, would have acted. Then it is possible to compare with this the actual course of action and to arrive at a causal explanation of the observed deviations, which will be attributed to such factors as misinformation, strategical errors, logical fallacies, personal temperament, or considerations outside the realm of strategy. Here, too, an ideal-typical construction of rational action is actually employed even though it is not made explicit.

The theoretical concepts of sociology are ideal types not only from the objective point of view, but also in their application to subjective processes. In the great majority of cases actual action goes on in a state of inarticulate half-consciousness or actual unconsciousness of its subjective meaning. The actor is more likely to "be aware" of it in a vague sense than he is to "know" what he is doing or be explicitly self-conscious about it. In most cases his action is governed by impulse or habit. Only occasionally and, in the uniform action of large numbers, often only in the case of a few individuals, is the subjective meaning of the action, whether rational or irrational, brought clearly into consciousness. The ideal type of meaningful action where the meaning is fully conscious and explicit is a marginal case. Every sociological or historical investigation, in applying its analysis to the empirical facts, must take this fact into account. But the difficulty need not prevent the sociologist from systematizing his concepts by the classification of possible types of subjective meaning. That is, he may reason as if action actually proceeded on the basis of clearly self-conscious meaning. The resulting deviation from the concrete facts must continually be kept in mind whenever it is a question of this level of concreteness, and must be carefully studied with reference both to degree and kind. It is often necessary to choose between terms which are either clear or unclear. Those which are clear will, to be sure, have the abstractness of ideal types, but they are none the less preferable for scientific purposes.

Max Weber
Economy and Society

ideal! not real!

We have in abstract economic theory an illustration of those synthetic constructs which have been designated as *"ideas"* of historical phenomena. It offers us an ideal picture of events on the commodity-market under conditions of a society organized on the principles of an exchange economy, free competition and rigorously rational conduct. This conceptual pattern brings together certain relationships and events of historical life into a complex, which is conceived as an internally consistent system. Substantively, this construct in itself is like a *utopia* which has been arrived at by the analytical accentuation of certain elements of reality. Its relationship to the empirical data consists solely in the fact that where market-conditioned relationships of the type referred to by the abstract construct are discovered or suspected to exist in reality to some extent, we can make the *characteristic* features of this relationship pragmatically *clear* and *understandable* by reference to an *ideal-type*. This procedure can be indispensable for heuristic as well as expository purposes. The ideal typical concept will help to develop our skill in imputation in *research*: it *is* no "hypothesis" but it offers guidance to the construction of hypotheses. It is not a *description* of reality but it aims to give unambiguous means of expression to such a description. It is thus the "idea" of the *histori-cally* given modern society, based on an exchange economy, which is developed for us by quite the same logical principles as are used in constructing the idea of the medieval "city economy" as a "genetic" concept. When we do this, we construct the concept "city economy" not as an *average* of the economic structures actually existing in all the cities observed but as an *ideal-type*. An ideal type is formed by the one-sided *accentuation* of one or more points of view and by the synthesis of a great many diffuse, discrete, more or less present and occasionally absent *concrete individual* phenomena, which are arranged according to those one-sidedly emphasized viewpoints into a unified *analytical* construct (Gedankenbild). In its conceptual purity, this mental construct (Gedankenbild) cannot be found empirically anywhere in reality. It is a *utopia*. Historical research faces the task of determining in each individual case, the extent to which this ideal-construct approximates to or diverges from reality, to what extent for example, the economic structure of a certain city is to be classified as a "city-economy". When carefully applied, those concepts are particularly useful in research and exposition. [...]

What is the significance of such ideal-typical constructs for an *empirical* science, as we wish to constitute it? Before going any further, we should emphasize that the idea of an ethical *imperative*, of a "model" of what "ought" to exist is to be carefully distinguished from the analytical construct, which is "ideal" in the strictly logical sense of the term. It is a matter here of constructing relationships which our imagination accepts as plausibly motivated and hence as "objectively possible" and which appear as *adequate* from the nomological standpoint.

Whoever accepts the proposition that the knowledge of historical reality can or should be a "presuppositionless" copy of "objective" facts, will deny the value of the ideal-type. Even those who recognize that there is no "presup-positionlessness" in the logical sense and that even the simplest excerpt from a statute or from a documentary source can have scientific meaning only with reference to "significance" and ultimately to evaluative ideas, will more or less regard the construction of any such historical "utopias" as an expository device which endangers the autonomy of historical research and which is, in any case, a vain sport. And, in fact, *whether* we are dealing simply with a conceptual game or with a scientifically fruitful method of conceptualization and *theory*-construction can never be decided *a priori*. Here, too, there is only one criterion, namely, that of success in revealing concrete cultural phenomena in their interdependence, their causal conditions and their *significance*. The construction of abstract ideal-types recommends itself not as an end but as a *means*. Every conscientious examination of the conceptual elements of historical exposition shows however that the historian as soon as he attempts to go beyond the bare establishment of concrete relationships and to determine the *cultural* significance of even the simplest individual event in order to "characterize" it, *must* use concepts which are precisely and unambiguously definable only in the form of ideal types. Or are concepts such as "individualism", "imperialism", "feudalism", "mercantilism", "conventional", etc., and innumerable concepts of like character by means of which we seek analytically and empathically to understand reality constructed substantively by the "presuppositionless" *description* of some concrete phenomenon or through the abstract synthesis of those traits which are *common* to numerous concrete phenomena? Hundreds of words in the historian's vocabulary are ambiguous constructs created to meet the unconsciously felt need for adequate expression and the meaning of which is only concretely felt but not clearly thought out. In a great many cases, particularly in the field of descriptive political history, their ambiguity has not been prejudicial to the clarity of the presentation. It is sufficient that in each case the reader should *feel* what the historian had in mind; or, one can content one's self with the idea that the author used a *particular* meaning of the concept with special reference to the concrete case at hand. The greater the need however for a sharp appreciation of the significance of a cultural phenomenon, the more imperative is the – FB need to operate with unambiguous concepts which are not only particularly but also systematically defined. A "definition" of such synthetic historical terms according to the scheme of *genus proximum* and *differentia specifica* is naturally nonsense. But let us consider it. Such a form of the establishment of the meanings of words is to be found only in axiomatic disciplines which use syllogisms. A simple "descriptive analysis" of these concepts into their components either does not exist or else exists only illusorily, for the question arises as to *which* of these components should be regarded as essential. When a genetic definition of the content of the concept is sought, there remains only the ideal-type in the sense explained above. It is a conceptual construct (*Gedankenbild*) which is neither historical reality nor even the "true" reality. It is even less fitted to serve as a schema under which a real situation or action is to be subsumed as one *instance*. It has the significance of a purely ideal *limiting* concept with which the real situation or action is *compared* and surveyed for the explication of certain of its significant components. Such concepts are constructs in terms of which we formulate relationships by the

-FB !

2. Constructing the object

application of the category of objective possibility. By means of this category, the adequacy of our imagination, oriented and disciplined by reality, is judged.

In this function especially, the ideal-type is an attempt to analyze historically unique configurations or their individual components by means of genetic concepts. Let us take for instance the concepts "church" and "sect". They may be broken down purely classificatorily into complexes of characteristics whereby not only the distinction between them but also the content of the concept must constantly remain fluid. If however I wish to formulate the concept of "sect" genetically, e.g., with reference to certain important cultural significances which the "sectarian spirit" has had for modern culture, certain characteristics of both become *essential* because they stand in an adequate causal relationship to those influences. However, the concepts thereupon become ideal-typical in the sense that they appear in full conceptual *integrity* either not at all or only in individual instances. Here as elsewhere every concept which is not purely classificatory diverges from reality.

Max Weber
The Methodology of the Social Sciences

a is "like" b (by ANALOGY?)

2.5 Model and theory

The summa and the cathedral: deep analogies, the product of a mental habit

The parallelism between the development of Gothic art and the development of Scholastic thought in the period between about 1130–1140 and about 1270 cannot be brought out unless one "brackets off phenomenal appearances" and seeks the hidden ? *analogies between the principles of logical organization of Scholasticism and the principles of construction of Gothic architecture. This methodological choice is dictated by the intention of establishing more than a vague "parallelism" or discontinuous, fragmentary "influences". Renouncing the semblances of proof which satisfy intuitionists or the reassuring but reductive circumstantial proofs which delight positivists, Panofsky is led to identify the historical convergence which provides the object of his research with a hidden principle, a* habitus or "habit-forming force".

31. E. Panofsky (1952)

What are the principles of EST? Axioms 1–5

During the "concentrated" phase of this astonishingly synchronous development, viz., in the period between about 1130–40 and about 1270, we can observe, it seems to me, a connection between Gothic art and Scholasticism which is more concrete than a mere "parallelism" and yet more general than those individual (and very important) "influences" which are inevitably exerted on painters, sculptors, or architects by erudite advisers. In contrast to a mere parallelism, the connection which I have in mind is a genuine cause-and-effect relation; but in contrast to an individual influence, this cause-and-effect relation comes about by diffusion rather than by direct impact. It comes about by the spreading of what may be called, for want of a better term, a mental habit—reducing this overworked cliché to its precise Scholastic sense as a "principle that regulates the act", *principium importans ordinem ad actum*[1] Such mental habits are at work in all and every civilization. All modern writing on history is permeated by the idea of evolution (an idea the evolution of which needs much more study than it has received thus far and seems to enter a critical phase right now); and all of us, without a thorough knowledge of biochemistry or psychoanalysis, speak with the greatest of ease of vitamin deficiencies, allergies, mother fixations, and inferiority complexes.

See the Skvarla papers

|| —D

— ho ho!

mathematics

Often it is difficult or impossible to single out one habit-forming force from many others and to imagine the channels of transmission. However, the period from about 1130–40 to about 1270 and the "100-mile zone around Paris" constitute an exception. In this tight little sphere Scholasticism possessed what amounted to a monopoly in education. By and large, intellectual training shifted from the monastic schools to institutions urban rather than rural, cosmopolitan rather than regional, and, so to speak, only half

[1] Thomas Aquinas, *Summa Theologiae*, I–II, qu. 49, art. 3, C.

ecclesiastic: to the cathedral schools, the universities, and the *studia* of the new mendicant orders—nearly all of them products of the thirteenth century—whose members played an increasingly important role within the universities themselves. And as the Scholastic movement, prepared by Benedictine learning and initiated by Lanfranc and Anselm of Bec, was carried on and brought to fruition by the Dominicans and Franciscans, so did the Gothic style, prepared in Benedictine monasteries and initiated by Suger of St.-Denis, achieve its culmination in the great city churches. It is significant that during the Romanesque period the greatest names in architectural history are those of Benedictine abbeys, in the High Gothic period those of cathedrals, and in the Late Gothic periods those of parish churches.

It is not very probable that the builders of Gothic structures read Gilbert de la Porrée or Thomas Aquinas in the original. But they were exposed to the Scholastic point of view in innumerable other ways, quite apart from the fact that their own work automatically brought them into a working association with those who devised the liturgical and iconographic programs. They had gone to school; they listened to sermons[2]; they could attend the public *disputationes de quolibet*[3] which, dealing as they did with all imaginable questions of the day, had developed into social events not unlike our operas, concerts, or public lectures[4]; and they could come into profitable contact with the learned on many other occasions. The very fact that neither the natural sciences nor the humanities nor even mathematics had evolved their special esoteric methods and terminologies kept the whole of human knowledge within the range of the normal, non-specialized intellect. [...]

[*Moreover, the social situation of the architect helps to explain how he came to be well placed to internalize the set of habits of thought characteristic of Scholasticism.*] The entire social system was rapidly changing toward an urban professionalism. Not as yet hardened into the later guild and "Bauhütten"

---

[2] See E. Gilson, "Michel Menot et la technique du sermon médiéval", in *Les idées et les lettres*, Paris: Vrin, 1932, pp. 93–154 (note by P. Bourdieu).

[3] *Disputationes ordinariae* and their literary version, *quaestiones disputatae*, were distinguished from *disputationes quodlibetales* and their written record, *quaestiones quodlibetales*. Each *disputatio ordinaria* unfolded as follows: on the first day, it was for the bachelor to respond, under the chairmanship of his master, to the *argumenta* and *objectiones* raised by the masters, bachelors or students present at this university ceremony, which took place at regular intervals. On the second day, the master ordered and grouped the arguments and objections and set against them, as *sed contra*, brief arguments drawn from reason and authority. Then he freely undertook to resolve the problem in full, relating it to its origins or its historical or speculative consequences, then formulating and demonstrating his definitive answer, called *determinatio magistralis*. Finally, on the basis of this, he answered the objections. Twice a year, before Christmas and Easter, there were exercises of discussion on various topics known as *disputationes de quolibet* because they touched on disparate questions and did not go so far in the resolution of the problems (see M. Grabmann, *Einführung in die Summa Theologiae des heiligen Thomas von Aquin*, Freiburg, 1919 [note by Pierre Bourdieu]).

[4] M. de Wulf, *History of Mediaeval Philosophy*, 3rd English ed. (E. C. Messenger, tr.), London, II, 1938, p. 9.

systems, it provided a meeting ground where the priest and the layman, the poet and the lawyer, the scholar and the artisan could get together on terms of near-equality. [...]

[The] professional architect was a man of the world, widely travelled, often well read, and enjoying a social prestige unequalled before and unsurpassed since. [...] The architect himself had come to be looked upon as a kind of Scholastic.

When asking in what manner the mental habit induced by Early and High Scholasticism may have affected the formation of Early and High Gothic architecture, we shall do well to disregard the notional content of the doctrine and to concentrate, to borrow a term from the schoolmen themselves, upon its *modus operandi*. The changing tenets in such matters as the relation between soul and body or the problem of universals vs. particulars naturally were reflected in the representational arts rather than in architecture. True, the architect lived in close contact with the sculptors, glass painters, wood carvers, etc., whose work he studied wherever he went (witness the "Album" of Villard de Honnecourt), whom he engaged and supervised in his own enterprises, and to whom he had to transmit an iconographic program which, we remember, he could work out only in close cooperation with a scholastic adviser. But in doing all this, he assimilated and conveyed rather than applied the substance of contemporary thought. What he who "devised the form of the building while not himself manipulating its matter[5] could and did apply, directly and *qua* architect, was rather that peculiar method of procedure which must have been the first thing to impress itself upon the mind of the layman whenever it came in touch with that of the schoolman.

Erwin Panofsky
Gothic Architecture and Scholasticism

[5] Thomas Aquinas, *Summa Theologiae*, I, qu. 1, art. 6, C.

The heuristic function of analogy

Pierre Duhem criticizes <u>the mechanical models</u> used by the English physicists of Lord Kelvin's school, <u>which reproduced the effects of a certain number of laws by means of mechanisms that functioned according to a quite different logic. He is careful to distinguish this imaginative recourse to superficial resemblances from the analogical procedure proper, which, moving from abstract relations to other abstract relations, provides the heuristic spring for generalizations and transpositions founded on a theory.</u>

32. P. Duhem   *Category theory*

It is well, if we wish to appreciate with accuracy the fruitfulness that the use of models may have, not to confuse this use with the use of analogy.

The physicist who seeks to unite and classify in an abstract theory the laws of a certain category of phenomena, lets himself be guided often by the analogy that he sees between these phenomena and those of another category. If the latter are already ordered and organized in a satisfactory theory the physicist will try to group the former in a system of the same type and form.

The history of physics shows us that the search for analogies between two distinct categories of phenomena has perhaps been the surest and most fruitful method of all the procedures put in play in the construction of physical theories.

Thus, it is the analogy seen between the phenomena produced by light and those constituting sound which furnished the notion of light wave from which Huygens drew such a wonderful result. It is this same analogy which later led Malebranche and then Young to represent monochromatic light by a formula similar to the one representing a simple sound.

A similar insight concerning the propagation of heat and that of electricity within conductors permitted Ohm to transport all in one piece the equations Fourier had written for the former to the second category of phenomena.

The history of theories of magnetism and dielectric polarization is simply the development of analogies seen for a long time by physicists between magnets and bodies which insulate electricity. Thanks to this analogy each of the two theories benefits from the progress of the other.

The use of physical analogy often takes a more precise form.

Two categories of very distinct and very dissimilar phenomena having been reduced to abstract theories, it may happen that the equations in which one of the theories is formulated are algebraically identical to the equations expressing the other. Then, although these two theories are essentially heterogeneous by the nature of the laws which they coordinate, algebra establishes an exact correspondence between them. Every proposition of one of the theories has its homologue in the other; every problem solved in the first poses and resolves a similar problem in the second. Each of these two theories can serve to *illustrate* the other, according to the word used by the English: "By physical analogy," Maxwell said, "I mean that partial resemblance between the laws of a science and the laws of another science which makes one of the two sciences serve to illustrate the other."

Of this mutual illustration of two theories, here is an example among many others:

The idea of a warm body and the idea of an electrostatically charged body are two essentially heterogeneous notions. The laws which govern the distribution of stationary temperatures in a group of good conductors of heat and the laws which fix the state of electrical equilibrium in a group of good conductors of electricity pertain to absolutely different physical objects. However, the two theories whose object is to classify these laws are expressed in two groups of equations which the algebraist cannot distinguish from each other. Thus, each time that he solves a problem about the distribution of stationary temperatures, he solves by that very fact a problem in electrostatics, and vice versa.

Now, this sort of algebraic correspondence between two theories, this illustration of one by the other, is an infinitely valuable thing: not only does it bring a notable intellectual economy since it permits one to transfer immediately to one of the theories all the algebraic apparatus constructed for the other, but it also constitutes a method of discovery. It may happen, in fact, that in one of these two domains which the same algebraic scheme covers, experimental intuition quite naturally poses a problem and suggests a solution for it, while in the other domain the physicist might not be so easily led to formulating this question or to giving it this response.

These diverse ways of appealing to the analogy between two groups of physical laws or between two distinct theories consist in bringing together two abstract systems; either one of them already known serves to help us guess the form of the other not yet known, or both being formulated, they clarify each other.

Pierre Duhem
The Aim and Structure of Physical Theory

1861 – 1916

Analogy, theory, and hypothesis

The role of analogy in scientific discovery may well have become a commonplace of epistemological reflection; but, with the aid of a logical analysis of the structure of theories conceived as the association of a lexicon and a syntax, Norman Campbell is able to show that analogy not only gives provisional assistance in the formulation of hypotheses, but is the mainspring of the explanatory power of a system of propositions functioning as a theory.* Contrary to the positivist representation of theory or, which amounts to the same thing, the "operationist" definition of the meaning of propositions, Campbell argues that the theoretical "meaning" of a system of propositions cannot be reduced to the meaning of another, logically equivalent, system of propositions.

33. *N. R. Campbell* (born 1871)
died 1949

There is nothing new in the suggestion that analogy with laws plays an important part in the development of theories. No systematic writer on the principles of science is in the least inclined to overlook the intimate connection between analogy and theories or hypotheses. Nevertheless it seems to me that most of them have seriously misunderstood the position. They speak of analogies as "aids" to the formations of hypotheses (by which they usually mean what I have termed theories) and to the general progress of science. But in the view which is urged here analogies are not "aids" to the establishment of theories; they are an utterly essential part of theories, without which theories would be completely valueless and unworthy of the name. It is often suggested that the analogy leads to the formulation of the theory, but that once the theory is formulated the analogy has served its purpose and may be removed and forgotten. Such a suggestion is absolutely false and perniciously misleading. If physical science were a purely logical science, if its object were to establish a set of propositions all true and all logically connected but characterised by no other feature, then possibly this view might be correct. Once the theory was established and shown to lead by purely logical deduction to the laws to be explained, then certainly the analogy might be abandoned as having no further significance. But, if this were true, there would never have been any need for the analogy to be introduced. Any fool can invent a logically satisfactory theory to explain any law. There is as a matter of fact no satisfactory physical theory which explains the variation of the resistance of a metal with the temperature. It took me about a quarter of an hour to elaborate the theory given [above]**; and yet it is, I maintain, formally as satisfactory as any theory

* It should be added that, even as a tool for inventing hypotheses, recourse to analogy is only fruitful if it is based on the effort to generalize or transpose already established theories. As M. Cohen and E. Nagel point out, "the unanalysed feeling of vague resemblance" with which, psychologically, the scientific process begins, leads to "an explicit analogy in structure or function" only when, after careful inquiry, the hypothesis is found to have "certain *structural analogies* to other, well-established theories" (M. Cohen and E. Nagel, *An Introduction to Logic and Scientific Method*, London; Routledge & Kegan Paul, 1964, pp. 221–222).

** In the previous pages, the author has tried his hand at formalizing a body of definitions and propositions giving a formal account of a set of experimentally established laws.

in physics. If nothing but this were required we should never lack theories to explain our laws; a schoolboy in a day's work could solve the problems at which generations have laboured in vain by the most trivial process of trial and error. What is wrong with the theory [above], what makes it absurd and unworthy of a single moment's consideration, is that it does not display any analogy; it is just because an analogy has (not) been used in its development that it is so completely valueless.

[...] It is never difficult to find a theory which will explain the laws logically; what is difficult is to find one which will explain them logically and at the same time display the requisite analogy. [...] To regard analogy as an aid to the invention of theories is as absurd as to regard melody as an aid to the composition of sonatas. If the satisfaction of the laws of harmony and the formal principles of development were all that were required of music, we could all be great composers; it is the absence of the melodic sense which prevents us all attaining musical eminence by the simple process of purchasing a text-book.

The reason why the perverse view that analogies are merely an incidental help to the discovery of theories has ever gained credence lies, I believe, in a false opinion as to the nature of theories. I said just now that it was a commonplace that analogies were important in the framing of hypotheses, and that the name "hypotheses" was usually given in this connection to the propositions (or sets of propositions) which are here termed theories. This statement is perfectly true, but it is not generally recognised by such writers that the "hypotheses" of which they speak are a distinct class of propositions, and especially that they are wholly different from the class of laws; there is a tendency to regard an "hypothesis" merely as a law of which full proof is not yet forthcoming.

If this view were correct, it might be true that the analogy was a mere auxiliary to the discovery of laws and of little further use when the law was discovered. For once the law had been proposed the method of ascertaining whether or no it were true would depend in no way on the analogy; if the "hypothesis" were a law, its truth would be tested like that of any other law by examining whether the observations asserted to be connected by the relation of uniformity were or were not so connected. According as the test succeeded or failed the law would be judged true or false; the analogy would have nothing to do with the matter. If the test succeeded, the law would remain true, even if it subsequently appeared that the analogy which suggested it was false; and if the test failed, it would remain untrue, however complete and satisfactory the analogy appeared to be.

A theory is not a law. But a theory is not a law; it cannot be proved, as a law can, by direct experiment; and the method by which it was suggested is not unimportant. For a theory may often be accepted without the performance of any additional experiments at all; so far as it is based on experiments, those experiments are often made and known before the theory is suggested. Boyle's

Law and Gay-Lussac's Law were known before the dynamical theory of gases
was framed; and the theory was accepted, or partially accepted, before any
other experimental laws which can be deduced from it were known. The
theory was an addition to scientific knowledge which followed on no increase
of experimental knowledge and on the establishment of no new laws; it cannot
therefore have required for its proof new experimental knowledge. The
reasons why it was accepted as providing something valuable which was not
contained in Boyle's and Gay-Lussac's Laws were not experimental. The
reason for which it was accepted was based directly on the analogy by which it
was suggested; with a failure of the analogy, all reason for accepting it would
have disappeared.

The conclusion that a theory is not a law is most obvious when it is such that
there are hypothetical ideas contained in it which are not completely
determined by experiment, such ideas for example as the m, n, x, y, z in the
dynamical theory of gases in its simple form. For in this case the theory states
something, namely propositions about these ideas separately, which cannot be
either proved or disproved by experiment; it states something, that is, which
cannot possibly be a law, for all laws, though they may not always be capable
of being proved by experiment, are always capable of being disproved by it. It
may be suggested that it is only because the theory which has been taken as an
example is of this type that it has been possible to maintain that it is not a law.
In the other extreme, when all the hypothetical ideas are directly stated by the
dictionary to "be" measurable concepts, the conclusion is much less obvious;
for then a statement can be made about each of the hypothetical ideas which, if
it is not actually a law, can be proved and disproved by experiment. [...]

The case which demands further consideration immediately is that in which
the dictionary relates functions of some, but not all, of the hypothetical ideas
to measurable concepts, and yet these functions are sufficiently numerous to
determine all the hypothetical ideas. In this case it is true that propositions can
be stated about each of the hypothetical ideas which can be proved or disproved by experiment. Thus, in our example, if one litre of gas has a volume
mass of 0·09 gm. when the pressure is a million dynes per cm.^{2} then, in virtue
of this experimental knowledge, it can be stated that v is $1·8 \times 10^5$ cm./sec. A
definite statement can be made about the hypothetical idea v on purely
experimental grounds. If the dictionary mentioned sufficient functions of the
other ideas, similar definite experimental statements might be made about
them. If the theory can thus be reduced to a series of definite statements on
experimental grounds, ought it not to be regarded as a law, or at least as a
proposition as definitely experimental as a law?

I maintain not. A proposition or set of propositions is not the same thing as
another set to which they are logically equivalent and which are implied by
them. They may differ in meaning. By the meaning of a proposition I mean
(the repetition of the word is useful) the ideas which are called to mind when it

is asserted. A theory may be logically equivalent to a set of experimental statements, but it means something perfectly different; and it is its meaning ← ! which is important rather than its logical equivalence. If logical equivalence were all that mattered, the absurd theory [given above] would be as important as any other; it is absurd because it means nothing, evokes no ideas, apart from the laws which it explains. A theory is valuable, and is a theory in any sense important for science, only if it evokes ideas which are not contained in the laws which it explains. The evocation of these ideas is even more valuable than the logical equivalence to the laws. Theories are often accepted and valued greatly, by part of the scientific world at least, even if it is known that they are not quite true and are not strictly equivalent to any experimental laws, simply because the ideas which they bring to mind are intrinsically valuable. It is because men differ about intrinsic values that it has been necessary to insert the proviso, "by part of the scientific world at least"; for ideas which may be intrinsically valuable to some people may not be so to others. It is here that theories differ fundamentally from laws. Laws mean nothing but what they assert. They assert that certain judgements of the external world are related by uniformity, and they mean nothing more; if it is shown that there may be a case in which these judgements are not so related, then what the law asserts is false, and, since nothing remains of the law but this false assertion, the law has no further value. We can get agreement concerning this relation and we can therefore get agreement as to the value of laws.

Norman R. Campbell
Foundations of Science

theories explain laws!

Part Three
Applied rationalism

3.1 The implication of operations and the hierarchy of epistemological acts

Theory and experimentation

[handwritten: My dissertation simulation experiments]

Because the meaning of a scientific act refers back to theory, and even to the whole history of theory, experimentations presented in isolation, without reference to the theory that made them possible or the theories they disprove, are epistemologically meaningless. *[handwritten: – FP]* *Citing the experiment in which "an isolated muscle, placed in a jar of water, contracts when excited by electricity, with no change in the level of the liquid", Canguilhem observes: "It is an epistemological fact that an experimental fact taught in this way has no biological significance."* One could go further: if the need for theoretical reorganization is suggested by the disconfirmations which the facts bring to the existing theories, or by the multitude of empirical data to be integrated, theories themselves do not flow directly from these facts but from previous theories, by reference to which they are constituted.* *[handwritten: – E-state]* *Thus only the history of theory can make it possible to fully understand both the prevailing theories and the empirical facts that they generate and organize.* *[handwritten: FP]*

34. G. Canguilhem

The nature of cell theory is such that it might well lead the philosophical mind to hesitate as to the character of biological science. Is it rational or experimental? Light waves are seen by the eyes of reason as waves, but it would seem that it is the eyes as sense organs that identify the cells of a cross-section of a plant. Cell theory would then be a collection of records of observation. The eye armed with the microscope sees microscopic life composed of cells, as the naked eye sees the macroscopic life which composes the biosphere. And yet the microscope is rather the extension of intelligence than the extension of *[handwritten: – Δ meaning]* sight. Moreover, cell theory is not the assertion that all beings are composed of cells, but first that the cell is the *only* component of *all* living beings, and then that every cell comes from a pre-existent cell. Now, it is not the microscope *[handwritten: ←]* that entitles us to say this. The microscope is at most one of the means of verifying it when one says it. But where did we get the idea of saying it before *[handwritten: !!]* verifying it? [...]

So long as biologists have been interested in the morphological constitution

---

* G. Canguilhem, *La connaissance de la vie*, op. cit., p. 18. Pierre Duhem gave the name "fictitious experiments" to the experiments the physicist is obliged to present without situating them in relation to theory, by a pedagogic device designed to justify propositions which these experiments cannot in themselves prove. See P. Duhem, *The Aim and Structure of Physical Theory*, op. cit., p. 201.

of living bodies, the human mind has oscillated between one or other of the two following representations: either a fundamental, continuous plastic substance, or a composition of parts, organized atoms, or grains of life. Here, as in optics, the two intellectual demands of continuity and discontinuity oppose each other.

In biology, the term "protoplasm" designates a constituent of the cell considered as an atomic element of composition of the organism, but the etymological meaning of the term sends us back to the conception of the initial formative liquid. The botanist Hugo von Mohl, one of the first authors who observed with precision the birth of cells by division of pre-existing cells, proposed the term "protoplasm" in 1843 to refer to the physiological function of a fluid preceding the first solid productions wherever cells are to be born. This is what Dujardin termed in 1835 "sarcoda", by which he meant a living jelly capable of organizing itself subsequently. Even for Schwann, who is regarded as the founder of cell theory, the two theoretical images interfere. According to Schwann, there is a substance without structure, cytoblasteme, in which nuclei are born, around which cells form. Schwann says that cells form in tissues where the nutritive fluid penetrates the tissues. This phenomenon of theoretical ambivalence in the very writers who did most to advance the cellular theory leads Klein to make the following observation, which is of great significance for our study: "So we find a small number of fundamental ideas returning insistently in authors who are working on the most varied objects and who start from very different standpoints. These authors certainly did not take the ideas from each other; these fundamental hypotheses seem to represent constant modes of thought which are a part of explanation in the sciences."[1] If we transpose this epistemological observation to the level of the philosophy of knowledge, we have to say, contrary to the empiricist commonplace, often uncritically adopted by scientists when they rise to the philosophy of their experimental knowledge, that *theories never proceed from facts*. Theories only proceed from earlier, often very ancient, theories. Facts are only the path, and rarely a straight one, along which theories proceed one from another. This filiation of theories from theories alone was brought out very well by Comte when he said that since a fact of observation presupposes an idea which orients one's attention, it is logically inevitable that false theories should precede true theories. But I have already indicated in what way Comte's conception seems to be untenable—in its identification of chronological anteriority with logical inferiority, which leads him, under the influence of an empiricism albeit tempered by mathematical deduction, to consecrate the theoretical value, which he sees as now definitive, of that logical monstrosity, the "general fact".

[1] M. Klein, *Histoire des origines de la théorie cellulaire*, Paris: Hermann, 1936.

To sum up, we must seek the real origins of cell theory elsewhere than in the discovery of certain microscopic structures.

Georges Canguilhem
La connaissance de la vie

It has to be acknowledged today that, as Brunschvicg put it, "the modality of physical judgements seems to us to be in no way different from the modality of mathematical judgements".[1] Empiricism could only present itself as the philosophy of experimental science in opposition to the claim of rationalism to present itself as the philosophy of mathematical science. The physicist's experiment could claim equivalence with sensory intuition only at a time when the reasoning of the mathematician claimed to depend in a definitive way on an intellectual intuition.

Contemporary epistemology does not recognize inductive or deductive sciences. It does not acknowledge the distinction, based on extrinsic characteristics, between *hypothetical* scientific judgements and *categorical* scientific judgements. It only recognizes *hypothetico-deductive* sciences. In this sense, there is no essential difference between geometry—a natural science (Comte, Einstein)—and mathematical physics. Nor is there for it a break between *reason* and *experiment*: one needs reason to conduct an experiment and an experiment to provide a reason. Reason appears not as a decalogue of principles but as a norm of systematization, capable of rousing thought from its dogmatic sleep.

So it will be admitted:

Against empiricism: that there is, strictly speaking, no inductive method. That which is induction, i.e. the invention of hypotheses in experimental science, is the clearest sign of the inadequacy of method to explain the progress of knowledge.

Against positivism: that there is no difference in certainty relative to laws and explanatory theories. There is no fact that is not informed by theory, no law that is not a momentarily stabilized hypothesis, so that the search for relations of structure is as legitimate as the search for relations of succession or similitude.

We cannot consider the hypothesis as an inadequacy of knowledge; it is not a second-best to which intelligence entrusts itself in the absence of categorical

---

[1] *Expérience humaine et causalité physique*, p. 606.

principles. Hypothesis is the anticipation of a relationship capable both of defining the concept implied in the perception of the phenomenon and of explaining it. (Example: Torricelli's hypothesis proposes, for the phenomenon observed, the concept of *pressure* and the explanation by the *equilibrium of fluids*.) If scientists make hypotheses, they do so in order to find, through them, the facts that will enable them to check them. *A hypothesis is a value judgement on reality.*[2] But what are the *logical* conditions for checking a hypothesis?

A fact can enter into a relation of agreement or disagreement with an *idea* only on one condition, that there is logical homogeneity between the fact and the idea. This means that if the idea is judgement—judgement to be judged—, then the fact must also be judgement—provisionally assured judgement. The idea—a hypothesis or law—is a universal judgement, the fact a particular judgement. A fact can therefore confirm or disconfirm a judgement only if the two judgements link the same concepts. *In experimental practice, the whole difficulty is to establish that the relationship is strictly the same, that the concepts have the same scope.* In order for a fact to contradict a hypothesis, the same method has to have determined the elements of the particular (the fact) and the universal (the hypothesis). The concepts that are interrelated have to proceed from the same techniques of detection and analysis. In biology, any action of a chemical substance on a tissue can only be correctly determined in terms of the dose. It is rarely possible, in biology, to extend to a whole species a conclusion relating to a particular variety of the species. At the same dose, caffeine has an effect on the striped muscle of the frog; but the mode of action is different in the green frog and the red frog.

Consequently, far from a perceived or observed fact being an argument for or against a hypothesis, simply because it is perceived or observed, it must first be criticized and reconstructed so that its conceptual translation makes it logically comparable to the hypothesis in question. A fact proves nothing so long as the concepts which state it have not been methodically criticized, rectified, and reformed. Only reformed facts provide information.

We thereby remove the objection of pragmatism which might arise from the fact of defining the hypothesis as a value judgement. What makes the value (the reality value) of a hypothesis is not the mere fact of concordance with the facts. It has to be possible to establish that the agreement or disagreement between a supposition and an experimental observation that is sought on the basis of the supposition taken as a principle is not due to coincidence, even repeated coincidence, but that one has indeed been led to the observed fact by the methods that the hypothesis implies.

So it is clear that it is not always misoneism or pride that makes a theoretician refuse to admit the validity of a fact as proof or disproof. Michelson

---

[2] "The great question is not whether an idea is true or false, not even whether it has a clearly statable meaning, but rather whether the idea will be the source of fertile work" (M. Planck, *Wege zur physikalischen Erkenntnis*, Leipzig: Hirzel, 1934, p. 280).

[handwritten margin note, top: "No ether detected"]

died firmly <u>believing</u> that his experiment was not conclusive and that <u>one had to be able to demonstrate the movement of the earth</u> by the anisotropic propagation of light relative to a terrestrial observer. <u>The same fact led Einstein, in 1905,</u> to revise the principles of classical <u>mechanics</u>. Faced with a contradiction between a fact and a theory, one may choose to doubt either the fact or the theory. This choice depends on the longevity of the theory and the number of facts that it has "crystallized" by systematizing them, or alternatively on its youth and its hesitations; it also depends on the intellectual audacity of the scientists. In any case, there is no knowledge that is not *polemical*; there is no brute fact so brutal that it forbids all suspicion concerning it. Let us confirm this by examining the methods of verification in more detail.

[handwritten margin note, right: "FP"]

<u>When a hypothesis explains and serves to predict a fact or a group of facts, it is not certain that it is the only true one that can do so.</u> When two hypotheses are possible, the only way to decide between them would be to predict, outside of all the facts that each can claim to explain interchangeably, a fact which only one of them would render intelligible. Such an experiment is called *crucial* (Bacon's *experimentum crucis*), for example Périer's experiment at Puy-de-Dôme, instigated by Pascal (Nature abhorring a vacuum or atmospheric pressure?). <u>Crucial experiments are no longer taken seriously.</u> Pierre Duhem showed in *The Aim and Structure of Physical Theory* that, strictly speaking if not in fact, <u>the possible hypotheses are always more numerous than the two alternatives.</u> For example, Foucault set up hypotheses which he supposed made it possible to decide between the emission hypothesis and the wave hypothesis concerning the nature of the luminous phenomenon (the propagation of light in air and water). <u>But Duhem shows that a third hypothesis, that of electromagnetism, was strictly present at the very moment when it was thought possible to pose the question in either/or terms.</u> In short, the exclusion of all hypotheses but one—an exclusion that would give a fully satisfactory proof—is an effectively unattainable ideal. As E. A. Poe says: "To show that certain data being given, a certain existing result might, or even *must*, have ensued, will fail to prove that this result *did* ensue *from the data*, until such time as it shall also be shown that there are, *and can be*, no other data from which the result in question might equally have ensued."[3] Even assuming that only two theories are in competition, the principles, within each theory, are multiple. One would have to be able to calculate separately the consequences that depend on each of these individual principles. But it is their totality that will be confirmed or disconfirmed by experiment.

[handwritten margin note, right: "FP?"]

While agreeing that a confirmation is never categorical and definitive, many logicians think that negation is decisive, that what is positive in an experiment is the negation of the theory tested in it. Jean <u>Nicod writes</u>: "<u>Confirmation provides only a probability, whereas disconfirmation creates a certainty.</u> Con-

[3] E. A. Poe, *Eureka*, in *The Centenary Poe*, London: Bodley Head, 1949, p. 382.

[handwritten margin notes, right side (vertical): "The decision on the disturbing of the quote)", "What is the 'result'?"]

[handwritten margin note, bottom: "due to error or chance?"]

firmation is only favourable, disconfirmation is fatal.'[4] Nicod seems to forget that it is impossible to give a fact a scientific value independent of the stage of scientific culture and the state of the techniques for detection and measurement. Newton had to confirm his theory with calculations which involved the length of the radius of the earth, necessarily inferred from measurement of the meridian. This measurement was crudely approximate at the time that the experiment—for that is what it was—contradicted the theory. Newton abandoned his theory until the day he learned the results of a new measurement of the meridian by Abbé Picard. The theory was then verified and Newton decided to publish it.

Although the negative experiment cannot be privileged with respect to the positive experiment, it must all the same be recognized that thought is more assured of the false than of the true. The true is the position that one thinks one can always hold; but enough errors of today are truths of yesterday to make us circumspect. By contrast, in the recognition of an error, there is the essential part of what we call truth, for accepted and recognized negation is justified by a more comprehensive affirmation; judgement abandons nothing that it does not justify itself in so doing. If the Puy-de-Dôme experiment made the abhorrence of a vacuum definitively an error, that was because in Torricelli's hypothesis the hitherto common unawareness of the effects of atmospheric pressure was both explained and excused.

We thus return to the definition proposed: the hypothesis is a value judgement on reality. Its value lies in the fact that it makes it possible to predict and construct new, often seemingly paradoxical facts, which the intelligence integrates with acquired knowledge the meaning of which is renewed in a coherent system. The realizations added to reality confirm natural causality by pragmatic efficacy, but an efficacy informed by intelligence. Pragmatism is right to demand that valid ideas should be creative ideas, but not to forget that authentic successes are calculable, if not always previously calculated, successes.

We should conclude that there is strictly speaking no experimental method, if this is taken to mean an investigative procedure distinct from the deductive method. Everything that is method is deduction, but no deduction and no method is sufficient to constitute a science. In this sense the relation to experiment is essential to the progress of knowledge, and this relationship, which is truly one of invention, cannot be codified in the rules of a method. The term "experimental" is ambiguous. Science is experimental insofar as it relates to experience, but not as a problem of which it wants to be the solution; it is truly science only because it takes the risk of being a solution, i.e. an intelligible system. The solution of empirical problems can only be rational; problems which call for rational solutions cannot be raised by Reason.

Georges Canguilhem
Leçons sur la méthode

[4] *Le problème logique de l'induction*, p. 24.

The favoured objects of empiricism

The overtly polemical nature of C. Wright Mills' analyses of the scientific abdications of American empiricist sociology too often prevents their readers from taking seriously the epistemological problem that they raise: there is a functional linkage between the research techniques of bureaucratic sociology and the problematics that it constructs—or avoids. Those whom Mills elsewhere calls "high-statisticians"* unconsciously produce "made to measure" facts and tend to choose to study those objects that best lend themselves to the application of the undiscussed techniques of routine surveys. Thus the sociology of diffusion and communication tends to be reduced to studies of public opinion, political sociology to analysis of electoral behaviour and the problem of social classes to study of the stratification of the inhabitants of small towns. At the end of this blind redefinition of the objects of science by techniques, "truth and falsehood are ground so fine that they become indistinguishable".** Unaware that it is a construction and refusing to question the procedures through which it constructs its facts, the canonical survey thereby denies itself the possibility of inventing other construction procedures and also of controlling the constructions it performs. The door is closed on, among other things, the historical comparison which alone could show whether the chosen field of study really makes it possible to apprehend the object that the sociologist claims to be dealing with.***

35. C. Wright Mills

Like grand theory, abstracted empiricism seizes upon one juncture in the process of work and allows it to dominate the mind. [...] The methodological inhibition stands parallel to the fetishism of the Concept.

I am not of course attempting to summarize the results of all the work of abstracted empiricists, but only to make clear the general character of their style of work and some of its assumptions. Accredited studies in this style now tend regularly to fall into a more or less standard pattern. In practice the new school usually takes as the basic source of its "data" the more or less set interview with a series of individuals selected by a sampling procedure. Their answers are classified and, for convenience, punched on Hollerith cards which are then used to make statistical runs by means of which relations are sought. Undoubtedly this fact, and the consequent ease with which the procedure is learned by any fairly intelligent person, accounts for much of its appeal. The results are normally put in the form of statistical assertions: on the simplest level, these specific results are assertions of proportion; on more complicated levels, the answers to various questions are combined in often elaborate cross-classifications, which are then, in various ways, collapsed to form scales. There are several complicated ways of manipulating such data, but these need

---

*   C. W. Mills, "I.B.M. plus Reality plus Humanism = Sociology", in *Power, Politics and People*, New York: Oxford University Press, 1963, p. 569.

** *Ibid.*

*** See for example S. Thernstrom, "Yankee City Revisited: the Perils of Historical Naïveté", *American Sociological Review*, vol. 30, no. 2, pp. 234–242, 1965.

not concern us here, for regardless of the degree of complication, they are still manipulations of the sort of material indicated.

Apart from advertising and media research, perhaps "public opinion" is the subject-matter of most work in this style, although no idea which re-states the problems of public opinion and communications as a field of intelligible study has been associated with it. The framework of such studies has been the simple classification of questions: who says what to whom in which media and with what results? The going definitions of the key terms are as follows:

> ... By "public" I mean to refer to the magnitude involved—that is, to non-private, non-individualized feelings and responses of large numbers of people. This charac- teristic of public opinion necessitates the use of sample surveys. By "opinion" I mean to include not only the usual sense of opinion on topical, ephemeral, and typically political issues but also attitudes, sentiments, values, information, and related actions. To get at them properly necessitates the use not only of questionnaires and interviews but also of projective and scaling devices.[1]

In these assertions, there is a pronounced tendency to confuse whatever is to be studied with the set of methods suggested for its study. What is probably meant runs something like this: The word public, as I am going to use it, refers to any sizable aggregate and hence may be statistically sampled; since opinions are held by people, to find them you have to talk with people. Sometimes, however, they will not or cannot tell you; then you may try to use "projective and scaling devices".

Studies of public opinion have mostly been done within the one national social structure of the United States and of course concern only the last decade or so. Perhaps that is why they do not refine the meaning of "public opinion", or reformulate the major problems of this area. They cannot properly do so, even in a preliminary way, within the historical and structural confinement selected for them.

The problem of "the public" in Western societies arises out of the trans- formation of the traditional and conventional consensus of medieval society; it reaches its present-day climax in the idea of a mass society. What were called "publics" in the eighteenth and nineteenth centuries are being transformed into a society of "masses". Moreover, the structural relevance of publics is declining, as men at large become "mass men", each trapped in quite power- less milieux. That, or something like it, may suggest the framework that is required for the selection and the design of studies of publics, public opinion, and mass communications. There is also required a full statement of the historical phases of democratic societies, and in particular, of what has been called "democratic totalitarianism" or "totalitarian democracy". In short, in this area the problems of social science cannot be stated within the scope and terms of abstracted empiricism as now practiced.

[1] Bernard Berelson, "The Study of Public Opinion", *The State of the Social Sciences*, edited by Leonard D. White, Chicago, Illinois: University of Chicago Press, 1956, p. 299.

Many problems with which its practitioners do try to deal—effects of the mass media, for example—cannot be adequately stated without some structural setting. Can one hope to understand the effects of these media—much less their combined meaning for the development of a mass society—if one studies, with whatever precision, only a population that has been "saturated" by these media for almost a generation? The attempt to sort out individuals "less exposed" from those "more exposed" to one or another medium may well be of great concern to advertising interests, but it is not an adequate basis for the development of a theory of the social meaning of the mass media.

In this school's study of political life, "voting behavior" has been the chief subject matter, chosen, I suppose, because it seems so readily amenable to statistical investigation. The thinness of the results is matched only by the elaboration of the methods and the care employed. It must be interesting to political scientists to examine a full-scale study of voting which contains no reference to the party machinery for "getting out the vote", or indeed to any political institutions. Yet that is what happens in *The People's Choice*, a duly accredited and celebrated study of the 1940 election in Erie County, Ohio. From this book we learn that rich, rural, and Protestant persons tend to vote Republican; people of opposite type incline toward the Democrats; and so on. But we learn little about the dynamics of American politics. *a bad metaphor?*

The idea of legitimation is one of the central conceptions of political science, particularly as the problems of this discipline bear on questions of opinion and ideology. The research on "political opinion" is all the more curious in view of the suspicion that American electoral politics is a sort of politics without opinion—if one takes the word "opinion" seriously; a sort of voting without much political meaning of any psychological depth—if one takes the phrase "political meaning" seriously. But no such questions—and I intend these remarks only as questions—can be raised about such "political researches" as these. How could they be? They require an historical knowledge and a style of psychological reflection which is not duly accredited by abstracted empiricists, or in truth, available to most of its practitioners. [...]

In so far as studies of stratification have been done in the new style, no new conceptions have arisen. In fact, the key conceptions available from other styles of work have not been "translated"; usually, quite spongy "indices" of "socio-economic status" have served. The very difficult problems of "class consciousness" and of "false consciousness"; of conceptions of status, as against class; and Weber's statistically challenging idea of "social class", have not been advanced by workers in this style. Moreover, and in many ways most grievously, the choice of smaller cities as "the sample area" for studies persists mightily, despite the quite obvious fact that one cannot add up any aggregate of such studies to an adequate view of the national structure of class, status, and power. [...]

In this short attempt to characterize studies in the abstracted empirical style

task-external status?

I have not merely been saying: "These people have not studied the substantive problems in which I am interested," or merely: "They have not studied what most social scientists consider important problems." What I have been saying is: They have studied problems of abstracted empiricism; but only within the curiously self-imposed limitations of their arbitrary epistemology have they stated their questions and answers. And I have not—I think—used phrases without due care: they are possessed by the methodological inhibition. All of which means, in terms of the results, that in these studies the details are piled up with insufficient attention to form; indeed, often there is no form except that provided by typesetters and bookbinders. The details, no matter how numerous, do not convince us of anything worth having convictions about.

Charles Wright Mills
The Sociological Imagination

3.2   The system of propositions and systematic verification

Theory as a methodological challenge

Hjelmslev shows, apropos of Saussure's analysis of a genetic problem, that scientific progress presupposes methodological challenges which are justified only by the economy of thought that they allow in the construction of the facts, and which can only be validated by the facts that they make it possible to discover. Proof is supplied not by a crucial experiment, but by the coherence of the indices that the theory makes it possible to see in hitherto scattered, insignificant facts. Here, the methodological decision to treat "formulae"—which are no more than abstractions "representing" linguistic correspondences that the traditional methods failed to interrelate—as a system makes it possible to give more coherence to the description of a hypothetical "linguistic state" (état de langue), which is subsequently confirmed by the phonetic facts.

TJF & JS & me

36. L. Hjelmslev

[*The work of Saussure has made it possible to advance the analysis of genetic problems (the history and formation of languages) by establishing the application of the structural method to these questions*]. Its distinctive feature is that, on the one hand, it treats the formulæ* as a system and draws all the consequences that follow, while on the other hand it does not attribute any other kind of reality to them and thus does not consider them as prehistoric sounds with a certain pronunciation which by gradual change became the sounds of the individual Indo-European languages.

[...] Precisely because Saussure treats the formulæ as a system and, moreover, as a system independent of any concrete phonetic definitions—in short, as a pure linguistic structure—he is led in this work to apply to the Indo-European parent language, the very stronghold of the theory of linguistic change, methods destined to set a pattern in the analysis of any état de langue, methods that can be taken as models of the way in which a linguistic structure should be analyzed. Saussure takes the system in and for itself and puts the question, How do I analyze it so as to obtain the simplest and most elegant explanation? In other words, What is the smallest number of formulæ or elements that I need to account for this entire mechanism?

And at this point Saussure came to do things with the Indo-European system that nobody had been able to do before, and thus to introduce a new method, a structural method into genetic linguistics.

---

* There is said to be a constant function between elements of expression in different languages when "the same correspondence is found in the same conditions in all the words in question". Thus, there is a function between the elements of expression *m* in Gothic, Celtic, Latin, Greek, Lithuanian, Old Slav, Armenian and Old Indian. For example, one finds: Latin *māter*, Greek *māter*, Lithuanian *mótė motė*, Old Slav *mati*, Armenian *mayr*, Old Indian *mātā*. This function is indicated by a single sign, called a "formula", which is thus an abstraction designating the series of elements that, in the different languages of the same family, are linked by a constant correspondence. (Note by P. Bourdieu et al.)

Let us take an example. We have observed above that Indo-European has a vowel alternation *e : *o : ø, which appears in diphthongs as *$ei̯$: *$oi̯$: *i, *$eu̯$: *$ou̯$: *u, etc. In addition, one finds in Indo-European a different kind of alternation—or something that might look like a different kind of alternation —namely, a shift between long vowel and *A. This is seen, for example, in

OI *sthi-táḥ* 'standing'	:	*ti-ṣthā-mi* 'I stand'
Lat. *sta-tus*	:	*stā-re* 'to stand'
IE root form *stA	:	*$stā$-

or in

OI *di-táḥ* 'given'	:	*dǎ-nam* 'a gift', *dá-dā-mi* 'I give'
Lat. *da-tus*	:	*dō-num*
IE root form *dA-	:	*$dō$-

(We recall that OI i = Lat. a is IE *A)

Now Saussure realized that if the long vowel in these alternations were interpreted as a combination of short vowel with *A, the two kinds of alternations, which had before looked entirely different, would become quite the same:

$$
\begin{array}{ccccc}
 & *ei̯ & : & *oi̯ & : & *i \\
\neq & *eu̯ & : & *ou̯ & : & *u \\
\neq & *eA & : & *oA & : & *A.
\end{array}
$$

[...] This reinterpretation [...] meant a sharp break with the previous method of reconstruction because a formula like Saussure's *oA is founded, not on the element-functions between the Indo-European languages, but on an internal function within the parent language. If the evidence were limited to the element-functions between the Indo-European languages known in Saussure's time, there would be no grounds for distinguishing between the $ō$ in *dō-num* and the $ō$ in *rhḗtōr*. If the $ō$ in *dō-num*, but not the $ō$ in *rhḗtōr*, can be interpreted as *oA, it is not because of a function between different languages, but because of a function between constituents of a single linguistic state. What has happened here is that one algebraic entity has been equated with the product of two others; the operation recalls that of the chemist who analyzes water as a product of hydrogen and oxygen. This kind of operation is required in the analysis of any linguistic state if the simplest possible description is to be achieved. [...]

To understand what is essential and important in these reductions from a methodological point of view, we must realize that they constitute a kind of resolution of the Indo-European entities into algebraic or chemical products.

This does not proceed directly from comparison of the several Indo-European languages, but from further treatment of the results of such comparison, from an analysis of those results. *Later*, long after the analysis had been made, it was discovered that there is an Indo-European language that distinguishes between *$\bar{o}$ alternating with *o and *$\bar{o}$ alternating with *A, namely Hittite, where the Polish linguist Kuryłowicz was able to show that h sometimes corresponds to IE *A. Moreover, Møller was able to confirm his theory by referring to Hamito-Semitic: that Hamito-Semitic has special consonants corresponding to the different Indo-European coefficients is, in fact, a cornerstone in his demonstration of the genetic relationship between Indo-European and Hamito-Semitic. These confirmations, obtained through consideration of previously unknown element-functions between the genetically related languages, are certainly of the greatest interest, especially in showing that the internal analysis of a linguistic structure like that of the Indo-European parent language bears strong realistic implications. It might be thought that this kind of analysis would lead us astray in a world of abstractions, but quite to the contrary, it puts us on the watch for element-functions remaining to be discovered. Through analysis of the linguistic state we have truly achieved a deeper understanding of the linguistic structure. On the other hand, these confirmations from Hittite and Hamito-Semitic are still merely confirmations, and the internal analysis of the element system of the parent language could be pursued without reference to them.

Louis Hjelmslev
Language

Circular arguments

The concern for dissimilation that arises from a mistaken conception of the methods of the natural sciences leads to epistemological blindness, which may be expressed as much in claims for the specificity of an intuitionist method as in timorous, servile imitation of the natural sciences. By contrast, Edgar Wind seeks, through a methodical comparison, to establish the specific form that the epistemological problems of the natural sciences take in the social sciences. Because it is only one aspect of the interdependence of theory and the operations of research, the "methodological circle" is not a logical circle. Progress in the theory of the object leads to progress in the method, the adequate application of which requires a refinement of the theory, which alone can control the application of the method and explain why, and in what respect, the method works. Thus a movement is set up which transforms the simple document into a scientific object and which does not suffer the static separation that positivism seeks to establish between facts and the interpretation of facts.

37. E. Wind

I shall confine myself to indicating some formal points of correspondence between these two worlds — or, to be more precise, between the scientific methods which render each of them an object of human knowledge and experience.

The mere assertion that there are such correspondences may appear heretical to many.[1] German scholars have taught for decades that, apart from adherence to the most general rules of logic, the study of history and the natural sciences are to each other as pole and antipole, and that it is the first duty of any historian to forswear all sympathy with the ideals of men who would like to reduce the whole world to a mathematical formula. This revolt was no doubt an act of liberation in its time. To-day it is pointless. The very concept of nature in opposition to which Dilthey proclaimed his *Geisteswissenschaft* has long been abandoned by the scientists themselves, and the notion of a description of nature which indiscriminately subjects men and their fates like rocks and stones to its "unalterable laws" survives only as a nightmare of certain historians.

Thus it need not be symptomatic of a sinful relapse into the method of thought so generously abused as "positivistic", if in what follows some examples are chosen to illustrate how the very questions that historians like to look upon as their own are also raised in natural science. The all too sedentary inhabitants of the "Globus intellectualis" may, it is true, think it incredible that their antipodes do not stand on their heads.

I. Document and Instrument
In defiance of the rules of traditional logic, circular arguments are the normal method of producing documentary evidence.

[1] The following refers in particular to the schools of Dilthey, Windelband, and Rickert.

An historian who consults his documents in order to interpret some political event can judge the value of these documents only if he knows their place within the very same course of events about which he consults them.

In the same way, an art-historian who from a given work draws an inference concerning the development of its author turns into an art-connoisseur who examines the reasons for attributing this work to this particular master: and for this purpose he must presuppose the knowledge of that master's development which was just what he wanted to infer.

This change of focus from the object to the means of inquiry, and the concomitant inversion of object and means, is peculiar to most historical studies, and the instances given may be multiplied *ad lib*. An inquiry concerning the Baroque, which uses Bernini's theoretical utterances as a source for explaining the style of his works, turns into a study of the role of theory in the creative process of Bernini. An inquiry concerning Caesar's monarchy and the principate of Pompey, making use of Cicero's writings as its main source, becomes a study of the part played by Cicero in the conflict between the Senate and the usurpers.

Generally speaking this might be termed the dialectic of the historical document: that the information which one tries to gain with the help of the document ought to be presupposed for its adequate understanding.

The scientist is subject to the very same paradox. The physicist seeks to infer general laws of nature by instruments themselves subject to these laws. For measuring heat, a fluid like quicksilver is chosen as a standard, and it is claimed that it expands evenly with increasing warmth. Yet how can such an assertion be made without knowledge of the laws of thermodynamics? And again, how can these laws be known except by measurements in which a fluid, e.g. quicksilver, is used as a standard?

Classical mechanics employs measuring rods and clocks that are transferred from one place to another; the assumption being that this alteration of place leaves untouched their constancy as measuring instruments. This assumption, however, expresses a mechanical law (viz. that the results of measurement are independent of the state of motion) the validity of which must be tested by instruments which, in their turn, are reliable only if the law assumed is valid.

The circle thus proves in science as inescapable as in history. Every instrument and every document *participates* in the structure which it is meant to reveal.

II. *The Intrusion of the Observer*

It is curious that Dilthey should have considered this *participation* as one of the traits which distinguish the study of history from the natural sciences. In his *Einleitung in die Geisteswissenschaften* he admits that the study of "social bodies" is less precise than that of "natural bodies". "And yet", he adds, "all this is more than counterbalanced by the fact that I who experience and know myself inwardly, am part of this social body... . The individual is, on the one hand, an element in the interactions of society,... reacting to its effects in conscious will-direction and action, and is at the same time the intelligence contemplating and investigating all this" (p. 46 sq.).

That human agents, who form the substance of what Dilthey calls "the socio-historical reality", experience and know themselves "inwardly" is a bold assertion. It transforms one of the most troublesome moral precepts ("Know thyself!") into a plain and ordinary matter of fact, which is contradicted by both ancient and modern experience. Whatever objections may be made to the current psychology of the unconscious, it is undeniable that men do not know themselves by immediate intuition and that they live and express themselves on several levels. Hence, the interpretation of historical documents requires a far more complex psychology than Dilthey's doctrine of immediate experience with its direct appeal to a state of feeling. Peirce wrote in a draft of a psychology of the development of ideas: "it is the belief men *betray*, and not that which they *parade*, which has to be studied."

Once the direct appeal to inner experience is abandoned, Dilthey's remark ceases to contain anything that a physicist might not apply to himself: "I myself, who am handling apparatuses and instruments, am a part of this physical world; the individual (i.e. the physical technician and observer) is, on the one hand, an element in the interactions of nature,... and he is at the same time the intelligence calculating and investigating all this."

Let it not be objected that by this "physical travesty" the meaning of Dilthey's statement is completely destroyed. True, the profundity has disappeared, and what remains seems to be rather trivial. But what the statement now conveys is not only simple, but also true: *The investigator intrudes into the process that he is investigating.* This is what the supreme rule of methodology demands. In order to study physics, one must be physically affected; pure mind does not study physics. A body is needed—however much the mind may "interpret"—which transmits the signals that are to be interpreted. Otherwise, there would be no contact with the surrounding world that is to be investigated. Nor does pure mind study history. For that purpose, one must be historically affected; caught by the mass of past experience that intrudes into the present in the shape of "tradition": demanding, compelling, often only narrating, reporting, pointing to other past experience which has not as yet been unfolded. Again, the investigator is in the first instance a receiver of signals to which he attends and which he pursues, but on whose transmission he has only a very limited influence. The registering and digesting of these signs, the functioning of this whole "receiving apparatus", cannot be reduced to the vague formula of traditional antitheses ("body and soul", "inward and outward"). The only antithesis that does apply is that between "part" and "whole". By his intrusion into the process that is to be studied, the student himself, like every one of his tools, becomes part-object of investigation; "part-object" to be taken in a twofold sense: he is, like any other organ of investigation, but a *part* of the whole object that is being investigated. But equally it is only a *part* of himself that, thus externalized into an instrument, enters into the object-world of his studies.

Edgar Wind
"Some Points of Contact between History and Natural Science"

Proof by a system of convergent probabilities

The reasoning with which Darwin indirectly establishes, through the subtle interplay of the likely and the unlikely, that all breeds of pigeon are descended from a single species, illustrates the risks and resources of individual discursiveness, which is perhaps closer to the laborious windings of the search for a proof in sociology than are the impeccable but rarely applicable programmes of pure methodology. Darwin composes and opposes systems and sub-systems of probabilities and improbabilities in order to prove what the real question that he encounters requires him to prove, on the basis of the material that it obliges him to take into account. As Kaplan, who quotes this text,* points out, Darwin shows that the hypothesis opposed to the one he proposes depends on a number of suppositions which are improbable if taken together but which might be more readily admitted if they were offered separately. Thus, by intertwining positive and negative reasons, some of which might not count for much in themselves, he puts together a system of proofs, "a concatenation of evidence", which is "stronger than its weakest links, stronger even than its strongest link".**

38. C. Darwin

Great as are the differences between the breeds of the pigeon, I am fully convinced that the common opinion of naturalists is correct, namely, that all are descended from the rock-pigeon (Columba livia), including under this term several geographical races or sub-species, which differ from each other in the most trifling respects. As several of the reasons which have led me to this belief are in some degree applicable in other cases, I will here briefly give them. If the several breeds are not varieties, and have not proceeded from the rock-pigeon, they must have descended from at least seven or eight aboriginal stocks; for it is impossible to make the present domestic breeds by the crossing of any lesser number: how, for instance, could a pouter be produced by crossing two breeds unless one of the parent-stocks possessed the character-istic enormous crop? The supposed aboriginal stocks must all have been rock-pigeons, that is, they did not breed or willingly perch on trees. But besides C. livia, with its geographical sub-species, only two or three other species of rock-pigeons are known; and these have not any of the characters of the domestic breeds. Hence the supposed aboriginal stocks must either still exist in the countries where they were originally domesticated, and yet be unknown to ornithologists; and this, considering their size, habits, and remarkable characters, seems improbable; or they must have become extinct in the wild state. But birds breeding on precipices, and good fliers, are unlikely to be exterminated; and the common rock-pigeon, which has the same habits with the domestic breeds, has not been exterminated even on several of the smaller British islets, or on the shores of the Mediterranean. Hence the supposed extermination of so many species having similar habits with the rock-pigeon seems a very rash assumption. Moreover, the several above-named domesti-

---

* A. Kaplan, *The Conduct of Inquiry*, San Francisco: Chandler, 1964, p. 245.
** *Ibid.*

cated breeds have been transported to all parts of the world, and, therefore, some of them must have been carried back again into their native country; but not one has become wild or feral, though the dovecot-pigeon, which is the rock-pigeon in a very slightly altered state, has become feral in several places. Again, all recent experience shows that it is difficult to get wild animals to breed freely under domestication; yet on the hypothesis of the multiple origin of our pigeons, it must be assumed that at least seven or eight species were so thoroughly domesticated in ancient times by half-civilised man, as to be quite prolific under confinement.

An argument of great weight, and applicable in several other cases, is, that the above-specified breeds, though agreeing generally with the wild rock-pigeon in constitution, habits, voice, colouring, and in most parts of their structure, yet are certainly highly abnormal in other parts; we may look in vain through the whole great family of Columbidæ for a beak like that of the English carrier, or that of the short-faced tumbler, or barb; for reversed feathers like those of the Jacobin; for a crop like that of the pouter; for tail-feathers like those of the fantail. Hence it must be assumed not only that half-civilised man succeeded in thoroughly domesticating several species, but that he intentionally or by chance picked out extraordinarily abnormal species; and further, that these very species have since all become extinct or unknown. So many strange contingencies are improbable in the highest degree.

Some facts in regard to the colouring of pigeons well deserve consideration. The rock-pigeon is of a slaty-blue, with white loins; but the Indian sub-species, C. intermedia of Strickland, has this part bluish. The tail has a terminal dark bar, with the outer feathers externally edged at the base with white. The wings have two black bars. Some semi-domestic breeds, and some truly wild breeds, have, besides the two black bars, the wings chequered with black. These several marks do not occur together in any other species of the whole family. Now, in every one of the domestic breeds, taking thoroughly well-bred birds, all the above marks, even to the white edging of the outer tail-feathers, sometimes concur perfectly developed. Moreover, when birds belonging to two or more distinct breeds are crossed, none of which are blue or have any of the above-specified marks, the mongrel offspring are very apt suddenly to acquire these characters. To give one instance out of several which I have observed:—I crossed some white fantails, which breed very true, with some black barbs—and it so happens that blue varieties of barbs are so rare that I never heard of an instance in England; and the mongrels were black, brown, and mottled. I also crossed a barb with a spot, which is a white bird with a red tail and red spot on the forehead, and which notoriously breeds very true; the mongrels were dusky and mottled. I then crossed one of the mongrel barb-fantails with a mongrel barb-spot, and they produced a bird of as beautiful a blue colour, with the white loins, double black wing-bar, and barred and white-edged tail-feathers, as any wild rock-pigeon! We can under-

stand these facts, on the well-known principle of reversion to ancestral characters, if all the domestic breeds are descended from the rock-pigeon. But if we
deny this, we must make one of the two following highly improbable suppositions. Either, first, that all the several imagined aboriginal stocks were coloured and marked like the rock-pigeon, although no other existing species is
thus coloured and marked, so that in each separate breed there might be a
tendency to revert to the very same colours and markings. Or, secondly, that
each breed, even the purest, has within a dozen, or at most within a score, of
generations, been crossed by the rock-pigeon: I say within a dozen or twenty
generations, for no instance is known of crossed descendants reverting to an
ancestor of foreign blood, removed by a greater number of generations. In a
breed which has been crossed only once, the tendency to revert to any character derived from such a cross will naturally become less and less, as in each
succeeding generation there will be less of the foreign blood; but when there
has been no cross, and there is a tendency in the breed to revert to a character
which was lost during some former generation, this tendency, for all that we
can see to the contrary, may be transmitted undiminished for an indefinite
number of generations. These two distinct cases of reversion are often con-
founded together by those who have written on inheritance.

Lastly, the hybrids or mongrels from between all the breeds of the pigeon
are perfectly fertile, as I can state from my own observations, purposely made,
on the most distinct breeds. Now, hardly any cases have been ascertained with
certainty of hybrids from two quite distinct species of animals being perfectly
fertile. Some authors believe that long-continued domestication eliminates this
strong tendency to sterility in species. From the history of the dog, and of
some other domestic animals, this conclusion is probably quite correct, if
applied to species closely related to each other. But to extend it so far as to
suppose that species, aboriginally as distinct as carriers, tumblers, pouters, and
fantails now are, should yield offspring perfectly fertile *inter se*, would be rash
in the extreme.

From these several reasons, namely,—the improbability of man having
formerly made seven or eight supposed species of pigeons to breed freely
under domestication;—these supposed species being quite unknown in a wild
state, and their not having become anywhere feral;—these species presenting
certain very abnormal characters, as compared with all other Columbidæ,
though so like the rock-pigeon in most respects;—the occasional re-
appearance of the blue colour and various black marks in all the breeds, both
when kept pure and when crossed;—and lastly, the mongrel offspring being
perfectly fertile;—from these several reasons, taken together, we may safely
conclude that all our domestic breeds are descended from the rock-pigeon or
Columba livia with its geographical sub-species.

Charles Darwin
The Origin of Species

3.3   Epistemological couples

Philosophy as dialogue

Bachelard often showed that the activity of modern science is guided by a "dual certainty" [bi-certitude] that is made explicit in the more or less close dialogue between the two philosophies of rationalism and realism.* Epistemology differs from the traditional philosophy of the sciences in taking as its object this twofold philosophy which runs through all the scientist's acts, instead of questioning them from the standpoint of a philosophy of knowledge. It can then be seen that "all philosophies of scientific knowledge arrange themselves in order starting from applied rationalism and technical materialism". The philosophies that are encountered in the two "weakened" perspectives which lead to naïve idealism and naïve realism lose their power to account for the scientist's work and to lend him theoretical assistance, precisely to the extent that they move away from the "philosophical centre where reflected experience and rational invention alike are grounded, in short, the area where contemporary science is working". If it were applied, mutatis mutandis, to the social sciences, this spectrum analysis of epistemological positions would show that fictitious dialogues between distant and sometimes colluding adversaries (such as formalism and intuitionism) are more frequent than intense exchanges between theory and experiment.

39. G. Bachelard

In fact, this crisscrossing of two contrary philosophies in action in scientific thought involves more numerous philosophies and we shall have to present dialogues that are perhaps less intense, but which extend the psychology of the scientific mind. For example, the philosophy of science would be misrepresented if one did not examine the positions of *positivism* or *formalism*, both of which undoubtedly have functions in contemporary physics and chemistry. But one of the reasons which make us believe in the correctness of our central position is that all philosophies of scientific knowledge arrange themselves in order starting from *applied rationalism*. The table below hardly requires any comment when it is applied to scientific thought:

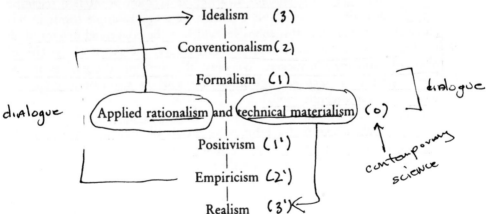

Idealism   (3)

Conventionalism (2)

Formalism   (1)

Applied rationalism and technical materialism (o)

Positivism (1')

Empiricism (2')

Realism   (3')

---

* See above, texts no. 1, p. 81 and no. 22, p. 157.

Let us simply indicate the two *weakened* thought-perspectives that lead, on the one hand, from rationalism to naive idealism and, on the other hand, from technical materialism to naive realism.

Thus, when one systematically interprets rational knowledge as the constitution of certain *forms*, as a mere toolkit of *formulae* capable of *informing* any experience, one sets up a *formalism*. This formalism may, at a stretch, receive the *results* of rational thought, but it cannot provide all the work of rational thought. Moreover, the line is not always drawn at a formalism. A philosophy of knowledge has been begun which weakens the role of experience. Some are close to seeing scientific theory as a set of *conventions*, a sequence of more or less *convenient* thoughts organized in the clear language of mathematics, which is no more than the Esperanto of reason. The convenience of conventions does not make them any less arbitrary. These formulae, these conventions, and this arbitrariness will fairly naturally be subjected eventually to an activity of the thinking subject. One thus arrives at an idealism. This idealism is not always spelt out in contemporary epistemology, but it played such a role in 19th-century philosophies of nature that it must still figure in a general examination of the philosophies of science.

We must also point out the inability of idealism to reconstitute a modern type of rationalism, an active rationalism capable of informing our knowledge of new areas of experience. In other words, the perspective that has just been described is not reversible. In fact, when the idealist establishes a philosophy of nature, he is content to set in order the *images* he has of nature, while concentrating on what is immediate in those images. He does not go beyond the limits of an elevated sensualism. He does not engage in a sustained experiment. He would be surprised to be asked to pursue the research of science in essentially instrumental experimentation. He does not think himself required to accept the *conventions* of other minds. He does not consent to the slow discipline that would *form* his mind on the lessons of objective experience. Idealism thus loses all possibility of giving an account of modern scientific thought. Scientific thought cannot find its hard and multiple forms in this atmosphere of solitude, this solipsism which is the congenital disease of all idealism. Scientific thought needs a social reality, the assent of the city of physicists and mathematicians. We must therefore place ourselves in the central position of *applied rationalism*, by working to institute a specific philosophy for scientific thought.

In the other perspective of our picture, instead of this evanescence which leads to idealism, we find a progressive inertia of thought which leads to realism, a conception of reality as a synonym for irrationality.

Indeed, in moving from the rationalism of the physical experiment, strongly bound to theory, to *positivism*, it seems that one immediately loses all the principles of *necessity*. At that point, pure positivism can scarcely justify the deductive power at work in the development of modern theories; it cannot account for the *coherence values* of contemporary physics. And yet, in comparison with pure empiricism, positivism at least appears as the guardian of the hierarchy of laws. It gives itself the right to set aside fine approximations, details, and varieties. But this hierarchy of laws does not have the capacity to organize the necessities clearly understood by rationalism. Moreover, by basing itself on judgements of utility, positivism is already close to declining into *pragmatism,* the heap of rules-of-thumb that constitutes *empiricism*. Positivism has nothing of what is required in order to decide orders of approximation, to feel the strange awareness of rationality that is given by second-order approximations, the more approximated, more debated, more coherent knowledge that we find in attentive examination of subtle experiments and which leads us to understand that there is more rationality in the complex than in the ✳ simple.

Moreover, taking a step beyond the empiricism that is engrossed in the recital of its successes, one comes upon the mass of facts and things that encumbers *realism* and gives it the illusion of richness. We shall subsequently show how contrary to scientific thought is the postulate, so readily accepted by some philosophers, that assimilates reality to a pole of irrationality. When we have brought back the philosophical activity of scientific thought towards its active centre, it will be clearly seen that active materialism has precisely the function of casting aside everything that might be called irrational in its matter, in the objects it deals with. Chemistry, guided by its rational *a prioris*, gives us *substances without accidents*, frees all matters of the irrationality of their origins. [...]

If one attempts a philosophical determination of active scientific notions, one soon sees that each of these notions has two sides, always two sides. Each ✗ precise notion is a notion that has been made precise [*précisée*]. It has been made precise in an attempt at idoneism, in Gonseth's sense of the term, an idoneism that can be taken further the more intense its dialectics are. But these dialectics are already awakened by the distant symmetries of the picture that — p. 24 we propose. Thus, a good many problems in the epistemology of the physical sciences would immediately be clarified by instituting the philosophical dialogue of formalism and rationalism. Formalism would instantly co-ordinate with considerable clarity all the mathematical points of view that inform the positive laws yielded by scientific experiment. Without having the apodictic ⎰ Estates nature of rationalism, formalism does have a logical autonomy.   ?

Between empiricism and conventionalism—philosophies which are no doubt too distended—it would again be possible to establish correspondences. Their dialogue would at least have the attraction of a twofold scepticism. They therefore have much success with modern philosophers who watch from a distance the progress of scientific thought.

As for the two extreme philosophies, idealism and realism, they have hardly any strength beyond their dogmatism. Realism is definitive and idealism is premature. Neither of them has the *actuality* that scientific thought demands. In particular, it is not clear how a scientific realism could be built up out of a vulgar realism. If science were a description of a given reality, it is not clear by what right science would *order* that description.

Our task will therefore be to show that rationalism is in no way bound up with the imperialism of the subject, that it cannot be formed in an isolated consciousness. We shall also have to prove that *technical materialism is in no way a philosophical materialism*. Technical materialism essentially corresponds to a transformed reality, a rectified reality, a reality which has precisely received the human mark par excellence, the mark of rationalism.

Thus we shall always be led back to the philosophical centre where reflected experience and rational invention alike are grounded, in short, the area where contemporary science is working.

Gaston Bachelard
Le rationalisme appliqué

Neo-positivism: sensualism coupled with formalism

It can be seen clearly in the case of the neo-positivism of the Vienna Circle that, contrary to the common representation which automatically attributes the properties of theoretical construction to every formal refinement, the most radical formalism calls for a submission to the "facts" of common sense, i.e. the sensualist theory that common sense implements when it represents facts to itself as data.

40. *G. Canguilhem*

It has often been pointed out that between empiricism and positivism there is a relation of filiation; the link between Comte and the 18th-century sensualist is d'Alembert. Positivism defines itself by the refusal to take into consideration any proposition whose content does not directly or indirectly sustain some correspondence with the facts observed. "By adding [to the term *philosophy*] the word *positive*, I announce that I consider this special discipline of philosophizing which consists in envisaging theories, in whatever realm of ideas, as having as its object the co-ordination of the facts observed."[1] It can immediately be seen how facts are here dissociated from the theory which is in a sense posterior and external to them; likewise in the schema of the positive method in which the human mind seeks to discover, "through the well-combined use of reasoning and observation", the effective laws of phenomena, i.e. the invariable relations of succession and similarity.[2] Elsewhere, Comte spells out the meaning of the word *positive* as "real, verifiable, useful".[3] The relationship between theoretical speculation and pragmatic utilization, which is already detectable in empiricism, is undeniable in positivism. It can be seen in the distinction, from the astronomical point of view, between the *universe* and the *world* (the solar system), which is alone worthy of human interest; in Comte's hostility to the use of methods or instruments making it possible either to determine the composition of the stars, or to complicate and correct simple forms of laws (such as Mariotte's law); or in his proscription of the calculation of probabilities in physics and biology. As for the general subordination of knowledge to action (knowing in order to foresee so as to be able to act), it is too well known to need emphasizing.

The same tendencies reappear in what is generally called the neo-positivism of the Vienna School, which paradoxically combines a radically sensualist theory of exploration of the real with a radically formalist (in the sense it has been given in recent work on axiomatics) theory of thought and language that is associated with two traditions as different as those symbolized by the names of Ernst Mach and Hilbert. The most authentic representatives of this school are Carnap, Schlick, and Neurath; one should also include Frank and, at a certain distance, Reichenbach, although he would deny that he belongs there.

---

[1] A. Comte, "Avertissement" to 1st edition of *Cours de philosophie positive*, 1830.
[2] *Cours de philosophie positive*, 1re leçon.
[3] *Discours sur l'ensemble du positivisme*, 1re partie.

The Vienna neo-positivists take over, with many restrictions, Wittgenstein's fundamental idea (in the *Tractatus Logico-Philosophicus*) that language is a copy of the world: the real is a set of "data" of which knowledge gives the description. Nouns correspond to objects and propositions to the effective relations between objects. Language has the same limits as the world; it cannot contain anything that is not in the world (for example, the notion of the boundary of the world is meaningless). Pursuing his argument to the limit —where Carnap refuses to follow him— Wittgenstein posits that there cannot be "propositions about propositions". The only aim of philosophy is to criticize language, to clarify propositions (in which case it has to be asked how one can work on propositions, if there can be no propositions about propositions).

So, when all due reservations have been made, the basis of science is, according to the Vienna School, propositions which bring the findings of observation to the level of language. Only propositions, and not isolated words, can have meaning. Now, *the meaning of a judgement about reality is always in relation to a method of verification*. A judgement that cannot be verified, i.e. related to an effective observation, has no meaning. For example, the concept of *simultaneity* has been given a meaning in relativity physics because Einstein has defined the conditions for a method of transmitting and receiving signals. Outside this experimental situation, the notion of simultaneity is meaningless.

According to Neurath, all the natural or cultural sciences are parts of a "unitary science" to be constructed, and this science is philosophy. This unitary science must be supplied with a universal language, which will be that of physics. Hence the term physicalism, which implies not that every scientific proposition must be reducible to physical theories which are currently admitted because currently verified, but that every proposition about the real world must be capable of being verified in the same way as the "protocol statements" or "observation propositions" (*Protokollsätze*) of physics. Every physical experiment amounts to saying that, in certain defined circumstances, a particular elementary fact (the displacement of a needle on a dial, the appearance or disappearance of a shadow or luminous band on a screen) has been noted by a particular experimenter. Every valid physical theory must lead to such observations; the faithful record of the observation is capable of transmitting to any person the authentic content and results of the observation; and the concordance of the observation statements derived from the theory (i.e. of the observations that one is *bound* to make) with the observation-propositions directly uttered by real observers guarantees the correctness of the theory.

Viennese neo-positivism will be examined here only as a *physicalism*.

According to Neurath and Carnap, it is necessary to clarify the meaning of the word *data* when referring to the relationship which gives its validity significance to any statement about reality. They think that in every observation-proposition one must say something relating to physical objects, for example, that one observes on a screen, at a particular point, a dark patch or a light circle. The consequence of this assertion is that the distinction maintained by all ontological philosophies between the "real" world and the "apparent" world is devoid of meaning. The real and the apparent differ from each other as "two experimental results obtained in different circumstances" (Frank). For example, the distinction between the apparent Na crystal and the real crystal (i.e. its molecular structure) amounts to the distinction between two ways of lighting it: in sunlight or lamplight the body is seen by the human eye as a compact body, but under a beam of Röntgen rays, a granular structure is seen on the photographic plate. It follows that the role of a physical theory is only to co-ordinate experimental data in accordance with a schema so as to orientate an expectation of certain observations to come. Thus, if one posits the identity of light and electricity, one cannot avoid citing, says Frank, at least one phenomenon observable as a consequence of a "real" identity of light and electricity. This *orientation of expectation* is the only real meaning that can be given to the principle of causality: "If we try to find out what is meant when, in everyday life, we speak of the principle of causality, we find that it is a particular way of associating the data of our experience with a view to adapting to the world that surrounds us and protecting ourselves against the anxiety produced by the most immediate future." It can be seen here how neo-positivism effects a "return to Hume", through Comte.

There is, however, a notable difference between sensualist empiricism and the positivism of the 19th or 20th centuries, namely that for the sensualist empiricists the chaos of "impressions" eventually finds an order within itself, through the links of association. Positivism, on the other hand, insists on the need to *bring order*, through a mathematical-type theory according to Comte, or through a formal schema according to the Viennese. But this is the *juxtaposition* of two demands (naturalism and rationalism), certainly not their synthesis. Both physical theory and the formal schema remain *posterior* and *external* to the data. So positivism acknowledges the initial adequacy of the immediate "given" to constitute matter of knowledge that can be informed subsequently by a demand for co-ordination. Gonseth has understood this very clearly; he says of the doctrine of the Vienna Circle that "it is the most summary, the least nuanced, realism".[4] The most summary, but also the most vulgar—that of the common sense which postulates, in the form of an absolute belief, the identity of sensation and knowledge.

It is this postulate or this belief that have to be judged. And I shall do so first by summarizing the thoughts, on this point, of one of the greatest contemporary physicists, Max Planck.

If it is accepted that sense perceptions are both a primitive datum and the only immediate reality, then it is incorrect to speak of sense illusions. Fur-

[4] B. Gonseth, *Qu'est-ce que la logique?*, p. 34.

thermore, if one cannot move beyond personal impression, then it is impossible to derive objective knowledge from it; there is no reason to sift or choose
between personal impressions: all have the same right. Positivism, taken to the
extreme, "rejects the existence or even the very possibility of a physics
independent of the individuality of the scientist".[5] Science is possible only if it
is posited that there is a real world, but that we cannot have immediate
knowledge of it. Scientific work is therefore an effort towards an inaccessible
goal: "the goal is metaphysical in nature, it is inaccessible".[6]

Positivism is right to see *measurements* as the basis of science, but it
seriously fails to understand that measurement is a phenomenon to which the
scientist, the instrument, and even the theory are internal. One notes the
similarity between Planck's criticisms and those which Meyerson makes of
positivism: the concept of reality, the concept of a "thing", is, says Meyerson,
indispensable to scientific research. The basic problem is in the end this: what
is the theoretical value of sense data?

First of all, they are only *data*. Then, sensualist or positivist epistemology
recognizes that if science is built up from sense data, it is built up by *moving
away from them*. For all his mathematicism, Comte remains faithful to empiricist realism: "Despite all arbitrary suppositions, luminous phenomena will
always remain a category *sui generis* necessarily irreducible to any other: a
light will be eternally heterogeneous to a movement or a sound. Even if there
were no other grounds, physiological considerations themselves would invinc-
ibly resist such a confusion of ideas, through the unalterable characteristics
which profoundly distinguish the sense of sight from the sense of hearing, or
the sense of touch or pressure."[7]

But the whole evolution of knowledge contradicts this assertion. Knowledge unifies what our sense perception specifies and distinguishes; it is the
effort to constitute a universe whose reality comes precisely from the fact that
it discredits the claims of sense perception to present itself as knowledge. It is
true that the explanatory theory maintains contact, the closest contact, with
experience, but only insofar as experience is *the problem to be unravelled* and
not the beginning of a solution. The relationship of theory to experience
guarantees that theory does not move away from the problem which gave rise
to it, but it in no way implies that the solution will be given in the form of the
initial experience.

Georges Canguilhem
"Leçons sur la méthode"

---

[5] M. Planck, "Positivismus und reale Außenwelt", in: *Wege zur physikalischen Erkenntnis*,
Leipzig: Hirzel, 1934, p. 216.
[6] M. Planck, *loc. cit.*, p. 217.
[7] *Cours de philosophie positive*, 33ᵉ leçon.

Formalism as intuitionism

Although it is conducted in terms of the particular principles—and presuppositions—of its author, Durkheim's critique of Simmel's attempt to found a formal sociology shows the link between formalism and intuitionism. The premature intention of giving sociology as its object social forms abstracted from their "content" necessarily leads to rash associations or to connections induced by the intuitions of common-sense. In depriving oneself of the knowledge and controls that would be required by the construction of more complex objects, one surrenders to "the fancy of the individual" and is condemned to a method in which example becomes the substitute for proof and eclectic accumulation the substitute for a system.

41. É. Durkheim

[Durkheim recalls the intention of Simmel's work: to give sociology a subject matter of its own by distinguishing within society the "content" from the "container". The container, that is, "the association within which such phenomena may be observed", constitutes the object of sociology, "the science of association in the abstract".]

But by what means is this abstraction given concrete form? If every human association develops with particular ends in view, how can one isolate association in general from the varied ends which it serves, and ascertain its laws?

> By putting together associations devoted to the most diverse purposes and eliminating what they have in common ... the differences, presented by the particular ends around which societies form, mutually cancel each other out, and the social form alone appears. A phenomenon—the formation of parties, for instance— may be observed in the world of art as well as in those of politics, industry, or religion; if we trace what occurs in all these milieus, irrespective of the diversity of ends and interests, it will be possible to determine the laws of this particular manner of grouping. The same method will allow us to study domination and subordination, the formation of hierarchies, the division of labor, competition, and so forth.[1]

It seems that in this fashion sociology is furnished with a clearly defined subject matter. We think, however, that in reality such a conception serves merely to keep it tied to metaphysical ideology when it actually shows an irresistible need to emancipate itself from this sphere. We do not contest the right of sociology to constitute itself by means of abstractions because there is no science that could be established otherwise. The abstractions must be methodically disciplined, however, and must separate the facts according to their natural distinctions; otherwise, they are bound to degenerate into fantastic constructions and vain mythology. The old political economy also claimed the right to make abstractions, and, in principle, it cannot be denied this right; but the use it made of it was vitiated because the basis of every one of its deductions was an abstraction that it had no right to make, that is, the

---

[1] "Comment les formes sociales se maintiennent", p. 72. [Cf. Simmel, "The Persistence of Social Groups", trans. Albion W. Small, *American Journal of Sociology*, III (1898), 663.—Translator's note.]

notion of a man who in his action was moved exclusively by his personal interest. This hypothesis cannot be determined at first sight from the beginning of the investigations; we are able to evaluate the impulsive force which personal interest can exercise on us only after repeated observations and methodical comparisons. Without them, there is no way of ascertaining whether there is in us something definite enough that it can be isolated from the other factors of our conduct and be considered apart from them. Who can say that between egoism and altruism there is the decisive separation which common sense unreflectively erects between them?

To justify the method advanced by Simmel, more is needed than to refer to the sciences that proceed by abstraction—namely, proof that the abstraction espoused is undertaken according to the principles with which every scientific abstraction must conform. By what right are the container and the content of society separated, and separated so radically? Only the container is claimed to be of a social nature; the content is not, or only indirectly so. Yet there is not a single proof to confirm such an assertion which, though far from being accepted as a self-evident axiom, may yet overwhelm a student.

To be sure, not all that happens in society is social; but this cannot be said of all that occurs in and through society. Consequently, in order to eliminate from sociology the various phenomena which constitute the web of social life, one has to demonstrate that they are not the work of the collectivity, but come from wholly different origins to place themselves within the general framework constituted by society. We do not know whether this demonstration has been attempted or whether the research that such a demonstration presupposes has been initiated. Yet it is immediately clear that the collective traditions and practices of religion, law, morality, and political economy cannot be facts less social than are the external forms of the collectivity; and if one deepens the study of these facts, one's first impression is confirmed: everywhere we find society at work elaborating them, and their effect on social organization is evident. They are society itself, living and working. What a strange idea it would be to imagine the group as a sort of empty form of trivial cast that can indifferently receive any kind of material whatever! The claim is that there are arrangements which are encountered everywhere, whatever the nature of the ends attained. But clearly, all these ends, despite their divergences, have characteristics in common. Why should only these common characteristics, and not the specific ones, have social value?

Such abstraction is not only unsystematic in that its effect is to separate things that are of the same nature, but the result of it, which is intended to be the subject matter of sociology, lacks all specificity whatever. Indeed, what are the meanings of the expression "social forms" and "forms of association in general"? If one wanted to speak only of the manner in which individuals are placed in contact with one another in association, of its external and morphological aspect—the notion would be definite; but it would be too restricted to constitute, by itself alone, the subject matter of a science. For it would be equivalent to reducing sociology to the exclusive investigation of the substratum on which social life rests. As a matter of fact, however, our author attributes to the term "social forms" a much more extended significance. By it he understands not only the modes of grouping, the static condition of association, but also the most general forms of social relations. The term refers to the largest forms of relations of every kind that mesh in society and to the nature of the phenomena with which we are presented as being directly pertinent to sociology—the division of labor, competition, imitation, or the state of the individual's liberty or dependence vis-à-vis the group.[2] Between these relations and the other, more special ones, however, there is only a difference of degree. How can a simple difference of this sort justify so definite a separation between two orders of phenomena? If the former constitute the subject matter of sociology, why must the latter, which are of the same kind, be excluded from it? The basis which the proposed abstraction seems to constitute when the two are opposed as container and content disappears once the significance of those words is more exactly specified, and it becomes clear that they are no more than metaphors, inexactly applied.

The most general aspect of social life is not, for that matter, either content or form, any more than it is any one of the special aspects which social life shows us. There are not two kinds of reality which, though intimately connected, are distinct and separable; what we have instead are facts of the same nature, examined at different levels of generality. And what, incidentally, is the degree of generality that such facts need in order to be classified among sociological phenomena? We are not told; and the question is one to which there is no answer. This suggests how arbitrary such a criterion is and how it gives us free rein for extending the boundaries of the science. While pretending that it defines research, it actually leaves it to the fancy of the individual. There is no rule for deciding in an impersonal manner where the circle of sociological facts begins and where it ends; not only are the boundaries mobile, which is quite legitimate, but it is not clear why they should be located at this point rather than at another. It must be added that in order to study the most general types of social actions and their laws, one has to know the laws of more special types, since the former cannot be investigated and explained without systematic comparison with the latter. In this respect, every sociological problem presupposes a profound knowledge of all those special sciences that should be placed outside sociology but which sociology cannot do without. And since such universal competence is impossible, one has to be satisfied with summary knowledge, which is rapidly gathered and cannot be subjected to any control. These are the characteristics of Simmel's investigations. We appreciate their subtlety and ingenuity, but we think it impossible to trace the main divisions of our science as he understands it in an objective manner. No connection can

[2] "Le problème de la sociologie", *Revue de Métaphysique et de Morale*, II (1894), p. 499.

be discovered among the questions to which he draws the attention of sociologists; they are topics of meditation that have no relation to an integral
scientific system. In addition, Simmel's proofs generally consist only of
explanations by example; some facts, borrowed from the most disparate fields,
are cited but they are not preceded by critical analysis, and they often offer us
no idea of how to assess their value. For sociology to merit the name of a
science, it must be something quite different from philosophical variations on
certain aspects of social life, chosen more or less at random according to the
leanings of a single individual. What is needed is the formulation of the
problem in a way that permits us to draw a logical conclusion.

Émile Durkheim
"Sociology and Its Scientific Field"

Conclusion
Sociology of knowledge and epistemology

Science and its worldly audience

By showing the interdependence between the fashionable enthusiasm for science and the scientists' indulgence of the whims of polite society that characterized the public life of physics in the 18th century, Bachelard identifies the more general logic whereby a scientific discipline is tempted to respond to the pressures of fashion so long as it fails to ✗ *complete its epistemological break with primary experience. His analysis of the social conditions of the impregnation of a science by the intellectual atmosphere of the day shows that only a "homogeneous, well-guarded scientific city" can defend itself against the seductions of "gala experiments".*

42. G. Bachelard

[*Nowadays, says the author, "scientific education has slipped a fairly accurate, fairly corrected book between nature and the observer."*] The same could not have been said in the pre-scientific period, in the 18th century. The book of science might be a good or a bad book. It was not *controlled* by official education. When it bore the mark of approval, it was often that of one of the [provincial Academies recruited from among the most muddled and worldly minds. Then the book *started out* from nature, it was interested in worldly life. It was a work of popularization for the popular mind, without the spiritual background which sometimes makes our popularizing works books of high quality. The author and the reader thought at the same level. Scientific culture was crushed beneath the mass and variety of second-rate works, which were much more numerous than works of value. By contrast, it is very striking that in our day works of scientific popularization are relatively rare.

Open a book of modern scientific education: science is there presented in relation with an overall theory. Its organic character is so evident that it would be very difficult to skip chapters. The first pages have hardly been read before there ceases to be talk of common-sense; nor is any more attention paid to the reader's questions. "Dear Reader" could easily be replaced by a stern admonition: pay attention, pupil! The book asks its own questions; it gives the orders.

Open a scientific work of the 18th century, and you will realize that it is rooted in everyday life. The author converses with his reader like a drawing-room lecturer. He espouses *natural* interests and concerns. Suppose, for example, that the question is to find the cause of thunder. The author will talk to the reader about the fear of thunder, will try to show him that this fear is ill-founded, will feel the need to repeat to him the old adage "When thunder claps, the danger is past", because only lightning can kill. Thus the Abbé Poncelet's book bears on its first page the Advertisement: "In writing on

Thunder, my principal intention has always been to moderate, if possible, the inconvenient impressions that this meteor habitually makes on an infinity of persons of all ages, sexes, and conditions. How many persons I have seen pass days in violent agitation, and nights in mortal anxiety!"[1] The author devotes a whole chapter, one of the longest, to Reflections on the terrors induced by thunder. He identifies four types of fear and analyses them in detail. [...]

The social quality of the readership sometimes brings a particular tone into the pre-scientific book. Astronomy for the upper classes has to incorporate society pleasantries. A scholar of great patience, Claude Comiers, starts his book on comets, a work much quoted in the 18th century, with these words: "Since in the Court it has been hotly debated whether Comet were male or female, and one of the Marshals of France, to put an end to the argument of the Scholars, has pronounced that this star's tail would have to be lifted, to see whether it has to be called he or she... ."[2] A modern scientist would probably not quote the opinion of a Marshal of France. He would not endlessly pursue jokes about the tail or beard of Comets: "As the tail, as the proverb says, is the hardest part of the beast to scotch, so that of the Comet has always been as hard to explain as the Gordian knot was to undo."

In the 18th century, the dedications of scientific books were, if this is possible, even more fulsome in their flattery than those of literary works. They are certainly more disconcerting to a modern scientific mind indifferent to the political authorities. [...]

Often there is an exchange of views between the author and his readers, between the "curious" and the *savants*. For example, a whole correspondence was published in 1787 under the title "Experiments on the properties of lizards, in flesh and in liquors, in the treatment of venereal and cutaneous diseases". A retired traveller in Pontarlier saw Negroes in Louisiana cure themselves of venereal disease "by eating anolis". He recommends this cure. A daily diet of three lizards leads to remarkable results which are related to Vicq d'Azyr. In several letters Vicq d'Azyr thanks his correspondent. [...]

The contemporary scientific city is so homogeneous and so well guarded that works by lunatics or deranged minds do not readily find a publisher. The same was not true a hundred and fifty years ago. [...]

These remarks on introductions to science perhaps suffice to indicate the difference in the first contact with scientific thought in the two periods that we seek to characterize. If we were to be accused of citing bad authors and forgetting the good ones, we should reply that the good authors are not necessarily those who were successful, and since we have to study how the scientific mind comes to birth in a free and quasi-anarchic—in any case unschooled—form, as it did in the 18th century, we are obliged to consider all

[1] Abbé Poncelet, *La Nature dans la formation du Tonnerre et la reproduction des Êtres vivants*, Paris, 1769.
[2] C. Comiers, *La Nature et présage des Comètes*, Lyon, 1665, pp. 7–74.

the false science which crushes true science, all the false science *against* which the true scientific mind has to constitute itself. To sum up, pre-scientific thought is "of the world". It is not *regular* like the scientific thought taught in official laboratories and codified in school books. We shall see the same conclusion emerge from a slightly different standpoint.

Mr. Mornet has shown, in a shrewd book, the worldly character of 18th century science. If we return to the question, it is simply in order to add a few details relating to the somewhat puerile *interest* then aroused by the experimental sciences, and to suggest a particular interpretation of this interest. Our thesis in this respect is the following: By giving immediate satisfaction to curiosity, multiplying the occasions for curiosity, far from encouraging scientific curiosity, one inhibits it. Knowledge is replaced by admiration, ideas by images.

— D

In trying to relive the psychology of the amused observers, we see the coming of an age of facility that takes away from scientific thought the *sense of the problem, and therefore the sinew of progress*. We shall take numerous examples from electrical science and we shall see how late and exceptional were the attempts at geometricization in the doctrines of static electricity since it was not until the *tedious* science of Coulomb emerged that one finds the first scientific laws of electricity. In other words, reading the numerous books devoted to electrical science in the 18th century, the modern reader will realize, in our view, the difficulty that was experienced in abandoning the picturesque aspect of the early observations, removing the exotic colour from the electrical phenomenon, ridding the experiment of its parasitic features, its irregular aspects. It will then appear clearly that the initial empirical grasp does not even give the correct *design* of the phenomena, not even a well-ordered, properly hierarchical description of the phenomena.

Once the mystery of electricity had been approved—and a mystery as such is always readily accepted—, electricity gave rise to a facile "science", very close to natural history, remote from the calculations and theorems which, since Huyghens, Newton, and others, had been progressively invading mechanics, optics, and astronomy. Priestley still writes, in a book published in 1769: "Electrical experiments are the clearest and most agreeable of all those that Physics offers."[3] Thus these primitive doctrines, which touched on such complex phenomena, presented themselves as easy doctrines, the indispensable condition for them to be entertaining and to interest a worldly audience. Or again, to speak as a philosopher, these doctrines presented themselves with the stamp of a *self-evident and deep-rooted empiricism*. It is so agreeable for idle intellects to confine themselves within empiricism, to call a fact a fact and forbid the search for a law! Even today, all the weakest students in the physics class "understand" empirical formulae. They readily believe that all formulae,

[3] J. Priestley, *The History and Present State of Electricity*, 2nd edn, London, 1769.

even those that derive from a strongly organized theory, are empirical formulae. They imagine that a formula is merely a set of numbers in waiting that simply have to be applied to each particular case. And then how seductive was the empiricism of early Electricity! It was not only a self-evident empiricism, but a *coloured empiricism*. It did not need to be understood, but just to be seen. For electric phenomena, the book of the World is a picture book. One has to leaf through it without trying to prepare one's surprise. In this domain, it seems so certain that one would never have been able to predict what one sees! Priestley rightly says: "Anyone who had been led to [predict the electric shock] by some reasoning, would have been regarded as a very great genius. But electrical discoveries are so much due to chance, that it is less the effect of genius than the forces of Nature which excite the admiration that we grant them." It is indeed a fixed idea of Priestley's that all scientific discoveries should be attributed to chance. Even when it is a question of his personal discoveries, patiently pursued with a very remarkable sense of chemical experimentation, Priestley modestly effaces the theoretical linkages which led him to assemble fertile experiments. He has such a commitment to empirical philosophy that thought is hardly more than an accidental cause of the experiment. If Priestley is to be believed, chance does everything. For him, chance comes before reason. So let us devote ourselves to the spectacle. Let us not concern ourselves with the Physicist who is merely the stage director. This is no longer true in our day, when the ingenuity of the experimenter, the theorist's brilliant insight, arouse admiration. And to show clearly that the phenomenon has a human origin, the name of the experimenter is attached— —probably for all eternity—to the *effect* he has constructed. So we have the Zeeman effect, the Stark effect, the Raman effect, the Compton effect, or indeed the Cabannes-Daure effect which might serve as an example of a, so to speak, *social* effect, produced by the collaboration of minds.

Pre-scientific thought does not labour over the study of a clearly circumscribed phenomenon. *It seeks not variation but variety.* And this is a particularly characteristic feature: the search for variety leads the mind from one object to another, without method. The mind then seeks solely the extension of the concepts. The search for variation focuses on a particular phenomenon, it tries to objectify all its variables, to test the sensitivity of the variables. It enriches the understanding of the concept and prepares for the mathematicization of the experiment. But let us see the pre-scientific mind in search of variety. One only has to run through the early books on electricity to be struck by the miscellaneous nature of the objects in which electrical properties are sought. Not that electricity is treated as a general property; paradoxically, it is regarded as an exceptional property though attached to the most diverse substances. In the first rank, naturally, are the precious stones; then sulphur, the residues of calcination and distillation, belemnites, smoke, and flames. An attempt is made to relate the electrical property to properties of superficial

appearance. Having made a *catalogue* of the substances capable of being electrified, Boulanger concludes that "the most brittle, and the most transparent
substances, are always the most electric".[4] Great attention is always paid to
what is *natural*. Electricity being a *natural* principle, there was a brief hope of
finding in it a means of distinguishing real from fake diamonds. The pre-
scientific mind always wants the natural product to be richer than the artificial
product.

To this scientific construction entirely made up of juxtaposition, everyone
can contribute. History testifies to the craze for electricity. Everyone is interested, even the King. In a "gala experiment", "the Abbé Nollet, whose name
is famous in electricity, gave the shock to one hundred and eighty of the
guards, in the King's presence; and at the grand convent of the Carthusians in
Paris, the whole community formed a line of nine hundred toises, by means of
iron wires between every two persons... and the whole company, upon the
discharge of the phial, gave a sudden spring, at the same instant of time, and all
felt the shock equally." This time the experiment gets its name from those who
contemplate it: "If a ring of persons take a shock among them, the experiment
is called the Conspirators."[5] When diamonds were successfully volatilized,
this feat was astonishing and even dramatic for persons of quality. Macquer
performed the experiment before an audience of seventeen. When Dercet and
Rouelle repeated it, 150 attended.[6]

The Leyden jar also provoked widespread amazement. "In the same year
that it was discovered, numbers of persons, in almost every country in
Europe, got a livelihood by going about and showing it. The vulgar of all ages,
sexes, and stations regarded this prodigy of nature with surprise and astonish-
ment."[7] "An Emperor would be content, for his revenue, with the sums paid
in shillings and small change to see the Leyden experiment performed." In the
course of scientific development, there will no doubt be fairground use of
some discoveries. But this use is now insignificant. The *demonstrators* of X-
rays who, thirty years ago, approached headmasters to offer a little novelty in
the classroom certainly did not make regal fortunes. They seem to have completely disappeared nowadays. An abyss now separates the charlatan from the
scientist, at least in the physical sciences.

In the 18th century, science interested every cultivated man. It was thought
instinctively, that a natural history collection and a laboratory were assembled
like a library, as the occasion suggested itself. There was trust: the chances of
individual serendipity were expected to coordinate themselves spontaneously.
Is not Nature coherent and homogeneous? An anonymous author, probably
the Abbé de Mangin, presents his *Histoire générale et particulière de l'électri-*

[4] *ibid.*, p. 124. (1769)
[5] *ibid.*, p. 534.
[6] *Encyclopédie*, article "Diamant".
[7] Priestley, *op. cit.*, p. 85.

cité with this symptomatic subtitle: "Or, the curious and entertaining, useful and interesting, delightful and amusing things said of it by some Physicists of Europe". He stresses the quite worldly interest of his work, for, if the reader studies his theories, he "will be able to say something clear and precise on the various debates which arise every day in the world, and on which even Ladies are the first to put forward questions... . A gentleman who might formerly have counted on his fine voice and elegant waist to make his name in society is now obliged to know at least something of his Réaumur, his Newton, and his Descartes".[8]

In his *Tableau annuel des progrès de la Physique, de l'Histoire naturelle et des Arts* for 1792, Dubois says of electricity (pp. 154–170): "Each physicist repeated the experiments, each wished to astonish himself... . M. le Marquis de X has, as you know, a very fine Physics display, but Electricity is his passion, and if paganism still reigned, he would raise electrical altars. He knew my taste, and was not unaware that I too was taken by *Electromania*. So he invited me to a supper where, he said, I should meet the leading electrifiers." One would like to know of these electrical conversations, which would no doubt tell us more about the psychology of the period than about its science.

We have more detailed account of the *electric dinner* enjoyed by Franklin and his friends in 1748. "A turkey was killed for their dinner by the electrical shock, and roasted by the electrical jack, before a fire kindled by the electrified bottle, when the healths of all the famous electricians in England, Holland, France, and Germany were drunk in electrified bumpers, under a discharge of guns from the electric battery."[9] The Abbé de Mangin, like so many others, describes this imposing dinner. He adds: "I think that if Mr. Franklin were ever to journey to Paris, he would lose no time in rounding off his magnificent meal with a well-electrified coffee."[10] In 1936 a minister inaugurated an *electrified* village. He too consumed an electric dinner and was none the worse for it. The press related the event in many columns, thus demonstrating that puerility belongs to all ages.

It can be seen, moreover, that this science dispersed over a whole educated society does not really constitute a *scientific city*. The laboratory of Mme la Marquise du Châtelet at Cirey-sur-Blaise, lauded in so many letters, has absolutely nothing in common with the modern laboratory in which a whole school works on a precise research project, such as those of Liebig or Ostwald, the cold laboratory of Kammerling Onnes or Mme Curie's radioactivity laboratory. The Cirey-sur-Blaise theatre is a theatre; the Cirey-sur-Blaise laboratory is not a laboratory. Nothing gives it coherence — neither the master nor the experiment. It has no other cohesion than good taste and the adjacent good table. It is a conversation piece for winter evenings or the drawing room.

---

[8] Anon., *Histoire générale et particulière de l'électricité*, Paris, 1752, Part II, pp. 2–3.
[9] B. Franklin, *Letters*, p. 35, quoted by Priestley, *op. cit.*, p. 541.
[10] *Histoire générale*, op. cit., Part I, p. 167.

More generally, 18th-century science is not a life, not even a profession. At the end of the century, Condorcet still contrasted in this respect the activities of the lawyer and the mathematician. The former provide a livelihood for their practitioner and so receive a consecration which the second lack. On the other hand, the scholastic line is, for mathematics, a well-graduated line of access which at least makes it possible to distinguish between pupil and master, to give the pupil an impression of the long, ungrateful task he has to provide. One only has to read the letters of Mme du Châtelet to have a thousand occasions to smile at her pretensions to mathematical culture. With condescending charm she would ask Maupertuis questions that a present-day school pupil of thirteen can solve without difficulty. This simpering mathematics is quite the opposite of a sound scientific training.

Gaston Bachelard
La formation de l'esprit scientifique

but see
Wikipedia
entry

For a reform of sociological understanding

Faults in method stem not so much from fidelity to a constituted theory as from an intellectual "disposition" that always owes something to the social characteristics of the intellectual world. For example, the separation of different types of explanation derives not so much from a theoretical reflection demonstrating the autonomy of the domain in question as from a mechanical attachment to the traditions of isolated disciplines that constitute so many insular domains of research. Epistemological errors are inscribed in institutions and social relationships (the tradition of a discipline, the expectations of an audience, etc.) in the form of temptations, incentives, or determinations, and they can never be reduced to simple individual blindness. Consequently, they cannot be corrected by a simple reflexive return by the researcher onto his own scientific procedure. Epistemological critique presupposes a sociological analysis of the social conditions of the various epistemological errors.

43. M. Maget

Ethnographic research, like any other, is not immune to affective pressures. Some vocations spring from the need for escape: escape towards other peoples, other social milieux, or the countryside, back to the good old days where the illusory stability of a golden age contrasts with the disconcerting turbulence of modern times. Then there are the aesthetic attraction for the exotic or the rustic, the ethical or political intentions of various kinds of traditionalism or regionalism, metaphysical vertigo and the obsession to rejoin or discover the essence of real humanity, filial attachment to the memory of ancestors, or the vestiges of the lifestyles which were theirs and expressed their being. And finally, there are the various forms of snobbery towards the curious and rare: travellers' tales vie with psychoanalytic tests as a pastime for winter evenings. [...]

Exaggerated and even exclusive use of intuition is no less formidable. Taking part in a ceremony, finding oneself in the atmosphere of a Basque pelota game or a Breton pardon, suggest to the spectator that he is in tune with the participants. Living their life, "putting oneself in their shoes", gives the hope that this adoption of a situation will automatically recreate the mental organization of the group, and some artists or inspired individuals seem to achieve this immediately.

In fact, intuition can be regarded as a ceaseless activity of every subject who seeks to understand the world and to discern the latent meanings and relationships on the basis of what is presently perceptible. The communication function appeals to it when one has to "read between the lines". The role of intuition has even been demonstrated in the field of mathematics. When attempting to recreate cultural systems, there is no reason radically to deny oneself the benefits of immersion in the milieu and the stimulations of mimeticism, *Einfühlung*, or empathy. At the same time, one has to control their products, and not regard the immediate data as irrevocably adequate knowledge but as hypotheses to be tested. Indeed, because of the very difference of culture, it is doubtful whether the observer can attain perfect coincidence. The intuitionist approach has the same disadvantages as introspection in general. Without verification (in this case, whenever possible, criticism by the subjects of the result of the investigations), how many chronic misunderstandings there are in everyday life, how many anthropomorphic, ethnocentric, or more simply egocentric errors in the euphoria of apparent communion.

Narrow specialization, closed to any external suggestion, is a source of errors that is no less often denounced. A branch of technology, or of regional arts, or costume, or architecture, is studied for its own sake without regard to the whole of which it is a part; the rural is studied independently of its relations with the contemporary urban world, and vice versa. This is not too serious so long as one keeps to morphological descriptions. Research, even when inspired by the best of intentions and anxious not to miss the connections with neighbouring levels, may be prevented by extra-scientific circumstances from fulfilling its programme. Inventories have thus been drawn up which are the only available documents on past eras, and they are positive contributions by these limited investigations, however truncated the picture they offer may be.

This compartmentalizing is much more damaging to attempts at explanation that confine themselves exclusively to the domain in question. It is true that in each order of phenomena one can define organizations, actual structures, and specific processes of transformation. Linguistics was one of the first disciplines to familiarize us with the notion of internal solidarity in phonetic or semantic systems. But at the same time it showed that their evolution cannot be explained without reference to the other levels of culture and the social equilibrium. Relative autonomy does not mean absolute independence.

The tendency towards a monopoly of explanation is strong, as is the hope of finding a universal characteristic. Exclusive determinisms aspire to hegemony, and no one is absolute immune to their seduction: geographism, biologism, diffusionism, functionalism... including ethnographism, as well as the too strictly antithetical attitudes which become equally erroneous and disappointing when they cease to be temporary polemical positions vis-à-vis an excess and tend to be stabilized as a categoric negation of realities whose defective interpretations alone were open to question.

Having pointed out the dangers of hasty generalization beyond the acquired data, the presumptions of exclusiveness or universality, hypostasis of concepts and their metaphysical substantification, we have reviewed the main dangers presented to our research by blind specializations, gaps in documentation, and the need for absolute, immediately accessible truths.

Reality rapidly takes its revenge, and as they make contact with it, schematic explanations, one-sided and exclusive determinisms, risky extrapolations and over-rigid divisions collapse one by one. Just as physical chemistry, bio-chemistry, bio-geography, and so on have emerged, so human geography, psychosomatics, social psychology, and genetic psychology — to mention only these — take their places on the boundaries which formerly divided humanity and its environment, mind and body, the individual and society, the biological and the cultural. The study of cultures advances as we gain more understanding of biology and the modelling process which shapes this "malleable wax". It is no longer conceivable, for example, in ignorance of the work in genetic psychology by Henri Wallon and Jean Piaget, who insisted on the need for psychology to take account of the characteristics of the environment. The newcomer, cybernetics, drawing on mechanical models much more complex than the automata contemporary with 18th-century associationism and sensualism, is casting new light on the relationship between the functioning of the central nervous system, internal physiology, and social communication. It is curious to observe the persistence of theoretical oppositions between history and an anthropology that is supposed to ignore historical phenomena. The science of the human race is inseparable from the history of the species, except through provisional methodological decrees defining organic specializations. Biology was quick to take up the notions of symbiosis, biological association, geotype, etc., showing its recognition of the phenomena of interaction between species and their environment, and early on placed considerable stress on the transformations of these species, which led to a complete renewal of this science. Even more so, cultural anthropology has to take account of the diachronic dimension of the phenomena that it studies, the conjunctures in which they emerge, mutate, or disappear.

This return to a richer conception of the complexity of anthropological questions and the burgeoning of linking disciplines, hypotheses, and discoveries have in turn inevitably produced some discomfort. We have already alluded to the schematization of concept and theories. Verbal fetishism and risky simplifications have already marked recent theories of electronic "brains" and communications, despite the circumspection of their promoters. The researcher, more prudent but carried away by this movement of convergence and this multiplicity of diverse activities, may think himself obliged to be *au fait* with everything, from the latest discoveries in electronics to those in psychosomatics or phonology. If recognition of interdependence slips into the assertion that everything is contained in everything, then a confused monadology is in the process of taking root, which will be as sterilizing as compartmentalization. It is liable to induce an inhibiting stupor by calling into question the right to proceed by successive levels and stages in the study of the totality which, it is postulated, has to be grasped as whole, and the right to refer to discontinuities and discriminations, for fear of missing the relationship between distinct levels and phenomena.

It is probably more necessary than ever to resist these exhilarating or inhibiting waves of vertigo and to set oneself precise tasks in association with the other scientific disciplines, the history and present situation of each of which can provide useful lessons and footholds for all the others.

The need to reduce the "personal equation", to benefit from the indispensable suggestions of intuition while controlling them without indulgence, to integrate induction and deduction, analysis and synthesis, the importance of statistics, both methodical—whether when dealing with electrons or stationary systems, individuals, or social conjunctures—and implicit in everyday life, the dialectical evolution of knowledge in extent and depth, of discrimination and assimilation, of classifications and typologies developing with discoveries, the necessary revision of concepts in the light of experience—these are not new problems. The most seasoned sciences have had to resolve them and work unceasingly at improving the answers they give them. They have also had to *Prondy* give up the claim to absolute and final truth, just when, in practical terms, they were obtaining the least contentious results. Likewise, the sciences of man can in their turn shed the crushing role of saying what man and society are in themselves, and devote themselves to the progressive study of them. At least as regards the fundamental problems, the unity of science is affirmed, from *?!* physics to psychology, from the natural to the human sciences.

The fundamental attitudes towards the object, the basic notions, the attempts at organization, are transposed from one science to another. Behaviorism—independently of the ontological postulates that are claimed for it—is setting the example of the refusal to yield in an uncontrolled way to the suggestions of introspection and the glamour of intuitive flashes. The notions of the unitary whole and the context have long been familiar to the psychology of form and linguistics; the notion of organism–environment interdependence is well established in biology and genetic psychology. Linguistics has helped to make explicit the relationship between synchronic and diachronic perspectives and the notion of structure, which has been boldly applied by Claude Lévi-Strauss in the area of social systems. These transpositions must of course not take place without a stringent critique of the conditions of validation particular to the domain in which one intends to implement them. While it is accepted, for example, that the definition of geotypes may indicate models usable for the *?* definition of relatively homogeneous cultural groups (which may by analogy be called ethno-types), the specific adaptability and sociability of mankind forbids their rigid application and requires one—without ignoring the permanence of certain environmental facilities or constraints—to loosen the relationship between man and his environment (geographical determinism) in favour of the social milieu and the rigour of inter-generational cultural transmission. Equally one should mistrust some forms of social chemistry or energetics without definitively rejecting the usefulness of valid analogies. It is not absolutely necessary to devote resources to rediscovering old problems to which solutions have already been found and can, with some critical adaptation and vigilance, be useful instruments for work in a new area.

Just as the separation between the natural and the human sciences is becoming more permeable to exchanges, so we can see a weakening of the notorious science/humanities divide whereby students initially trained in indifference or even disdain for scientific activities found themselves some years later in a difficult position vis-à-vis disciplines which at least in some respects were turning into sciences.

Basic training in epistemology, on-going information and contact can only facilitate the specialization that is indispensable in the co-operation of disciplines that are increasingly conscious of their organic solidarity as they better define their specific tasks and free themselves of the preoccupation or pretension of knowing everything or explaining everything, and of the fear of wandering in solitary error.

1953!

Marcel Maget
Guide d'étude directe des comportements culturels

This could/should have been put up first!

Cross-checks and the transitivity of critiques

Exposing the illusion of an objectivity based solely on the commitment to objectivity, Michael Polanyi shows that a common adherence to common norms, overriding specialist frontiers, is obtained through the social mechanisms of cross-control and not through the miracle of scientists' scientific goodwill. Similarly, a general consensus on the scientific value of particular works is guaranteed by a kind of circular delegation of the power of control.

44. M. Polanyi

Each scientist watches over an area comprising his own field and some adjoining strips of territory, over which neighbouring specialists can also form reliable first-hand judgments. Suppose now that work done on the speciality of B can be reliably judged by A and C; that of C by B and D; that of D by C and E; and so on. If then each of these groups of neighbours agrees in respect to their standards, then the standards on which A, B and C agree will be the same on which B, C and D agree, and on which also C, D and E agree, and so on, throughout the whole realm of science. This mutual adjustment of standards occurs of course along a whole network of lines which offers a multitude of cross-checks for the adjustments made along each separate line; and the system is amply supplemented also by somewhat less certain judgments made by scientists directly on professionally more distant achievements of exceptional merit. Yet its operation continues to be based essentially on the "transitiveness" of neighbouring appraisals—much as a marching column is kept in step by each man's keeping in step with those next to him.

By this consensus scientists form a continuous line—or rather a continuous network—of critics, whose scrutiny upholds the same minimum level of scientific value in all publications accredited by scientists. More than that: by a similar reliance of each on his immediate neighbour they even make sure that the distinction of scientific work above this minimum level, and right up to the highest degrees of excellence, is measured by equivalent standards throughout the various branches of science. The rightness of these comparative appreciations is vital to science, for they guide the distribution of men and subsidies between the different lines of study, and they determine, in particular, the crucial decisions by which recognition and assistance are granted to new departures in science or else withheld from them. Though it is admittedly easy to find instances in which this appreciation has proved mistaken, or at least sadly belated, we should acknowledge that we can speak of "science" as a definite and on the whole authoritative body of systematic knowledge only to the extent to which we believe that these decisions are predominantly correct.

Michael Polanyi
Personal Knowledge: Towards a Post-Critical Philosophy

"Meanwhile, I have come to know all the diseases of sociological understanding"

An interview with Pierre Bourdieu, by Beate Krais

1968
↓
1988

B.K.: When you wrote this book, you already had some experience of sociological research. At what point in your work did you find it useful or necessary to perform the sociological reflection that appears in *The Craft of Sociology*? I ask you that, because you have much more experience now... but all the same, you had already done a good deal of work by that time.

P.B.: The book started to take shape in 1966. By then, the École des Hautes Etudes had set up an intensive training programme in sociology. Passeron and I had taught a course on epistemology, and putting the book together was a way of perpetuating the course without having to repeat it every year. So, at the starting point, there was a didactic intention and the book presented itself as a manual: but, at the same time, there was a broader ambition. Writing a manual was a way of writing a treatise on sociological method in a modest form.

B.K.: But it was also a work of reflection on what had already been done.

P.B.: Yes. There was a didactic intention, but also a desire to draw up a balance-sheet of a decade of fieldwork, first in ethnology and then in sociology. I had done a lot of work in Algeria with people from the Algiers Institute of Statistics and I had the sense that I was putting into practice a methodology that had not been made explicit. This feeling that it absolutely had to be made explicit was strengthened by the fact that it was then the high-water mark of the "Lazarsfeldian" invasion in France. Lazarsfeld—we're talking about the 1960s—had come to Paris and given solemn lectures at the Sorbonne that all the French sociologists attended, except me. I stayed away quite deliberately. I thought that, symbolically, I didn't need to take lessons from Lazarsfeld (you only had to read the books). Through some interesting techniques, which needed to be learned and which I had learned, he was also imposing something else, an implicit positivistic epistemology that I didn't want to accept. And that was the real intention of *The Craft of Sociology*. In fact, there's a note at the beginning that says roughly: people will say this book is written against empirical sociology, but that's not true. It's designed to give a theoretical basis to another way of doing empirical research, by applying a technology that Lazarsfeld had undeniably done much to advance, in the service of a different epistemology. That was the real intention of the book. At the time, I saw two contrasting errors against which sociology had to define ✗ *itself*

itself. The first one, which could be called theoreticist, was symbolized by the Frankfurt school, in other words, people who, without doing any empirical research, denounced the positivist danger everywhere (Lucien Goldmann was the French representative of that current). The second, that could be called positivist, was symbolized by Lazarsfeld. It was the Lazarsfeld/Adorno dyad, on which I've written a note in the Appendix to *Distinction*. Against these two tendencies, I wanted to produce an empirical sociology that was theoretically grounded, a sociology that could have critical intentions (like every science) but which had to be performed empirically.

B.K.: What were the epistemological traditions that you could draw on at the time to realize that intention?

P.B.: At the time, there was first of all my own experience... I had worked in Algeria with people from the Institute of Statistics, with all my friends from INSEE, Alain Darbel, Claude Seibel, Jean-Paul Rivet, with whom I learned statistics "on the job". It was a real stroke of luck. They belonged to a very rigorous tradition of statistics that stood comparison with the Anglo-American version but which was unknown to the sociologists. At the same time, while being very strict as regards sampling or mathematical models, they were locked in a bureaucratic-positivist tradition that prevented them from questioning the elementary operations of research. Shortly before writing this book, I was teaching sociology at the École Nationale de la Statistique et des Études Économiques. Teaching those future statisticians, I found that I had to teach them not only how to process data but also how to construct the object with reference to which it was collected. Not only how to code, but also how to draw out the implications of a coding; not only how to draw up a questionnaire, but also how to construct a system of questions on the basis of a problematic, and so on. So that was my experience.

Apart from that, I had my training, and in the course of my studies in philosophy, I had been particularly interested in the philosophy of the sciences, epistemology, and so on. I tried to transpose into the field of the social sciences a whole epistemological tradition represented by Bachelard, Canguilhem, Koyré, for example, little known abroad, except by people like Kuhn, through Koyré—so that Kuhn's theory of scientific revolutions did not strike me as a scientific revolution... . That tradition, which cannot easily be labelled with an "ism", has as its common basis the primacy given to construction. The fundamental scientific act is the construction of the object; you don't move to the real without a hypothesis, without instruments of construction. And when you think you are without any presuppositions, you still construct without knowing it and, in that case, almost always inadequately. In the case of sociology, this attention to construction is particularly necessary because the social world constructs itself in a sense. Our heads are full of preconstructions. In everyday experience, as in much work in the social sciences, our thinking applies instruments of knowledge which serve to construct the object when they should be taken as the object. Some of the ethnomethodologists were discovering that at about the same time, but they failed to arrive at the idea of the necessary *break* that is set out by Bachelard. That's why, in defining social science as a simple "account of accounts", they ultimately remain in the positivist tradition. This can be seen clearly today with the vogue for discourse analysis (which has been enormously strengthened by the development of tools for recording, such as video). Their attention to discourse taken at face value, as it presents itself, with a philosophy of science as a *recording* (rather than a construction), led them to ignore the social space in which discourse is produced, the structures that determine it, and so on.

B.K.: This idea of the construction of the object seems to me to be extremely important. It may be banal nowadays in the natural sciences, but no one can say it is part of the tool kit of social science researchers, as a precondition for all scientific procedure.

P.B.: The need to break with preconstructions, prenotions, spontaneous theory, is particularly imperative in sociology, because our minds, our language, are full of preconstructed objects, and I think that three-quarters of research simply converts social problems into sociological problems. There are countless examples: the problem of old age, the problem of women, at least if raised in a certain way, the problem of young people... . There are all sorts of preconstructed objects that impose themselves as scientific objects; being rooted in common-sense, they immediately receive the approval of the scientific community and a wider public. For example, a good number of divisions of the object correspond to bureaucratic divisions: the major divisions of sociology correspond to the division into ministries, with the Ministry of Education, the Ministry of Culture, the Ministry of Sport, and so on. More generally, many instruments used to construct social reality (like occupational categories, age groups, and so on) are bureaucratic categories that no one has thought through. As Thomas Bernhard says in *Alte Meister*, we are all more or less "servants of the State", functionaries, insofar as we are products of the educational system, teachers... . And, to break away from pre-thought objects, you need a terrific energy, an iconoclastic violence that you find more often in writers like Bernhard or artists like Hans Haacke than in professors of sociology, however "radical" in intention.

The problem is that these preconstructed objects seem to be self-evident, so that scientific work based on a break with common sense runs up against a whole host of difficulties. For example, the most elementary scientific operations become extremely difficult. So long as you take it as you find it, as it presents itself, the social world offers ready-made data, statistics, discourses that can easily be recorded, and so on. In a word, when you question it as it asks to be questioned, it has a great deal to say for itself, it tells you whatever you want to know, it gives you figures... . It likes sociologists who *record*, who reflect it, who function as mirrors. Positivism is the philosophy of science as a mirror... .   *"... the mirror of Nature"?*

B.K.: But aren't you close to a positivist position when you say that one knows nothing in sociology until the sociologist has collected his "scientific data" through scientific work, as in the natural sciences? I can see that in social science you can't take things, "social facts", as they present themselves. But it has to be admitted that agents are also 'experts 'on their own lives, that they have an awareness and a practical knowledge of the social world, and that this practical knowledge is more than a simple illusion.

P.B.: Among the preconstructions that science has to call into question, there is a certain idea of science. On the one hand, there is common-sense, which has to be mistrusted, because social agents do not have innate wisdom, *la science infuse*, as we say in French. One of the obstacles to scientific knowledge — I think Durkheim was quite right to say it — is the illusion of immediate knowledge. But secondly, it is true that the conviction of having to construct against common-sense may in turn favour a scientistic illusion, the illusion of absolute knowledge. That illusion is very clearly expressed in Durkheim's approach: agents are in error, which is deprivation; deprived of knowledge of the whole, they have a first-degree, entirely naïve knowledge. Then along comes the scientist who grasps the whole and who is a sort of God compared to the mere mortals who understand nothing. The sociology of sociology, which, for me, is an integral part of sociology, is indispensable for calling into question both the illusion of absolute knowledge which is inherent in the scientist's position, and the particular form that this illusion takes depending on the position that the scientist occupies in the space of scientific production. I've stressed this point in *Homo Academicus*. In the case of a study of the academic world, the danger is particularly strong; scientific objectification can be a way of putting oneself in the position of God-the-Father vis-à-vis one's competitors. That was perhaps the first thing I discovered in my ethnological work: there are things you no longer understand until you take as your object the scientific stance itself. The fact of not understanding oneself as a scientist, of not knowing what is implied in the situation of the observer, the analyst, generates errors. Structuralism, for example — as I tried to show in *The Logic of Practice* — is based on the illusion of putting into the agents' heads the thoughts the scientist works out about them.

B.K.: There was the Adorno/Lazarsfeld dyad, representing the Scylla and Charybdis of sociology. But you also allude to sociological humanism in *The Craft of Sociology*, and I rather wonder what this humanism is or was, in sociology, which you presented as one of the dangers.

P.B.: Empirical sociology partly emerged, in France, after the war, from people who were linked to the Christian-left social movements (for example, there was Révérend Père Lebret, who ran a movement called "Économie et Humanisme"). They conducted what you might call... charitable sociology. Very well-meaning people, who wanted to do good in the world... . There's a famous remark by André Gide that "good sentiments make bad literature"; you might equally say that good sentiments make bad sociology. In my view, the whole Christian-humanist or humanitarian-socialist movement was leading sociology into a dead-end.

B.K.: But that humanism perhaps isn't necessarily Christian? You can see parallels in some would-be left-wing sociology, it can be a sociology inspired by an ideal of social work—in fact, that's an important strand in Anglo-Saxon sociology, you only have to think of the Webbs—or a sociology which wants the sociologist to conduct his research from a "Klassenstandpunkt", siding with the proletariat.

P.B.: Unfortunately, the empirical sociology on leisure, work, or cities was done by people who were perfectly human, but, if I might say so, all too human... . The break is also made against all that. You don't do sociology in order to enjoy yourself by suffering with those who suffer. One had to have the courage to say no to all that. I can remember that when I was working in Algeria, in the midst of the war, surrounded by things that touched me greatly, I tried to keep a kind of distance that was also a way of respecting people's dignity... . The model that comes to mind here is Flaubert, someone who looks at reality with a distant gaze, who sees things with sympathy, but without letting himself be caught up in them. That is probably why I have exasperated many people; I have refused *"prêchi-prêcha"*, as we say in French, good intentions, humanistic niceness. One example of this attitude would be my use of the idea of *interest*. Obviously I don't use the word interest in Bentham's sense. I've spent a lot of time explaining that. But it was a way of breaking with that kind of humanism, of pointing out that even the humanist enjoys calling himself a humanist.

B.K.: OK, but when you have this critical gaze, you're presupposing that the agents are the accomplices of what's going on. Otherwise, you have to see the agents as puppets whose strings are pulled by social structures quite external to them, such as capitalism... .

P.B.: Sociology is a very difficult science. You're always steering between two opposite dangers, you can easily jump from the frying-pan into the fire. That's why I've spent my life demolishing dualisms. One of the points I would stress more strongly than I did in *The Craft of Sociology* is the need to move beyond couples of oppositions, which are often expressed by concepts ending in "ism". For example, on the one hand, you have humanism, which at least has the merit of inciting one to move closer to people. But they are not real people. On the other hand, you have theoreticians who are a million miles away from reality and from people as they are. The Althusserians were typical of that attitude. Those *normaliens,* often of bourgeois origin, who had never seen a worker, or a peasant, or anything, produced a grand theory without agents. That theoreticist wave came just after *The Craft of Sociology* was published. In every period, the *Craft* would need to be written differently. Epistemological propositions are generated by reflecting on scientific practice—a reflection that is always governed by the dangers that are uppermost at the moment in question. As the principal danger changes in the course of time, so the emphasis of the discourse has to change too. At the time when the *Craft* was written, it was necessary to strengthen the theoretical pole against positivism. In the 1970s, when the Althusserian wave was sweeping France, I would have wanted to strengthen the empirical pole against this theoreticism which reduces agents to the state of *Träger,* "bearers" of the structures. A whole aspect of my work, for example *The Logic of Practice,* is radically opposed to this ethnocentrism practised by scientists who claim to know the truth of people better than those people themselves and to be able to make them happy despite themselves, in accordance with the old Platonic myth of the philosopher-king (modernized in the form of the cult of Lenin). Ideas like those of habitus, practice, and so on, were intended, among other things, to point out that there is a practical knowledge that has its own logic, which cannot be reduced to that of theoretical knowledge; that, in a sense, agents know the social world better than the theoreticians. And at the same time, I was also saying that, of course, they do not really know it and the scientist's work consists in making explicit this practical knowledge, in accordance with its own articulations.

B.K.: So theoretical or scientific knowledge isn't really different from practical knowledge, because it is *constructed,* like practical knowledge, but constructed explicitly: it reconstructs practical knowledge in an explicit way and so "raises it to consciousness", as we say in German. At the same time, it has to be remembered that what is reconstructed with the means of science is the same "thing", it's not an "object" or a reality that belongs to another world, inaccessible to the agents... . But how does object-construction work? How is it done, how do you gain the necessary distance without immediately rising above those poor agents who "know not what they do"?

P.B.: I believe more than ever that the most important thing is constructing the object... . All through my work I've seen how everything, including the technical problems, hangs on the preliminary definition of the object. Obviously, this object-construction is not a kind of initial act, and constructing an object is not the same thing as drawing up a "research project". One could usefully do a sociology of the "research proposals" that sociologists have to produce in the United States in order to get grants. You have to define in advance your objectives and methods, to prove that what you are going to do is new in relation to previous work, and so on. The rhetoric that has to be mobilized to generate the "methodological appeal" that Adam Przeworski and Frank Salomon refer to in their guide for beginners (*On the Art of Writing Proposals*, New York: Social Science Research Council, 1981), contains an implicit, socially sanctioned epistemology. So much so that when a piece of empirical research does not present itself in accordance with the norms of that rhetoric, many sociologists, in the USA and elsewhere, have the impression that it is not scientific. Whereas, in fact, that mode of presentation of a scientific project is the exact opposite of the real logic of the work of constructing an object, work which is not done once and for all at the beginning, but in every moment of research, through a multitude of small corrections. All of which does not mean that one confronts the object totally disarmed. You have some general principles of method that are in a sense inscribed in the scientific habitus. The sociologist's *métier* is exactly that—a theory of the sociological construction of the object, converted into a habitus. When you possess this *métier*, you master in a practical state everything that is contained in the fundamental concepts: habitus, field, and so on. It means for example that you know that, in order to have some chance of constructing the object, you have to make explicit the presuppositions, to construct sociologically the preconstructions of the object; or again, that the real is relational, that what exists is relationships, something that you can't see, in contrast to individuals and groups. Let's take an example. Suppose I have a project of studying the *grandes écoles*. Right at the start, by saying "the *grandes écoles*", I've already made a decisive choice... . Every year there's an American who comes over to study the *École Polytechnique* from the origins to the present day, or another one who wants to do the *École Normale*... . Everyone finds that perfectly reasonable. A very manageable task—the objects are already constituted, the archives readily available, and so on. In reality, in my view—though it would take time to spell this out—, you can't study the *École Polytechnique* independently from the *École Normale* and the *École Nationale d'Administration*, it's located in a space. So these people are studying an object which is no object at all. And here we come back to what I was saying a moment ago: the more naïve the object you study, the more easily the data present themselves to be studied. On the other hand, as soon as I say the *constructed object* is the whole set of *grandes écoles*, I'm faced with innumerable problems—noncomparable statistics, for example. And I'm liable to be seen as less scientific than those who stick with the apparent object, because there are such difficulties to be overcome to empirically grasp the constructed object.

B.K.: I'd like to ask you about the second volume of *The Craft of Sociology*. Why was it not written? In the Preface to the second French edition, you say there should have been three volumes—the epistemological preliminaries, which is the book that exists, a second book on constructing the object, and a third one that was to contain a critical catalogue of tools. I can very well imagine the third volume, but I find it hard to imagine what a book on constructing the sociological object would look like.

P.B.: The first volume was able to be an original book disguised as a manual because there was nothing else on the question; and I think that even today there isn't much... . With the second part, things got much more difficult. Either we would compile a classic manual, using the headings that you expect to find in a sociology primer (structure, function, action, etc.), or we would do the same thing as in the first part, that's to say write an original treatise that would have been a general theory. Personally, I had no desire to produce a traditional-style manual, taking up a position on "functions and functionalism". It would have been a purely scholastic exercise. The third part, on the sociologist's tools, could have been useful, but it would have amounted to recognizing the theoretical/empirical division that is the equivalent of the disastrous opposition between theory and methodology in the Anglo-Saxon tradition. We said in *The Craft of Sociology* that the various statistical techniques contain implicit social philosophies that need to be made explicit. When you perform a regression analysis, a path analysis, or a factorial analysis, you need to know what social philosophy you are bringing in, and more especially what philosophy of causality, action, the mode of existence of social things, and so on. You choose one technique rather than another on the basis of a problem and a particular construction of the object. For example, I make a lot of use of the analysis of correspondences, because I think it's an essentially relational technique whose philosophy entirely corresponds to what social reality is in my view. It's a technique that "thinks" in terms of relationships, as I try to do with the idea of the field. So you can't separate object-construction from the instruments of object-construction, because, to move from a research programme to scientific work, you need instruments, and these instruments are more or less appropriate depending on what you're looking for. If I'd wanted to explain the factors determining the differential success of students in the different schools, then—assuming that I had been able to prove the independence of the different fundamental variables, which is not the case, in my view—I could have made use of multiple regression analysis.

B.K.: So we come back to the problem of the construction of the object, this time in connection with the instruments, which have to be adapted to the specific objects. If I've understood correctly, the sociologist's work is greatly determined by the properties of the specific object, its history... .

P.B.: It's the problem of the particularity of objects. Given my conception of scientific work, it's clear I can only work on a situated, dated object. Suppose I want to study how professorial judgement operates. I assume that the judgements that teachers make of their pupils and their work are the product of the implementation of the incorporation of mental structures such as, for example, the division into disciplines. To resolve this very general problem, I work on the *Concours général* prizewinners or on the pupil records that a particular teacher kept, in the 1960s, and bring out the categories that are involved in ⟵ ! them. If I publish that today, people will say: "These data are out of date, all that is over, humanities teachers are no longer dominant, now it's the maths teachers," and so on. In fact, my object is the mental structures of a person who holds one of the most socially influential positions in our society, who has the power to symbolically condemn (you're stupid or worthless) or con-   ⁓ ⟩ secrate (you're intelligent). It's a very important object, which can be observed everywhere. Through my analysis of a historical case, I offer a programme for   ✳ other empirical analyses conducted in situations different from the one I've studied. It's an invitation to a generative reading and to the theoretical induction which generalizes from a well-constructed particular case. Having got a programme in this way (it's a matter of making explicit mental structures, principles of classification, taxonomies that are very likely to be expressed in adjectives), one only has to repeat the survey at another moment and in another place, looking for invariants. Those who criticize the "French"   ⎧ character of my findings fail to see what is important, which is not the findings ✳ ! but the process through which they are found. "Theories" are research programmes which call not for "theoretical discussion" but for practical implementation, which refutes or generalizes. Husserl used to say that one has to immerse oneself in the particular case in order to discover the invariant within it; and Koyré, who had attended Husserl's lectures, shows that Galileo did not need to repeat the experiment of the inclined plane a thousand times to understand the phenomenon of falling bodies. He simply had to construct the model, against appearances. When the particular case is well constructed, it ceases to be particular and, normally, everyone ought to be able to make it work.

B.K.: Twenty years have gone by since the first French edition of *The Craft of Sociology*, and in those two decades, sociology has evolved considerably. In particular, it's evolved regarding empirical research; and you have also done a lot more work. You have a lot more experience now. If you were rewriting the *Craft* now, what would you change? Would you want to add anything?

P.B.: Above all, I would put things differently. It's a programmatic text. I had some experience behind me, but above all I needed to express my dissatisfaction with the official discourse on scientific practice. Now I understand better and more practically what was then put forward as a programme. At bottom, the *Craft* remains a book by a teacher. And there are a lot of negative things in it, which is typical of a teacher: don't do this, don't do that... . It's full of warnings. It's both programmatic and negative. It's rather as if one offered a manual of grammar as a way of teaching people how to talk... . Although *Le Métier de sociologue* constantly refers to *métier* in the French sense ("*avoir du métier*" means having a "habitus", a practical mastery), it presents a didactic discourse which is thereby somewhat ridiculous. It constantly repeats that one has to construct, but without ever showing practically how one constructs. I think it's a book that also did some harm. It woke people up, but it was immediately used in a theoreticist sense. One of the many ways of not doing sociology is to intoxicate yourself with fine-sounding words and perform endless sacrifice to the "epistemological preliminaries". The *métier* is largely transmitted through practice, and to be capable of transmitting it, one has to have internalized it very profoundly. I often say in my seminar that I'm rather like an old doctor who knows all the diseases of the sociological understanding. There are propensities to error that vary according to sex, social origin, and intellectual background. Male students are more often theoreticist, whereas female students are socially disposed to be too modest, too prudent, too pernickety, taking refuge in empirical detail, minutiae, and they need to be encouraged to have more audacity, theoretical *chutzpah*... . But these dispositions themselves vary according to social origin: theoretical arrogance is less probable among first-generation intellectuals... . Having said that, there's a whole series of classical diseases that you can recognize. My experience as a research supervisor, to which I can add the experience of all the diseases I've had myself, at one moment or another in my career, and all the mistakes I've made, enables me, I think, to teach the principles of object-construction in practice, like an old craftsman, and that's the great difference from what you find in *The Craft*. If I had to write the book again, I would present a series of examples, or "master works", as mediaeval craftsmen did. As an example of object-construction, I would give what appears in the appendix to *Homo Academicus*, the analysis of a list of "outstanding authors". I'd say: There's the material, in front of you; it's available to everyone. Why is it badly constructed? What does this questionnaire mean? What would you do with it? The second one is an appendix to *Distinction*, called "Associations". One day I came across an issue of the journal *Sondages*, published by the opinion-polling organization IFOP, which gave statistical tables of the distributions of the various attributes that the respondents had assigned to a number of politicians (Giscard, Marchais, Chirac, Servan-Schreiber, etc.). The commentary was limited to simple paraphrases: Marchais is associated with the pine tree, and so on. You could give the raw material (the *Sondages* article) to the students and then, as an exercise, ask them what they could get out of it, and then show them what can be got out of it. In both cases, it's a question of bringing out the hidden conditions of the construction of the preconstructed object that underlies the naïvely presented results. In the first case, you have to question the sample: who are the judges whose judgements led to this list of best authors? How were they chosen? Isn't the set of authors implied in the list of judges chosen and in their categories of perception? In the second case, you have to question the questionnaire (in fact, questionnaires should always be questioned...). The people who asked the questions put into them unconscious categories of thought (such as: pine is dark, gloomy, the wood used for coffins, associated with death, and so on), and they then got the respondents to apply equally unconscious categories which happened to be roughly the same. There was communication of unconsciousnesses. And so an idiotic survey, of no scientific value, can provide a fascinating scientific object if, instead of reading the results at face value, one reads the categories of thought projected in the results they produced. In both cases, you're dealing with already published results that needed to be re-constructed. That's often what happens. In other words, I'd give three or four examples of extreme cases where it's only by doing in practice what is said theoretically in the *Craft* that you get an object rather than a simple artifact, or nothing at all. I'd present specimens of empirical work, with some commentary.

Another thing I'd reinforce is the sociology of sociology. It's mentioned at the end, but very abstractly. Since then, that side has been developed a lot, especially with *Homo Academicus*. But apart from that, the great difference would be in the way of putting things.... I haven't reread it... , but I think that many things in it might exasperate me now.... I'm sure I'd say: This is so arrogant! When you're young, you're arrogant, out of insecurity... .

B.K.: I started by asking you to situate *The Craft of Sociology* in the context of twenty years ago. If you were writing a new *Craft* now, what would be the context? What debate would the book enter? And what are the specific problems or barriers that have arisen in these two decades of work and research?

P.B.: The essential features of the landscape haven't changed enormously. The "positivist" paradigm is still very strong. People are still doing empirical research without theoretical imagination, with problems that are much more the product of "scientific" common-sense than of genuine theoretical reflection; on the other side, there is grand theory, eternal grand theory, completely cut off from empirical research. In fact, the two go very well together, in other words, one can carry on empirical research of a positivist type while producing theoretical theory. What is nowadays called theory is often commentaries on canonical authors (in Germany, Britain, and the United States, there are a number of "catch-all theories" modelled on that of Parsons) or big trend-reports produced for teaching purposes (often based on notes made by students). As it happens, I have on my desk two ideal-typical examples: an article by Robert Wuthnow and Marsha Witten, entitled "New Directions in the Study of Culture" (*Annual Review of Sociology*, 1988, 14, pp. 49–67) and one by Judith R. Blau, "Study of the Arts; A Reappraisal" (*ibid.*, pp. 269–292). The state of theoretical theory is probably explained by the fact that these disparate and insubstantial products of a sort of academic rapid-reading, which is often associated with the application of equally absurd academic categories of classification, exerts a brain-washing effect. Faced with this theory conceived of as a speciality in its own right, there is "methodology", the series of recipes or precepts that you have to respect, not in order to know the object but in order to be recognized as knowing the object.

Having said that, the situation has changed greatly and I would write quite differently.... . I think that a good proportion of the producers of sociology in the United States have freed themselves from the positivist paradigm. There have been movements like interactionism and ethnomethodology which have had beneficial effects, and they were saying things that are fairly close to what is said in *The Craft of Sociology* (for example, with their reflection on presuppositions, folk theories, and so on). There has also been the development of "historical" currents that have brought the historical dimension back into sociological analysis, especially analysis of the state. And there was Kuhn, who brought in something of the European tradition of the philosophy of science, saying things close to the themes developed in the *Craft*: science constructs and is itself socially constructed, etc. I think that there is now a possibility of a reception for the *Craft*, whereas when it was written, there was no hope; it was impossible to see who in the world would be interested in that. That's why, whereas we then had a lot of difficulty in finding texts by sociologists that illustrated our points, it would probably be a lot easier today.

I think there have been big changes, especially in the United States. Alongside the central orthodoxy, the one defended by the Capitoline triad, Parsons, Merton and Lazarsfeld, all sorts of new currents have developed. More critical —and self-critical—forms of research have emerged (even if, in Europe, and especially in Germany where the dualism of grand theory and positivist empiricism persists, people seem not to have noticed; the heartland is changing, but in the outposts of the American cultural empire, it's business as usual). Having said that, when the critique of speech strategies, or observation and interviewing strategies, becomes an end in itself, it leads to a kind of nihilistic and even obscurantist abdication, which is in every way the opposite of the preliminary epistemological critique as put forward in the *Craft*, which aimed to help to advance the scientificity of sociology.

B.K.: There's an irrationalist current which says: "All that is useless! What is science, anyway? Just another way of earning a living!"

P.B.: Yes, and that is why epistemology is always very difficult. I don't think that anyone wants to see the social world as it is. There are several ways of denying it; one of them is art, of course. But there is even a form of sociology that achieves the remarkable feat of talking about the social world as if it were not talking about it—formalistic sociology, which interposes a screen of equations, generally ill-constructed ones, between the researcher and the real. That's another form of nihilism. Denial, *Verneinung* in Freud's sense, is a form of escapism. When you want to escape from the world as it is, you can be a musician, or a philosopher, or a mathematician. But how can you escape it as a sociologist? Some people manage to. You just have to write some mathematical formulae, go through a few game-theory exercises, a bit of computer simulation. To be able to see and describe the world as it is, you have to be ready to be always dealing with things that are complicated, confused, impure, uncertain, all of which runs counter to the usual idea of intellectual rigour.

December 1988

$$23 + 12$$
$$= 35 \text{ years ago}$$

List of texts

Suggestions for further reading

Works which seemed to us particularly useful in assisting the pedagogic use of this book are indicated by one or two asterisks.

Aron, R., *German Sociology*, trans. M. and T. Bottomore, New York: Free Press, 1964.

Bachelard, G., *Essai sur la connaissance approchée*, Paris: Librairie philosophique J. Vrin, 1927.

——*Le matérialisme rationnel*, Paris: P.U.F., 1953.

——**La formation de l'esprit scientifique: contribution à une psychanalyse de la connaissance objective*, 4th edn., Paris: Librairie philosophique J. Vrin, 1965 (1st edn. 1938).

——*Le rationalisme appliqué*, 3rd edn., Paris: P.U.F., 1966 (1st edn. 1949).

——*The Philosophy of No: A Philosophy of the New Scientific Mind*, trans. G. C. Waterson, New York: Orion Press, 1968.

——*The New Scientific Spirit*, trans. A. Goldhammer, Boston: Beacon Press: 1984 (1st French edn. 1934).

Bernard, C., *Introduction à l'étude de la médecine expérimentale*, Paris: Hachette, 1943 (1st edn. 1865).

Bierstedt, R., "The Limitation of Anthropological Methods in Sociology", *American Journal of Sociology*, 54, pp. 22–30, 1948.

Borel, E., *Probabilité et certitude*, Paris: P.U.F., 1950.

Brunschvicg, L., *Les étapes de la philosophie mathématique*, Paris: Alcan, 1912.

Campbell, N. R., *What is Science?*, New York: Dover, 1952 (1st edn. 1921).

Canguilhem, G., "Le problème des régulations dans l'organisme et dans la société", *Les cahiers de l'alliance israélite universelle*, no. 92, pp. 64–81, 1955.

——*La connaissance de la vie*, 2nd edn., Paris: Librairie philosophique J. Vrin, 1965.

——*La formation du concept de réflexe aux XVIIe et XVIIIe siècles*, Paris: P.U.F., 1955.

——"The Role of Analogies and Models in Biological Discovery", in A. C. Crombie (ed.), *Scientific Change: Historical Studies in the Intellectual, Social and Technical Conditions for Scientific Discovery and Technical Invention, from Antiquity to the Present*, Symposium on the History of Science, London: Heinemann, 1963, pp. 507–520.

——*Le normal et le pathologique*, Paris: P.U.F., 1966 (first published 1943).

——"Le tout et la partie dans la pensée biologique", *Les études philosophiques*, nouvelle série, 21, pp. 13–16, 1966.

Carnap, R., "Les concepts psychologiques et les concepts physiques sont-ils foncièrement différents?", *Revue de synthèse*, vol. 10, no. 5, pp. 43–53, 1935.

——"Testability and Meaning", *Philosophy of Science*, no. 3, 1936, pp. 419–471 and no. 4, 1937, pp. 1–41.

——"Empiricism, Semantics and Ontology", *Revue internationale de philosophie*, no. 4, 1950.

——*The Logical Structure of the World*, trans. R. A. George, London: Routledge and Kegan Paul, 1967.

Cassirer, E., "Le langage et la construction du monde des objets", *Journal de psychologie normale et pathologique*, vol. 30, pp. 18–44, 1933.

——"The Influence of Language upon the Development of Scientific Thought", *The Journal of Philosophy*, vol. 33, pp. 309–327, 1936.

——*Philosophy of Symbolic Forms*, 3 vols, trans. R. Manheim et al., New Haven: Yale University Press, 1953–57.

Cohen, M. R., *Studies in Philosophy and Science*, New York: Holt, 1949.

Cohen, M. R. and E. Nagel, *An Introduction to Logic and Scientific Method*, London: Routledge and Kegan Paul, 1934.

Cohen, P. S., "Models", *British Journal of Sociology*, vol. 17, no. 1, pp. 70–78, 1966.

Comte, A., *Introduction to Positive Philosophy*, ed. with introdn. and revd. transln. by F. Ferré, Indianapolis, Indiana: Bobbs-Merrill, 1970.

Cournot, A., *Considérations sur la marche des idées et des événements dans les temps modernes*, Paris: Hachette, 1872.

——*Essai sur les fondements de nos connaissances et sur les caractères de la critique philosophique*, Paris: Hachette, 1912 (1st edn. 1851).

Duhem, P., *The Aim and Structure of Physical Theory*, New York: Atheneum, 1974.

Durkheim, É., *The Elementary Forms of the Religious Life: A Study in Religious Sociology*, trans. J. W. Swain, London: Allen & Unwin; and New York: Macmillan, 1915.

——*The Division of Labor in Society*, trans. G. Simpson, New York: Free Press; and London: Macmillan, 1933.

——*Leçons de sociologie: physique des mœurs et du droit*, Paris: P.U.F., 1950.

——*Suicide: A Study in Sociology*, trans. J. A. Spaulding and G. Simpson, edited with introduction by G. Simpson, Glencoe (Ill.): Free Press, 1951; and London: Routledge and Kegan Paul, 1952.

——*Sociology and Philosophy*, trans. D. F. Pocock with introduction by J. G. Peristiany, London: Cohen & West; and Glencoe (Ill.): Free Press, 1953.

——*Education and Sociology*, trans. S. D. Fox with introduction by S. D. Fox and foreword by T. Parsons, Glencoe (Ill.): Free Press, 1956.

——*Émile Durkheim, 1858–1917: A Collection of Essays, with Translations and a Bibliography*, trans. and ed. K. H. Wolff, Columbus (Ohio): Ohio State University Press, 1960.

——"Sociology and the Social Sciences", (1909) in *Emile Durkheim on Institutional Analysis*, ed., transl. and introduction by M. Traugott, Chicago and London: University of Chicago Press, 1978, pp. 71–87.

——*The Rules of Sociological Method* (2nd French edition, 1901), trans. W. D. Halls, New York: Free Press, 1982.

Fauconnet, P. and M. Mauss, **"Sociologie", in La Grande Encyclopédie, Paris: Société anonyme de la Grande Encyclopédie, vol. XXX, pp. 165–176.

Feigl, H. and H. Brodbeck (eds.), *Readings in the Philosophy of Science*, New York: Appleton-Century-Crafts, 1953.

Festinger, L. and D. Katz (eds.), *Research Methods in the Behavioral Sciences*, New York: Holt, Rinehart, and Winston, 1953.

Gardiner, P., *The Nature of Historical Explanation*, Oxford: Oxford University Press, 1952.

Gonseth, B., *Les fondements des mathématiques: de la géometrie d'Euclide à la relativité générale et à l'intuitionnisme*, Paris: Blanchard, 1926.

Gross, L. (ed.), *Symposium on Sociological Theory*, London and Evanston (N.Y.): Harper & Row, 1959.

Hammond, P. E. (ed.), *Sociologists at Work: Essays on the Craft of Social Research*, New York: Basic Books, 1964.

Kahl, R. (ed.), *Studies in Explanation: A Reader in the Philosophy of Science*, Englewood Cliffs (N.J.): Prentice-Hall, 1963.

Kaplan, A., *The Conduct of Inquiry: Methodology for Behavioral Science*, San Francisco: Chandler, 1964.

Kendall, P. L. and P. F. Lazarsfeld, "Problems of Survey Analysis", in P. F. Lazarsfeld and R. K. Merton (eds.), *Continuities in Social Research: Studies in the Scope and Method of "The American Soldier"*, Glencoe (Ill.): Free Press, 1950, pp. 133–196.
Koyré, A., *Etudes d'histoire de la pensée scientifique*, Paris: P.U.F., 1966.
Lazarsfeld, P. F. and R. K. Merton (eds.), *Continuities in Social Research: Studies in the Scope and Method of "The American Soldier"*, Glencoe (Ill.): Free Press, 1950.
Lazarsfeld, P. F. and M. Rosenberg, *The Language of Social Research: A Reader in the Methodology of Social Research*, Glencoe (Ill.): Free Press, 1955.
Lévi-Strauss, C., *Race and History*, Paris: UNESCO, 1952.
——*Structural Anthropology*, trans. C. Jacobson and B. G. Schoepf, New York and London: Basic Books, 1963.
——*Introduction to the Work of Marcel Mauss*, trans. F. Baker, London: Routledge and Kegan Paul, 1987.
Linton, R., *The Study of Man*, London: Owen, 1965 (1st ed. 1936).
Lipset, S. M. and N. J. Smelser (eds.), *Sociology: The Progress of a Decade*, Englewood Cliffs (N.J.): Prentice-Hall, 1961.
Maget, M., *Guide d'étude directe des comportements culturels*, Paris: CNRS, 1953.
Malinowski, B., *Argonauts of the Western Pacific*, London: Routledge and Kegan Paul, 1922.
Marx, K., **Grundrisse: Foundations of the Critique of Political Economy*, trans. with a foreword by M. Nicolaus, Harmondsworth: Penguin, 1973.
——*Capital*, Harmondsworth: Penguin (3 vols.), 1976–1981.
Mauss, M., *Sociologie et anthropologie*, Paris: P.U.F., 1950.
——*Œuvres*, Paris: Editions de Minuit, 3 vols., 1968–69.
Merton, R. K., *Social Theory and Social Structure*, New York: Free Press (3rd edition, revised and enlarged), 1968.
Mills, C. W., *The Sociological Imagination*, New York: Oxford University Press, 1959.
Nagel, E., *Logic without Metaphysics*, New York: Free Press, 1956.
——*The Structure of Science: Problems in the Logic of Scientific Explanation*, New York: Harcourt, Brace and World, 1961.
——"Verifiability, Truth and Verification". *Journal of Philosophy*, vol. 31, 1934.
Nagel, E. and C. G. Hempel, "Problems of Concepts and Theory in the Social Sciences", Symposium, in *Language, Science and Human Rights*, Papers of the American Philosophical Association, Eastern Division, I, Boston: University of Pennsylvania Press, 1952.
Piaget, J. (ed.), *Logique de la connaissance scientifique*, Paris: Gallimard, 1967.
Poincaré, H., *La science et l'hypothèse*, Paris: Flammarion, 1902.
Polya, G., *Mathematics and Plausible Reasoning*, Princeton (N.J.): Princeton University Press, 1954.
Popper, K. R., *The Logic of Scientific Discovery*, London: Hutchinson, 1959.
Sapir, E., *Culture, Language and Personality*, Berkeley and Los Angeles: University of California Press, 1956.
de Saussure, F., *Course in General Linguistics*, London: Duckworth, 1983.
Simiand, F., *Statistique et expérience: remarques de méthode*, Paris: Rivière, 1922.
——*Le salaire, l'évolution sociale et la monnaie*, Paris: Alcan, 1932.
Weber, M., *Essays in Sociology*, trans. H. H. Gerth and C. W. Mills, London Routledge & Kegan Paul, 1948.
——*The Protestant Ethic and the Spirit of Capitalism*, trans. T. Parsons, New York: Charles Scribner's Sons, 1958.

——***The Methodology of the Social Sciences*, trans. and ed. E. A. Shils and
H. A. Finch, foreword by E. A. Shils, New York: Free Press, 1949.
——*Economy and Society: An Outline of Interpretive Sociology*, ed. G. Roth and
C. Wittich, New York: Bedminster Press, 1968.
Whitehead, A. N., *Science and the Modern World*, London: Macmillan, 1925.
Wittgenstein, L., *Tractatus Logico-Philosophicus*, London: Routledge and Kegan Paul,
1961.
——*Philosophical Investigations*, Oxford: Blackwell (2nd edition, revised), 1958.
Zetterberg, H. L., *On Theory and Verification in Sociology*, Stockholm: Almqvist and
Wiksell; New York: Tressler Press, 1954.

Index of names[1]

[1] The page numbers in italics refer to text extracts.

Niklas Luhmann
Political Theory in the Welfare State
Translated by John Bednarz, Jr.
1990. 13,5 x 20,5 cm. VI, 239 pages. Cloth.   ISBN 3-11-011932-3;
0-89925-554-X (U. S.)

Hans Haferkamp (Editor)
Social Structure and Culture
1989. 15,5 x 23 cm. VIII, 340 pages. Cloth.   ISBN 3-11-011310-4;
0-89925-363-6 (U. S.)

Joel Best (Editor)
Images of Issues
Typifying Contemporary Social Problems
1989. 15,5 x 23 cm. XXII, 257 pages. Cloth.   ISBN 3-11-012358-4;
0-202-30352-7 (U. S.) Paper.   ISBN 3-11-012359-2; 0-202-30353-5 (U. S.)
(Social Problems and Social Issues – An Aldine de Gruyter Book Series)
Aldine de Gruyter

Dennis Brissett, Charles Edgley (Editors)
Life as Theater
A Dramaturgical Sourcebook
2nd Edition. 1990. 15,5 x 23,5 cm. XVI, 462 pages. Cloth.   ISBN 3-11-012558-7;
0-202-30362-4 (U. S.) Paper.   ISBN 3-11-012557-9; 0-202-30363-2 (U. S.)
(Communication and Social Order – An Aldine de Gruyter Book Series)
Aldine de Gruyter

Malcolm Spector, John I. Kitsuse
Constructing Social Problems
1987. 15,5 x 23,5 cm. VIII, 184 pages. Paper.   ISBN 3-11-011555-7; 0-202-30337-3 (U. S.)
(Social Problems and Social Issues – An Aldine de Gruyter Book Series)
Aldine de Gruyter

Bruce Luske
Mirrors of Madness
Constructing Psychic Reality
1990. 15,5 x 23,5 cm. VIII, 130 pages. Cloth.   ISBN 3-11-012749-0; 0-202-30422-1 (U. S.)
Paper.   ISBN 3-11-012748-2; 0-202-30423-X (U. S.)
(Social Problems and Social Issues – An Aldine de Gruyter Book Series)
Aldine de Gruyter

de Gruyter · Berlin · New York

de Gruyter & Co., Genthiner Str. 13, D-1000 Berlin 30, Tel.: (0 30) 2 60 05-0, Fax (0 30) 2 60 05-251
de Gruyter, Inc., 200 Saw Mill River Road, Hawthorne, N.Y. 10532, Tel. (914) 747-0110, Fax (914) 747-1326

Lavuelle .

3749456
6139961

9 783110 119404